EVOCATIONS OF GRACE

EVOCATIONS OF GRACE

*The Writings of Joseph Sittler on
Ecology, Theology, and Ethics*

Edited by

Steven Bouma-Prediger *and* Peter Bakken

WILLIAM B. EERDMANS PUBLISHING COMPANY
GRAND RAPIDS, MICHIGAN / CAMBRIDGE, U.K.

To the memory of my father, Curtis Prediger,
and of his father, Joseph Prediger

To my father, Stewart Bakken,
and in memory of my mother, Marion Bakken

© 2000 Wm. B. Eerdmans Publishing Co.
All rights reserved

Wm. B. Eerdmans Publishing Co.
255 Jefferson Ave. S.E., Grand Rapids, Michigan 49503 /
P.O. Box 163, Cambridge CB3 9PU U.K.

Printed in the United States of America

05 04 03 02 01 00   7 6 5 4 3 2 1

Library of Congress Cataloging-in-Publication Data

Sittler, Joseph.
Evocations of grace: the writings of Joseph Sittler on ecology, theology, and ethics /
edited by Steven Bouma-Prediger and Peter Bakken.
p.   cm.
Includes bibliographical references.
ISBN 0-8028-4677-7 (pbk.)
1. Human ecology — Religious aspects — Lutheran Church. 2. Lutheran Church —
Doctrines. I. Bouma-Prediger, Steven. II. Bakken, Peter W., 1957– III. Title.

BX8074.H85 S58 2000
261.8′362 — dc21
00-032152

www.eerdmans.com

Contents

CONTENTS

Foreword

Picture a shuffler, virtually blind, who has to "see" with his inner eye. Picture him black coat clad under black beret, with white flecks of dried skin and dandruff he cannot see to dust off. He does not only shuffle; he can stride and lope, but usually he looks lost, at least lost in thought. If we could picture his inmost heart, we would know it to have been heavy. For years his beautiful musician-spouse lies passively at home, a victim of multiple sclerosis. He also looks lonely, unless he is being followed by overhearing students who track him around theology school campuses in Chicago's Hyde Park. You have heard that people make some fuss over him and that he is worth fussing over. You wonder why, and how that can be.

Then you hear him speak in a classroom or chapel and see him half-smile. Almost at once your curiosity about this figure is satisfied. This is Joseph Sittler, theologian, rhetor, teacher, exemplar. And after hearing him you know you want to follow up on him through what will become his legacy, his writings. Disappointment follows. Sittler has written several important small books, but there is no large corpus — how he would have loved to play with that term in respect to his writings! — so there cannot be as much plumbing of his depths as you might like.

Fortunately, Sittler was born just late enough for tape-recorders to capture him, and he was surrounded by enough note-takers and transcribers to assure that a significant number of his lectures and classroom presentations survive. Finally, some of those influenced by him have begun writing dissertations about Sittler and his theology and, better for us, have gathered and edited writings. I am happy to say that *Evocations of Grace* is the most significant venture of this sort to date, and one can only hope for more like it.

I once read a now fugitive line by a Dutch or Belgian phenomenologist whose name eludes me. I know the English edition was bound in bright red. (Noticing that but not remembering names and publishing details is a nice Sittlerian touch.) The philosopher said something like this: "The great person is one who sees already what others do not see as yet." On those terms, Sittler was a great person.

Since the editors introduce this book and its contents quite systematically and satisfactorily, I will try to put "Joe" Sittler's endeavor and their achievement in a context.

Never heard of him? Some of us are chilled at the thought that the effect and recall of a theologian who spoke more than he wrote might before long be forgotten. He might pass into oblivion with the two generations that followed him, many of them already gone and others on the exit ramp. This book helps assure that he will continue to have effect, and to reach people for whom he will be only a literary name and not a rhetorician or a presence.

Hear of him, as you will "hear" him on these pages. Years ago I recall discussing Jewish theologians with some critics. We got to talking about Abraham Joshua Heschel. His juniors made efforts to categorize him. Conclusion: he was essentially a rhetorical theologian. Sittler is his Christian counterpart.

We can still play with categories. I didn't know until I read the introduction to this book that he had been hired at the University of Chicago to be a "biblical theologian." He was that. But not so if that meant that he had joined the company of biblical scholars who exegete texts, molecule of ink by molecule of ink. Think of him more as a "diviner" of scriptures, who worked with them the way water-witches walk over surfaces until their device is pulled magnetically, as it were, to the flowing sources. I've heard of Origen and Luther belonging to such a school of biblical theology. Sittler lived in, was engulfed by, walked in the light of, and ransacked elements of biblical worlds, but look for no precise and formal "biblical theology" here.

When he taught at Chicago we liked to speak of people in his area and discipline as "systematic" or "constructive" theologians. Sittler was not systematic. Repeat: Sittler was not systematic. That fact probably cost him some points against some of those who were given to scrupulosity and protectiveness about their disciplinary definition. He was not a member of the club. Here and there one can sense that he felt a bit left out of their company, but he chose the route he took and knew there'd be a price for him to pay. Fortunately for us, he paid it. This is not a slam at systematic theology so much as a bow to the notion that theology can take numerous forms.

Constructive theologian? Yes, very much so. He could never read texts and let them lie there. He had to shape and build out of what he read, be it a Gerard Manley Hopkins sonnet or the Gospels. He constructs a whole theology of nature and grace on the pages you are now opening.

An ethicist? He wrote on ethics, and there are pages here where he acknowledges that he is stepping into the role of the moral theologian. But here as so often he does not follow the rules, and no more turns moralist than he is able to stand back and discuss ethical principles from a distance.

The editors speak of him at one point as being a practical theologian, and he was that, by emergent more than by historic definitions. True, he could also "theologize" on the basis of a psalm, a glimpse of nature, a Richard Wilbur poem, loving the result the way the art-for-art's sake and poetry-for-poetry's sake people do. There is intrinsic beauty and value in the effort and product. It is hard to picture a reader not simply enjoying Sittler enjoying creation. But one also finds Sittler saying little about a theological truth without running it through the wringer of *praxis,* or seeing anything happening in practice that did not demand and deserve some theorizing. Yes, he was a practical theologian.

Not desperately urgent about categorizing but hoping to be of help to readers, I would go back to the Heschel parallel and speak of Sittler's rhetorical theology. He did speak and write to persuade. Sittler knew the *pathos,* the situation of a suffering humanity that was not simply looking for grace but dealing with a dis-graced nature. He embodied *ethos,* the character of a credible respondent to situations in the natural world as well as in the questing heart. And Sittler was ready with *logos:* content, having something to say.

We co-taught a course of restless seminarians in the 1960s, when relevance was to be the norm for all that we transacted. One day he said to the class, "We give you all the instruments for being relevant, for getting society's ear. And when you get it, you haven't the faintest idea what to say into it." "Saying" became urgent.

Once I was on a program with Sittler during an occasion when he had the audience in tears because this would be his "last" such appearance. He often said that, but would then take new commitments and show up again. Someone in response to his talks queried: if Sittler were asked to put into one sentence the first step for the reform of the church today, what would it be? "Watch your language!" he barked, and that was it. This shows up on page 89 where he quotes Alfred North Whitehead's aphorism that "style is the morality of the mind." One reads it in the marvelous sub-chapters on the rhetoric of recollection, the rhetoric of participation and reenactment, the rhetoric of cosmic extension. Of the middle of these three he writes on page 101: "This type of rhetoric proposed that in the actual life, obedience, suffering, death, and resurrection of Jesus Christ is concentrated both the reality of alienation and its conquest by the grace of God."

I've pointed to them in other portraits of Sittler but must revisit some lines (condensed from Sir Arthur Quiller-Couch, here on page 161) that get close to Sittler's appeal as a rhetorical theologian. The mighty works of literature on which he so consistently drew "traffic not with cold, celestial certainty, but with men's hopes and fears and breakings of the heart, all that gladdens, saddens, maddens us men and women in this brief and mutable traject" of life in what Sittler calls "the creation which is our home for a while, the anchorage of our actual selves." He used to complain that much literature did well with the phenomenology of evil, but that we needed a phenomenology of grace. You will find it hinted at and pointed to on the pages that follow.

Sittler had, and has, a lot to say into society's ear. And, as this collection makes clear, when he deals with "ecology, theology, and ethics," it all gravitates to, gets focused on, and deals with both "nature" and "grace." The editors are most helpful in introducing that theme, but there is little danger that the unintroduced newcomer could forget it for a minute or a page.

What is the big deal? Sittler grew up in a "grace" tradition of Saint

Paul, Saint Augustine, and Martin Luther, the masters of grace-talk and experience. But from the same writers he lifted up for view a neglected theme — "nature," and how grace related to it. In doing so, as early as 1954, before semi-secular savants were saying it, he was noticing the threat to nature, the unheeding practice of most citizens and believers, and the urgency of the task of alerting all to "care of the earth."

Sittler was in his prime during the fading but still dominant times of Protestant neo-orthodoxy, which tended to sever nature from grace, unbiblically, he thought. When he made the most important speech of his life at the World Council of Churches at New Delhi in 1961 he was met, as the editors point out, with cheers from some (e.g., Eastern Orthodox), jeers from others (e.g., neo-Orthodox), and incomprehension from still others. Joe saw already what they did not see as yet. His "cosmic Christology" was so new to them that they did not remember that it was as old as Paul's Letter to the Colossians or Irenaeus, or Augustine and Martin Luther on their good days. But they began to learn, and we keep learning.

The editors like to point out that Sittler's reflections on the environment date from the time when Rachel Carson and her kith and kind were only beginning to waken the world from its ecological slumber. One notes happily that they do not dwell long on the "who was there first" theme, which gets boring after a paragraph or two. They move instead and at once to the more important question: What is in it for us today, if it is still ahead of us, if it still has promises of what we do not see or have not seen "as yet"? To see that get disclosed, it is time for me to turn you over to capable editors, in whose debt we are, and to Joseph Sittler, in whose debt they are as well.

MARTIN E. MARTY
Fairfax M. Cone Distinguished Service Professor Emeritus
The University of Chicago

Acknowledgments

The editors gratefully acknowledge a generous grant from the Hunger Education Program of the Evangelical Lutheran Church in America, which made the publication of this book possible. We thank especially Dr. Job Ebenezer, Director of Environmental Stewardship and Hunger Education for the ELCA.

Our thanks also to the Au Sable Institute of Environmental Studies for providing institutional support for this project.

Many thanks to Ryan Atwell for compiling the index in a timely fashion.

We are grateful to the following for granting permission to reprint essays and quoted material in this volume:

Portions of this edition licensed by special permission of Augsburg Fortress.

Scripture quotations marked RSV are from the Revised Standard Version of the Bible, copyright 1946, 1952 and 1971 by the Division of Christian Education of the National Council of Churches and are used by permission.

Scripture quotations marked NEB are from the New English Bible, © The Delegates of the Oxford University Press and the Syndics of the Cambridge University Press, 1961, 1970.

From *Age of Anxiety,* by W. H. Auden. Copyright © 1947 by W. H. Auden and renewed 1975 by Monroe K. Spears and William Meredith, Executors of the Estate of W. H. Auden. Reprinted by permission of Random House, Inc.

Lutheran School of Theology at Chicago, for Joseph Sittler, "Commencement Address," *Chicago Lutheran Theological Seminary Record* 64, no. 4 (November 1959): 34-37.

The World Council of Churches, for "Called to Unity," *The Ecumenical Review* 14 (January 1962): 177-87.

"Advice to a Prophet" from *Advice to a Prophet and Other Poems,* copyright © 1959 and renewed 1987 by Richard Wilbur, reprinted by permission of Harcourt, Inc.

Mr. Franklin H. Littell, for Joseph Sittler, "The Care of the Earth," in *Sermons to Intellectuals from Three Continents,* ed. Franklin Littell (New York: The Macmillan Company, 1963), 18-28.

The lines from "i thank You God for most this amazing," copyright 1950, © 1978, 1991 by the Trustees for the E. E. Cummings Trust. Copyright © 1979 by George James Firmage. From *Complete Poems: 1904-1962 by E. E. Cummings,* edited by George J. Firinage. Reprinted by permission of Liveright Publishing Corporation.

Indiana University Press, for "The Role of the Spirit in Creating the Future Environment," in *Environment and Change,* ed. William R. Ewald, Jr. (Bloomington, Ind.: Indiana University Press, 1968), 55-68.

Blackwell, Publishers for Joseph Sittler, "Ecological Commitment as Theological Responsibility," *Zygon* 5 (June 1970): 172-81.

Excerpt from "Objects," in *The Beautiful Changes and Other Poems,* copyright © 1947 and renewed 1975 by Richard Wilbur, reprinted by permission of Harcourt, Inc.

From *W. H. Auden: Collected Poems,* by W. H. Auden, edited by Edward Mendelson. Copyright © 1944 and renewed 1972 by W. H. Auden. Reprinted by Random House, Inc.

"The Waking," copyright 1953 by Theodore Roethke. From *The Collected Poems of Theodore Roethke,* by Theodore Roethke. Used by permission of Doubleday, a division of Random House, Inc.

Interpretation: A Journal of Bible and Theology, for Joseph Sittler, "The Scope of Christological Reflection," *Interpretation* 26 (July 1972): 328-37.

St. Olaf College, for Joseph Sittler, "The Context: Nature and Grace in Romans 8," in *Faith, Learning and the Church College: Addresses by Joseph Sittler,* ed. Connie Gegenbach (Northfield, Minn.: St. Olaf College, 1989), 15-26, 37-39.

Nature as a Theater of Grace:
The Ecological Theology of Joseph Sittler

PETER W. BAKKEN

I t is easy to assume that ecological theology (or theology of ecology, eco-theology, environmental theology, or whatever label one wishes to use) as such did not exist before the publication of medieval historian Lynn White Jr.'s essay, "The Historical Roots of Our Ecological Crisis," in 1967. The thesis of that essay was that Christianity, with its transcendent God in whose image humanity alone was made and its endorsement of the biblical commandment to "have dominion" over the earth, bears a "huge burden of guilt" for the current environmental crisis.[1] The charge quickly became accepted as almost axiomatic by many persons inside and outside of Christianity. The ensuing surge of articles and books by Christians in the early 1970s — whether defending Christian teaching and the Bible as supportive of environmental stewardship, or calling for Christian repentance and a "new theology of nature"[2] — has contributed to the suspicion of many that "eco-theology" is only another

---

1. Lynn White Jr., "The Historical Roots of Our Ecological Crisis," *Science* 155 (10 March 1967): 1203-4.

2. H. Paul Santmire, "Toward a New Theology of Nature," *Dialog* 25 (Winter 1986): 43-50; Joseph K. Sheldon, *Rediscovery of Creation: A Bibliographical Study of the Church's Response to the Environmental Crisis* (Metuchen, N.J.; London: The American Theological Library Association; The Scarecrow Press, 1992); Peter W. Bakken, Joan Gibb Engel, and J. Ronald Engel, *Ecology, Justice and Christian Faith: A Critical Guide to the Literature* (Westport, Conn.: Greenwood Press, 1995).

episode in the frantic pursuit of relevance, a desperate attempt to retrofit Christianity in self-defense against its secular critics.

As a rough generalization, the late and breathless arrival of theologians on the environmental scene cannot be denied. But it is not the whole story. Alarm at the havoc that modern industrial society has wrought on the life-supporting services of the earth predates Earth Day 1970 — and even the publication of Rachel Carson's *Silent Spring* in 1962. In the 1940s and 50s, a handful of theologians were arguing that environmental degradation is a profoundly spiritual matter. Among them was the American Lutheran theologian, Joseph Sittler (1904-1987).[3]

The Environmental Crisis as a Theological Issue

Joseph Sittler was born in 1904 in Upper Sandusky, Ohio, the son of a Lutheran pastor. As he later said, his experiences in the rural Midwestern congregations his father served disposed him, from an early age, toward theology that attends to the whole creation and "that can penetrate the ordinary problems of human existence, including the care of the earth."[4] He graduated from Wittenberg University (Springfield, Ohio)

3. For other pioneers in relating theology to environmental (or conservation) concerns, see: Liberty Hyde Bailey, *The Holy Earth* (New York: C. Scribner's Sons, 1915); V. A. Demant, "Christian Strategy," in *Malvern 1941: The Life of the Church and the Order of Society; Being the Proceedings of the Archbishop of York's Conference* (London: Longmans, Green and Company, 1942), pp. 121-49; W. C. Lowdermilk, "The Eleventh Commandment," *American Forests* 46 (January 1933): 12-15; and Daniel Day Williams, "The Good Earth and the Good Society," in *God's Grace and Man's Hope* (New York: Harper and Brothers, 1949), pp. 158-77.

4. Joseph Sittler, "Closing Address: Creating a Rhetoric of Rural Values," in "Preliminary Report: A Family Farm Action Agenda," xeroxed booklet from "A Time to Choose: An Ecumenical Event on the Future of Family Farm Agriculture in Wisconsin," (8-9 March 1985) (Madison, Wis.: Wisconsin Conference of Churches, 1985), p. 38. For general biographical information on Sittler, see Jerald C. Brauer, "In Appreciation of Joseph Sittler," *Journal of Religion* 54 (April 1974): 97-101; Moira Creede, "Logos and Lord: A Study of the Cosmic Christology of Joseph Sittler" (Ph.D. Dissertation, Louvain, 1977); Sonia Groenewold, "Theologian Joseph Sittler, 83, Dies," *The Lutheran* (ELCA) 1, no. 2 (27 January 1988): 22-23; Joseph Sittler, *Grace Notes and Other Frag-*

in 1927 with a major in biology and English, and from Hamma Divinity School in 1930. From 1930 to 1943 he served as pastor of Messiah Lutheran Church in Cleveland Heights, Ohio. While a pastor, he continued his education at the University of Heidelberg, at Case Western Reserve, and at Oberlin Theological School. In 1943 he became professor of Systematic Theology at Chicago Lutheran Seminary in Maywood, Illinois. While teaching at Maywood, Sittler studied at the University of Chicago (although he never did complete a Ph.D.).

Preaching at the University of Chicago's Rockefeller Chapel one Sunday in the early 1950s, Sittler cited Fairfield Osborne's *Our Plundered Planet,* one of several postwar books raising environmental concerns about the booming American postwar economy and its plethora of new technologies.[5] Sittler began with a forceful statement of the spiritual relevance of such concerns:

> It is necessary for the preservation of man's body, the sanity of his mind, and the salvation of his soul that he be related to nature in a right way. The quest for this proper relationship is an ancient one, and two contemporary discussions have brought it to the attention of our day. The title of one of these books, *Our Plundered Planet,* may suggest an exaggerated sense of crisis, and the discussion may in detail be open to criticism. But the principal problem is not. That problem is this: When man relates himself to nature as one who plunders her, he ultimately destroys what he uses. When nature is regarded only as an inexhaustible warehouse of oil, ore, timber and all other materials, then she is ruthlessly plundered. This problem cannot be solved by economics, for the disposition to plunder is not an economic problem at all. It is the creation of a lust grown rapacious; and lust and rapacity are problems of the spirit of man before they ever become events of economic history.[6]

---

ments, ed. Robert M. Herhold and Linda Marie Delloff (Philadelphia: Fortress Press, 1981), pp. 125-26.

5. Fairfield Osborne, *Our Plundered Planet* (Boston: Little, Brown and Co., 1948).

6. Joseph Sittler, "God, Man and Nature," *The Pulpit* 24, no. 3 (August 1953): 16 (published under the rather banal editorial blurb, "A timely sermon for summer").

The essays in this volume, as well as additional pieces listed in the bibliography, document Sittler's continuing preoccupation with this theme throughout his career.[7]

Sittler not only recognized resource conservation as a serious societal problem at a time when such concern tended to be dismissed as irresponsible fear-mongering,[8] but also saw it as a fundamentally *spiritual* — and thus theological — problem. Thus we have, in Sittler himself, an indication of how an earth-affirming theology has roots that go deeper than the desire to defend Christianity against the charge that it is ultimately responsible for the environmental crisis.

Nature and Grace

If Sittler had only been one of the first of many theologians to address the environmental issue, the writings in this volume might be of merely historical interest. However, Sittler had a distinctive approach to the subject. His rubric of choice for reflecting on the environmental problematic was the ancient theological dialectic of nature and grace. Immediately following the paragraph already quoted, Sittler sounded what was to be the keynote of his theology of ecology throughout his career:

7. Although the latest piece included here is from 1975, Sittler continued to reflect on these issues until his death in 1987. By the mid-1970s, Sittler's failing eyesight meant that he could no longer write out his theological musings, but had to rely on his considerable gifts of memory and extemporaneous eloquence. Thus, most of his publications from his retirement from the University of Chicago Divinity School in 1973 until his death were in fact transcriptions by others of his oral remarks. With the exception of "Nature and Grace in Romans 8" we have not included such transcriptions; while they contain much that is of interest and testify to the continuing vitality of Sittler's mind, he was not able to rework and refine them to his satisfaction in the way that he could his written compositions. For examples of these later transcribed works, see Joseph Sittler, *Gravity and Grace: Reflections and Provocations,* ed. Linda Marie Delloff (Minneapolis: Augsburg, 1986) and idem, "The Sittler Speeches," in *Center for the Study of Campus Ministry Yearbook 1977-78,* ed. Phil Schroeder (Valparaiso, Ind.: Valparaiso University, 1978), pp. 10-61.

8. See Hans Huth, *Nature and the American: Three Centuries of Changing Attitudes* (Lincoln: University of Nebraska Press, 1957), pp. 193-94.

Many of you must be reading with delight and instruction the other book that bears, although indirectly, upon our problem — Rachel Carson's *The Sea Around Us.* What sets this book apart from and above similar descriptions is a quality of wonder in the manner of it. The lady writes of plankton and the turning of the tides with a positive, spiritual grace. She stands beside her massive and venerable subject as a receiving child, reverent before its enduring mystery. To stand in wonder before what I did not make and whose processes and rhythms I can neither alter nor arrest may be a means of grace, a path to understanding.[9]

Sittler deliberately cast environmental ethics in terms of highly charged religious doctrines central to Christian, particularly Lutheran, piety — namely, grace and christology — rather than in terms of teachings that are less central (but more commonly connected to environmental concerns), such as creation and stewardship. The "Commencement Address" reprinted in this volume, delivered at Maywood on May 8, 1959, is an early expression of Sittler's effort to develop a dynamic, capacious theology of nature and grace. "Nature" in this essay is not merely "human nature," the motions and structures of the human spirit as tending toward or away from God, but also encompasses the whole of society and the physical environment, "artificial" as well as "natural." Likewise, the reality of grace is not simply that divine acceptance whereby an individual's sins are forgiven, but a disturbing, even violent energy that is a living and active presence in the whole of creation. It is grace not against or above or identical with nature, but grace *transforming* nature.[10] The social and cosmic turbulence of grace surfaces again and is amplified in such later reflections as "The Role of Spirit" and "Nature and Grace in Romans 8."

9. "God, Man and Nature," 16. All but the first two paragraphs (quoted in full here and above) of this sermon were incorporated into Joseph Sittler, "A Theology for Earth," *The Christian Scholar* 37 (September 1954): 367-74. (Reprinted in this volume, pp. 20-31.) The sermon continues with the sentence beginning, "There is a meaning in the nonhuman world of nature . . ." in that essay (see p. 24 of this volume) and includes about half of the material in section II (excluding the portions referring to neo-orthodoxy, Keats, and Goethe's *Faust*) and all of the material in sections III and IV.

10. See James M. Gustafson, *Protestant and Roman Catholic Ethics: Prospects for Rapprochement* (Chicago: University of Chicago Press, 1978), pp. 120-25.

The Cosmic Christ

Grace, for Christian theology and experience, is focused in the person of Jesus Christ, "the point, as it were, at which God becomes historically present, radiant, incandescent, available for our knowing and historical reality."[11] Thus, to examine ecological issues in the context of nature and grace raises the question of Christ and the cosmos. Sittler not only raised that question as few others in this century had (notably Teilhard de Chardin, whose works were at that time only beginning to be widely known), but he did so in the widest forum available: the World Council of Churches. Sittler thought big. It is as if so vast a problem could only be effectively and adequately addressed within the whole global Christian communion itself, and only such an all-embracing topic as humanity's relationship to the universe in the light of Christ could provide a common ground upon which the far-flung and diverse churches could pursue the unity they sought.

After joining the Federated Theological Faculty of the University of Chicago in 1957 as a professor of biblical theology, Sittler continued the active participation in ecumenical and denominational studies that he had begun at Maywood. From 1951 to 1966 he was a member of the Faith and Order Commission of the World Council of Churches, and a delegate to several Faith and Order Conferences and WCC Assemblies. Sittler's ecumenical involvement was, by his own account, the crucible for the maturation of his thought as well as a forum for its expression.[12] "Called to Unity," his address to the World Council of Churches General Assembly in New Delhi in 1961, was by far the most public and influential of his statements, and is widely regarded as a milestone in ecumenical theology.[13] In that address, Sittler appealed to the witness of the

11. Sittler, *Gravity and Grace*, p. 19.

12. Joseph Sittler, *Essays on Nature and Grace* (Philadelphia: Fortress Press, 1972), pp. 7-11. (That chapter is not reprinted in this volume.)

13. For studies placing the address in the context of the ecumenical movement, see Conrad Simonson, *The Christology of the Faith and Order Movement,* Oekumenische Studien, no. 10 (Leiden: E. J. Brill, 1972), especially pp. 94-95 and 179; Moira Creede, "Logos and Lord," especially pp. 94-98; and J. A. Lyons, *The Cosmic Christ in Origen and Teilhard de Chardin: A Comparative Study,* Oxford Theological Monographs (New York: Oxford University Press, 1982), pp. 59-68. For a contemporary perspective, see "The Ecumenical Century," *Time* magazine, 8 Dec. 1961, pp. 76-80.

New Testament — especially in the letter to the Colossians — to "the cosmic Christ" to ground his claim that the sphere of grace and redemption can be no smaller than the sphere of creation itself. Only a christology of such dimensions can adequately address the depth and magnitude of contemporary humans' capacities to know, to manipulate — and to destroy — the creation. In contrast to some "green theologies" current today, Sittler argued not for a shift from "redemption-centered" theology to "creation-centered" theology, but for an expansion of the *circumference* of redemption to embrace the whole of creation.

The address resonated with the theological orientations and concerns of some in his audience: Eastern Orthodox, whose cosmic christology and spirituality were powerful influences on Sittler's own thinking; Anglicans whose theology placed special stress on the incarnation; and members of Free Churches who appreciated its ethical implications. Some hearers were excited by the new theological directions opened up by the address, while others were unsure of what Sittler was saying, or were put off by his somewhat idiosyncratic terminology. Existentialist theologians were particularly critical of Sittler's cosmological focus as too remote from human experience and a temptation to irresponsible speculation and mysticism, just as some Lutherans were suspicious of its lack of traditional language of sin and justification and the novelty of its expansive understanding of grace.[14] As Paul Santmire has said, "The response to Sittler's address at New Delhi was mainly one of polite indifference, along with some shocked resistance on the part of representatives from the then reigning theological guilds in Europe."[15]

Undeterred, Sittler continued to argue for rethinking the relationship between nature and grace in a contemporary context. It was almost another decade before that relationship — in the form of the relationship between Christian faith and the environmental crisis — entered the consciousness of a significant number of theologians.

14. Simonson, *The Christology of the Faith and Order Movement*, p. 179.
15. H. Paul Santmire, "Toward a Christology of Nature: Claiming the Legacy of Joseph Sittler and Karl Barth," *Dialog* 34 (fall 1995): 270.

The Care of the Earth

Sittler's interpretation of nature and grace, defined by the belief that the whole of creation is capable of bearing the grace of God's presence, had a definite ethical import. Humans should deal with creation with reverence and respect, for abuse and manipulation of the earth are, in a profound sense, dis-graceful. This is the heart of Sittler's theology of "the care of the earth." Sittler was already reflecting on these issues while at Maywood (as early as 1953, as we have seen) but they came into full flower during his tenure at Chicago, when ecological issues came to the forefront of public consciousness — and even began to penetrate the inner sanctums of academic theology and the churches.

The year before his New Delhi address, Sittler preached on "The Care of the Earth" at Eisenhower Chapel, Pennsylvania State University.[16] As with the 1953 sermon on "God, Man and Nature," the scripture for the sermon was ostensibly Psalm 104, Sittler's beloved "ecological doxology." But the real text was Richard Wilbur's poem, "Advice to a Prophet" (published in *The New Yorker* in early April, 1959). Sittler returned to that poem again and again to illuminate the deep interior filaments binding the human spirit to the natural, "nonhuman" world. Here, he used it as a springboard for articulating an environmental ethic based on his theology of nature and grace. The proper use of creation depends on its proper enjoyment: "Abuse is use without grace; it is always a failure in the counterpoint of use and enjoyment."[17] The same "ethic of appreciation" appears, with some changes in terminology, in later writings such as "Ecological Commitment as Theological Responsibility" and the final chapter of *Essays on Nature and Grace*.[18] In the latter, Sittler speaks of a "gracious regard" for the natural world which corresponds to the reality of that world as the "theater of God's grace." Such gracious

16. Joseph Sittler, "The Care of the Earth," in *The Care of the Earth and Other University Sermons* (Philadelphia: Fortress Press, 1964), pp. 88-98. First published in: *Sermons to Intellectuals from Three Continents,* ed. Franklin Littell (New York: The Macmillan Company, 1963), pp. 18-28. (Reprinted in this volume, 51-58.)

17. Sittler, "The Care of the Earth," p. 97 (p. 57 in this volume).

18. Joseph Sittler, "Ecological Commitment as Theological Responsibility," *Zygon* 5 (June 1970): 175 (pp. 76-86 in this volume); *Essays on Nature and Grace* (Philadelphia: Fortress Press, 1972), pp. 121-22 (pp. 87-190 in this volume).

regard which respects the God-given integrity of creation, Sittler argued, is essential for the survival and flourishing of human beings as well as that of the natural world.

Much environmental advocacy, secular as well as religious, tends toward apocalypticism and moralism. But though he could speak powerfully of the torment of creation under human rapaciousness and disregard, Sittler grounded environmental responsibility in joy, appreciation, and celebration rather than in guilt, fear, and obligation.

Moreover, Sittler made an integral connection between the gospel and the capacity for such appreciation. For the Christian, it is Jesus Christ — as the "incandescent" focal point of God's self-giving — that discloses the fundamentally gracious character of all reality. But in Christ we are not only enabled to see the grace that inheres in the world as God's creation: God's action in Christ can give us the capacity to respond appropriately to creation-as-grace. The Gospel's declaration of God's acceptance of human beings in Christ liberates us from the anxious and egocentric grasping that strives to possess the world and plunder it. In a sermon on Paul's letter to the Philippians, published with "Care of the Earth" in a collection of his sermons in 1964, Sittler said,

> The Gospel of Jesus Christ proposes something shockingly new, and promises to deliver it to the man who accepts God's acceptance of him and understands himself and the world in the light of that center. This new bestowal to heart and understanding can be indicated in several propositions. . . .
>
> . . . When the world is received as a gift, a grace, an ever astounding wonder, it can be rightly enjoyed and justly used.
>
> . . . The peace of God as rest in God's acceptance of man is not a knowledge that the world can deliver, is not in fact concerned with the world at all. But this same peace ("not as the world giveth . . .") matures to turn upon the world with a deep constructive joy, knows that the peaceless world is precisely the place for the working out of God's will for truth, justice, purity, beauty.[19]

19. Joseph Sittler, "Peace as Rest and as Movement," in *The Care of the Earth and Other University Sermons,* pp. 38-39.

9

A few years earlier (1958), Sittler had published *The Structure of Christian Ethics,* which described Christian ethics as "the engendered response" to "the engendering deed" of God's action in Christ.[20] He did not there discuss environmental or conservation issues, but the themes of Christocentrism, the ecological structure of human life in society and nature, ethics as creative responsiveness, and Christian responsibility in and for the world God has created strongly resonate with both the New Delhi address and the Pennsylvania sermon.

The Ecology of Justice

Sittler continued to pursue and elaborate the themes of nature and grace and Christ and the cosmos through the later 1960s and early 1970s. During that period, "ecology" burst upon the popular consciousness and also found its way, alongside issues of war, race, and poverty, onto the agenda of Christian social concern. And it began — in part as a result of Lynn White Jr.'s essay — to be taken seriously as a subject for theological reflection in its own right. Sittler became less of a lone maverick and was increasingly acknowledged as a prophet and pioneer in articulating a theological basis for the growing Christian concern for the environment.

Modern thought — including and perhaps especially twentieth-century theology — has tended to posit dualisms of nature and history and nature and culture. The vision of the whole of creation as the theater of God's grace, however, allows no such polarization. "Nature" as Sittler used it encompassed not only the biological and physical world, but also the "artificial" world of art, architecture, technology, and social structures. Culture as well as "nature" is an integral part of creation, and therefore the products of human creativity are also capable of manifesting God's grace — but Sittler did not thereby reduce nonhuman nature to a mere prologue to or raw material for culture. "Ecology" was Sittler's metaphor for the complex webbed interconnectedness binding together church and world, self and society, spirit and nature, theology and cul-

20. Joseph Sittler, *The Structure of Christian Ethics* (Baton Rouge, La.: Louisiana State University Press, 1958; reprint, Library of Theological Ethics, Louisville, Ky.: Westminster/John Knox Press, 1998).

ture as the context within which Christian faith must find ever renewed expression.[21] He saw the natural environment as itself an integral factor in the shaping of culture, as his adaptation of Frederick Jackson Turner's "frontier hypothesis" — that the existence of an expanding frontier placed a peculiar stamp upon American culture — in "The Role of Spirit in Shaping the Future Environment" and other essays[22] shows. Elsewhere, he used the images of nature as the life-giving womb or placenta of human selfhood,[23] and he repeatedly pointed out how poets and writers seem to need to draw images from nature in order to express the depths of the human heart.[24]

Nor does the cosmically inclusive scope of grace permit an ultimate opposition between the environmental movement and movements for justice and equality. For Sittler, the struggles for ecological integrity and for racial and economic justice were manifestations of the same dynamic: The quest is for a gracious response to the grace encountered in God's creation, human and nonhuman. "What pollution is to natural ecology, injustice is to social ecology,"[25] namely, ". . . all abuse is a dis-

---

21. In spite of the title — and its occasional appearance on "theology and ecology" bibliographies — Sittler's *The Ecology of Faith* (Philadelphia: Muhlenberg Press, 1961) does not deal in any direct way with environmental issues. "Ecology" is used in the metaphorical sense just described, with specific attention to the situation of preaching in contemporary culture.

22. Joseph Sittler, "Eschatology and the American Mind" in *Charisteria Iohanni Kopp: Octogenario Oblata,* ed. J. Aunver and A. Vööbus (Stockholm: Estonian Theological Society in Exile, 1954); this essay, with portions of "The Role of Spirit," was partially incorporated into "An Aspect of American Religious Experience," *Proceedings of the Twenty-Sixth Annual Convention of the Catholic Theological Society of America* 26 (14-17 June 1971), which in turn was reprinted in slightly shortened form as "Space and Time in American Religious Experience," *Interpretation* 30 (January 1976): 44-51.

23. For "womb," see Joseph Sittler, "Two Temptations — Two Corrections," *National Parks and Conservation Magazine: The Environmental Journal* 45 (December 1971): 21; for "placenta," see Joseph Sittler, "The Scope of Christological Reflection," *Interpretation* 26 (July 1972): 333 (below, p. 196), and *Essays,* p. 108 (below, p. 175).

24. See, e.g., *Gravity and Grace,* p. 18, and *Essays,* pp. 107-8 (below, pp. 175-76).

25. [Joseph Sittler], "The New Creation," Chap. 6 in *The Human Crisis in Ecology,* ed. Franklin L. Jensen and Cedric W. Tilberg ([Philadelphia]: Board of Social Ministry, Lutheran Church in America, 1972, p. 96. (In the Foreword, p. ix, Sittler is credited with "primary responsibility" for this chapter, and it is definitely written in his distinctive style.)

tortion of right use, for persons as for all things. What is not regarded as a grace will be disgraced into use without care."[26] The theme recurs in "Ecological Commitment as Theological Responsibility," where Sittler rejects white paternalism in favor of the celebration of the grace-fulness of human ethnic diversity as a response to what he (unfortunately) terms "the black problem."[27] Sittler worked on the Lutheran Church in America's social statements on Racism (adopted 1964) as well as the one on "The Human Crisis in Ecology" (adopted 1972).[28] In the same way that he named human degradation of the nonhuman creation "blasphemy" in "Ecological Commitment"[29] and elsewhere, the proposed draft of the racism statement he helped draft declared that to pray for an end to hatred and prejudice while practicing racial discrimination was to commit an act of "devout blasphemy."[30]

A Rhetoric of Grace

Sittler's efforts to elaborate and defend his understanding of grace culminated in *Essays on Nature and Grace,* published in 1972. There he reviewed the career of the relationship between creation and grace from the Old Testament, through the New Testament, the Patristic period, the Reformation, the Enlightenment, and into the present. He argued for the necessity and possibility of relocating grace within a secularized, managed contemporary existence from which a sense for the world as graced seems to be excluded. Insights from scripture, tradition, and contemporary art and literature were brought to bear on the environmental crisis. One can see in *Essays* and other of his later writings (such as "The

26. Sittler, *Essays,* p. 133 n. 5 (below, p. 185, n. 77).

27. Sittler, "Ecological Commitment," pp. 180-81 (below, pp. 85-86).

28. Christa R. Klein with Christian D. von Dehsen, *Politics and Policy: The Genesis and Theology of Social Statements in the Lutheran Church in America* (Minneapolis: Fortress Press, 1989), pp. 46-53, 124-27.

29. Sittler, "Ecological Commitment," p. 179 (p. 84 in this volume).

30. Klein and von Dehsen, *Politics and Policy,* p. 48. Both formulations have been regarded by some as fudging the distinction between faith and ethics, law and Gospel — bifurcations for which Sittler had as little patience as he did for that of nature versus history. See ibid., pp. 48-50.

Scope of Christological Reflection") not only an elaboration of this thesis and the bolstering of his case with citations from Irenaeus, Athanasius, Augustine, and Eastern Orthodoxy, but efforts to respond to those who believed that he was going beyond what a sober study of the text could warrant or straying too far from traditional understandings.

He was also compelled to defend his style of writing and his use of literature. Inseparable from the content of his theology was his use of language — his own characteristic style, and his use of quotes from poetry and literature. He insisted that his loose, unsystematic manner of exposition was appropriate to the dynamic and interrelated character of experience, and to the concrete particularity of occasions of grace.[31]

Literary quotations were not just embellishments to his writing, but were integral to his own unique form of argumentation. Throughout his career, and on whatever topic, Sittler's theological explorations were informed by the human self- and world-knowledge expressed in secular culture as well as by scripture and tradition. In addition to literature, music (jazz as well as Bach) and contemporary architecture were of particular interest. Sittler drew upon these resources for the understanding of contemporary culture that theology and preaching need in order to meaningfully address men and women. The importance for Sittler of literature, as both a theological resource and a stylistic influence, was enormous.

Secular art and literature (especially poetry), was the "unaccredited witness" to the human longing for, and occasional experience of, God's grace. Sittler's use of secular art as a theological resource was itself testimony to his belief in the universal scope of grace. He sought to combine openness to the radically novel situation of modern thought and experience disclosed in these sources with a faithful obedience to the Bible and the traditions of the church, showing how each can enrich, deepen, and illuminate the other in a kind of "counterpoint." He was particularly attentive to the way in which each of these resources can inform us about human relationships to the natural world. He approached the environmental problematic by examining how human interiority is affected by our interactions with the world of nature — our "sense for the world" — and how that sense has been broadly and profoundly affected by science,

---

31. Sittler, *Essays,* pp. 2-5 (pp. 88-91 in this volume).

technology, and other forms of cultural change. Poetry articulated exactly his conviction that grace comes to us in the particular, concrete occasions of our ordinary lives. It is not surprising that the writers he credited with making him an "ecological theologian" were poets and nature writers: Richard Wilbur, Loren Eiseley, Rachel Carson, and Aldo Leopold.[32]

Like the poetry he quoted, his own writing employed vivid, earthy, almost palpable words and memorable turns of phrase. Few other theologians are such a pleasure to read for the way in which they express their insights. On the other hand, many have found Sittler's unsystematic mode of exposition frustrating, or at least challenging. It is often difficult to pin down one of his statements to a clear, determinate meaning. Yet therein lies much of their charm, and continuing value. Like the calculated ambiguity of a great work of art, Sittler's texts continually invite repeated reading, deeper reflection, further exploration. Sittler did not clearly articulate or rigorously argue for a particular theology of grace or cosmic christology, but he did powerfully communicate a sense of how the world would look if you had such a theology; he conveyed the feeling-tone of a truly incarnational Christianity. He evoked more than explained, suggested more than stated, pointed more than presented. His language operates at the level of the *perception* of value — or grace — in nature, not (as in much contemporary environmental philosophy) at the level of elaborating a non-anthropocentric conception or theory of value.[33]

Grace in Action

An ethic is worthless unless it gives rise to effective, concrete action. Sittler accordingly emphasized (in, for example, "Evangelism and the Care of the Earth") that the churches' witness to God's grace in creation must be in deeds as well as words. In the final chapter of *Essays on Nature and Grace,* he even proposed that the vision of the natural world as the

32. Sittler, "Creating a Rhetoric of Rural Values," p. 43.
33. On this distinction, see Erezim Kohák, "Perceiving the Good" in *The Wilderness Condition,* ed. Max Oelschlaeger (Washington. D.C.: Island Press, 1992), pp. 173-87.

creature and theater of grace can be pragmatically verified by the life-sustaining consequences of *acting* on that belief.[34]

What does Sittler suggest for how to practically address the ecological problematic? As *The Structure of Christian Ethics* makes clear, his response-oriented ethic is not amenable to codification in terms of principles or rules. The appropriate response to grace is as free and unpredictable as are the occasions of grace itself. Nonetheless, Sittler's theology directs our ethical attention in some specific directions.

The first direction follows directly from the immediately preceding section: attending to rhetoric. Sittler once commented that, while Christian theology has elaborated an elaborate rhetoric of sin, we have no correspondingly well-developed rhetoric of grace.[35] Devising such a rhetoric, which can foster the sort of "beholding" of creation that can call forth and direct appropriate responses, may be a necessary part of any effective effort to increase public motivation to care for creation. At a conference on rural values and the family farm crisis in the 1980s, Sittler suggested that

> You've got to help yourself find a way to verbalize what you mean by value, by loss, by re-cog-nition — that is, to bring, to articulate, statements about the unrecognized memories. . . .
>
> . . . The farther our children get from existential experience of the land, the more necessary this kind of rhetoric of grace about the world has got to be used in our preaching and teaching and in our listening.[36]

A second directive is to pay attention to the concrete particulars, including — and perhaps especially — the "little" things. Sittler's own environmental praxis (from what little I know of it) seems to have embodied the notion that grace is in the details: that the ordinary and even the seemingly trivial material elements of our daily life have a dimension of transcendent significance. For example, when I was parish secretary at Augustana Lutheran Church in Chicago (where Sittler had served

34. Sittler, *Essays*, pp. 120-22 (pp. 188-90 in this volume).
35. Sittler, "The Sittler Speeches," p. 44.
36. Sittler, "Creating a Rhetoric of Rural Values," p. 43.

as interim pastor after his retirement from the University of Chicago Divinity School in 1973, and which he continued to attend afterwards), Sittler would come by at Christmastime with a bottle of *good* wine for Holy Communion on Christmas Day. He did not have to explain his rationale; Christianity (as Archbishop Temple said) is a "materialistic" religion; the feast commemorating the Word become flesh is fitly celebrated with a symbol that sensorily communicates the goodness of the material creation.

The Lutheran School of Theology at Chicago, where Sittler remained as Distinguished Theologian in Residence until his death in 1987, is housed in a boxy structure of glass and black metal. "Bauhaus laid *this* egg," Sittler once remarked to me.[37] So Sittler did his best to humanize and naturalize it: at his insistence, a slight curve was added to the concrete bases of the pillars that support the building. He also lobbied to have the building's lawn punctuated by small flower garden plots. When my wife came to Chicago to attend seminary in the early 1980s, she came across Sittler planting crocuses in the L.S.T.C. lawn. By that point, he was too blind ever to be able to see them, but he knew that the flowers — like the architectural curves — would add a "grace note" to the grounds in the spring.

The environmental crisis will not be solved, and hardly ameliorated, by flower plantings, architectural details, or good wine at Christmas. Yet it cannot be adequately met without the sensibility that recognizes the value of the seemingly unimportant. "Grace note" was one of Sittler's favorite terms (it was the name of his column in the Chicago Lutheran Theological Seminary *Record* in the 1940s and 1950s, and of the parish newsletter begun during his pastorate at Augustana in the 1970s). According to Philip Hefner, a student of Sittler's, the term refers to one of the notes in a musical composition which are not part of the main melody, but which subtly signal the direction in which it is headed.[38] Grace, Sittler is telling us, often manifests itself to us in the same way: in the seemingly dispensable details and nuances that are

---

37. Sittler was far from condemning the Bauhaus style or modern architecture as such; it was a matter of the appropriate use of form and materials. See *Gravity and Grace*, pp. 90-93.

38. Philip Hefner, personal communication.

commonly regarded as separate from the "real business" of making a living, being productive, getting ahead. It could be argued that the environmental crisis is at least partly rooted precisely in our tendency to ignore such grace notes — to see environmental values and nonhuman creatures as at best incidental to the "real business" of human salvation or economic progress, rather than as vital clues to the meaning of God's purposes for the whole creation, and of our place within it.

Further, Sittler urges us to remember that creation is a dynamic and interrelated whole. We cannot hope to restore a lost "golden age" of harmonious human-nature relationships, nor can we put the brakes on all social or technological change. But neither are we to blindly swallow every promise made by those who speak for "development" or "progress" at the price of destroying what we know to be good and valuable. We cannot pursue ecological integrity apart from social justice, but neither can we treat nature as merely a human possession and raw material for projects of human progress or liberation. Our environmental ethic must enable us both to preserve the integrity and diversity of the earth and its creatures, and to use them gently and respectfully; and we must cultivate the sensitivity and discernment to the concrete particulars of specific situations so that we enact forms of preservation or use that are appropriate to a given case. We cannot set nature against humanity, or the cultural against the natural, but we must appreciate and enjoy the unique graces that belong to each. In the face of unprecedented situations we need to develop creative responses that are faithful both to our inheritance from the past and to the promise of the future; we need to find new modes of symbiosis between human beings and the rest of nature that are true to the divine intentions for the unity of creation.

Sittler's directives for environmental action are more matters of motivation, attention, and framing rather than formulation of rules or goals. Sittler urges us to respond out of wonder, joy, delight, and amazement rather than out of fear or a sense of obligation; to view the world, at least in part, through the lenses of poetry and art as well as science and experience; to pay attention to nuances of the biblical and everyday language that speaks the world to us, and to the concrete particulars that make up the rich and subtle texture of creation. Sittler's writings also suggest that we try "reframing" environmental issues not, or not only, in terms of values, interests, or rights, but in terms of *grace*. How might our ecological perceptions be changed by viewing the concrete instances of the fecundity, integrity, beauty, diversity, and dynamism of creation — including human beings and their culture — as manifestations of grace, as gifts pointing beyond themselves to their source in the ultimate and all-encompassing reality of the free, faithful, and self-giving love of God? What creative responses might be made possible by viewing particular environmental problems as occasions for new embodiments of grace in nature? What potentialities for life-enhancing symbiosis might appear if we truly believed that God, humanity, and nature are, in Sittler's words, "meant for each other"?[39]

Why Read Sittler Now?

Sittler remained on the faculty of the Divinity School until his retirement in 1973. In spite of his failing eyesight, he continued to reflect theologically in public speaking and private conversation until the year of his death. Most of his publications during this period were in fact transcripts of interviews or talks he gave without benefit of notes. He was Distinguished Professor in Residence at the Lutheran School of Theology at Chicago from 1980 until his death from cancer in December of 1987, at age 83.[40] Characteristically, he made the experience of aging and approaching death a subject for his latest meditations — but he also addressed the global threat of nuclear war.[41]

Sittler's loose and allusive style sometimes makes it difficult to determine exactly what he thought or meant by a particular word, phrase, or sentence. Nonetheless, his writings provide paths to follow, directions to explore, a sensibility to strive to emulate. They drive us back to the *experience* of nature as creation, nature as graced, especially as attested by poetry, art, and literature; and to the rich resonances of the language and imagery of the Bible and the Christian tradition. His writings are a good

39. Sittler, "A Theology for Earth," p. 373 (p. 30 in this volume).

40. Kenan Heise, "Rev. Joseph Sittler, Theology Prof," *Chicago Tribune,* 30 December 1987, sec. 2, p. 11; "Rev. Joseph Sittler, 83, Theologian and Author," *Chicago Sun-Times,* 30 December 1987, p. 56.

41. Joseph Sittler, "Moral Discourse in a Nuclear Age;" idem, "Aging: A Summing Up and a Letting Go," in *Gravity and Grace,* pp. 108-18; 119-27.

antidote to the repetitiveness, dullness, and stridency of much Christian ecotheological writing. During his life, Sittler was "mentor to many" as their pastor, teacher, and colleague. Through his writings, he has been and can continue to be a mentor to many more.

This volume is offered in the hope that the encounter with these essays will be productive of fresh insights as we join Sittler in probing the resources of the Christian tradition, brooding over the troubles and turmoil of society and nature, and beholding, in delighted amazement, the shining forth of God's grace in the variegated creation.

Editorial Note

The essays reprinted here originally appeared with varying degrees of footnoting and documentation. To aid the reader and give the essays a more consistent style in this regard, we have tried to provide additional footnotes and more complete citation information where possible. Where we do not know the exact source used by Sittler for a reference or quotation, we have sometimes given a standard edition or used an edition cited by him elsewhere. We have also occasionally corrected typographical errors appearing in the original publications and, very rarely, made slight changes where we strongly suspect that Sittler's intended words were altered in publication. We have refrained from making other changes, such as making the language more gender-inclusive or correcting the somewhat garbled astrophysics on p. 216.

Original publication data for these essays can be found in the bibliography at the end of this book. Essays reprinted here are marked in the bibliography with an asterisk.

[1954]

A Theology for Earth

Within five years there have appeared notable works dealing with the relation of Christianity to culture. Professors Reinhold and Richard Niebuhr, Professor Richard Kroner, Professor John Bennett, and others have produced careful studies. As a grateful reader of these works, I feel incompetent directly to address myself to the problem which in them is so amply and responsibly discussed. I should, in fact, not be moved to utter a word on the subject were it not for the invitation to make a contribution to the pages of *The Christian Scholar.* Having, however, accepted such an invitation, I propose to discharge its responsibility in this way: To set down as clearly as I can the substance of what I have missed in the contemporary discussions; and, to make an effort to articulate a vague but general discontent.

What I am setting down here, therefore, is not by any means a positive criticism of what I have read, nor a systematic substitute for works which I have not the brains to emulate! This article is rather in the nature of a familiar essay, a verbalization of various ponderings about this matter of the relation of Christian faith and nature. I adopt this mode for two reasons: It permits, in fact invites, the kind of mental and emotional meandering which at the moment is the only just representation of my thought and feeling; and it has by virtue of discursive form no resemblance to such a calculated theological utterance as commonly calls forth more refutation than deliberation. There is a third reason, too, but I state it here in a soft voice for I am a little ashamed of it, and would not dare mention it at all save in the friendly company of fellow-teachers who have invited and presumably will read these lines. I am not an architectural systematic theologian at all! When I look at systematically wrought works like those of Tillich, Aulen, Niebuhr — my first reaction is one of thundering astonishment! Examination of what they have done is a response secondary to my admiration for the fact that they have done it at all! What I have of intellect is so permeated by its involvement with sense, emotion, and remembrance — a feeling for the blend of consonance and dissonance in life, an intuition of wholeness, and a sense of humor called forth by all vigorous proposals of the partial, that it will forever be beyond my compass to produce a system about anything!

In the instance of the discussion presently being carried forward in these pages, however, I cannot feel that the admission of such an essay as this is either irrelevant or impertinent. For it is precisely in this area that the systematicians have historically made pretensions of the most massive asininity, betrayed the most broad-backed insensitivity, and have been most blind to the revelatory fact. Culture is a function of spirit, and spirit's productions are always a fusion of freedom and material. The man who discusses culture only in terms of its palpable achievements does violence to the prior thrust toward expression which is the fire of all culture, and the man who discusses culture in extrapolation from its achievements moves about in a wide windy abode where the actual carriers and creators of culture would gasp for air. All systematic constructions have got to be preceded in my opinion by exposure to the creative chaos, the promising apprehension of emergent meaning as I hope in a moment to deploy it. For, "All that's passing is but sign and symbol," and for the appreciative grasp of symbolic meaning an open imagination is necessary.

We have given, then, a Professor of Christian Theology. The poor man, unless he be a hod-carrier for a closed tradition or have a human soul carved of alabaster, will be alive and responsible to double vocation: a vocation to work at the task of Christian theology, and a vocation to citizenship in the twentieth century. The first vocation binds him to history, history in general and ecclesiastical history in particular. In obedience to this first vocation he must always look back and look down with responsibility, with gratitude, and in complete teachableness. In obedience to his second vocation (and this vocation is from God, too — for he was born a man on earth before he was called to a professorship on a theological faculty), he must look his day full in the face, participate in the joyous thud of ideas in collision, listen to its multiple voices, become a creature of its vitalities and torments. But as a man of this day he cannot avoid coming to terms with the fact that what he has to communicate is so radically strange to the symbolical mentality of his time that he can scarce find hooks to hang it on, allusions to convey it with, or a matrix of association to bear it forth. The full extent of this destruction of symbols of communication in our time is described by Suzanne Langer in her *Philosophy in a New Key:*

> The mind, like all other organs, can draw its sustenance only from the surrounding world; and metaphysical symbols spring from reality. Such adaptation always requires time, habit, tradition, and intimate knowledge of the way of life. If, now, the field of our unconscious symbolic orientation is suddenly plowed up by tremendous changes in the external world and in the social order, we lose our hold, our convictions, and therewith our effectual purposes. In modern civilization there are two great threats to mental security: the new mode of living, which has made the old nature symbols alien to our mind, and the new mode of working, which makes personal activity meaningless, unacceptable to the hungry imagination.[1]

I

This uprooted life with its resultant desymbolization of our culture may be illustrated on a very common level. Most American people have no home that is the symbol of their childhood: their unfolding memory does not gather the felt stuff of common experience about a core-place. That in life which blooms with significance — granted a material thread of continuity — is hopelessly blasted by the mores of our tran-

---

1. Suzanne Langer, *Philosophy in a New Key: A Study in the Symbolism of Reason, Rite and Art* (Cambridge, Mass.: Harvard University Press, 1942), p. 291.

sient existence. A young man is born in Ohio, goes to school in Massa-
chusetts, marries a girl from Virginia. Their first child is born in the
Bronx, baptized in a church that knew them not as children and will not
see them in old age. The young father goes to work in Manhattan for a
corporation chartered in Delaware, writes advertisements for the consumption of people he never sees and for whom he has no immediate responsibility. And at any time he may and probably will be ordered to
move in two weeks to Dallas, Texas, there to pick up certain contacts
(how expressive a word, that, for the way we moderns meet one another!)
that will be useful to him when after two years he is transferred to Seat-
tle, Washington. This brutalizing rootlessness of the life of an increasing
number of our citizenry produces a creeping symbolic starvation; the
very matrix of small meaningfulness in life which can become the womb
of profounder and vaster structures of meaning is rendered anemic, becomes sour and brittle.

The response and tactic of the Roman Church as she confronts the
convulsion and transformation of this cultural era is astonishingly subtle
and multiform. She moves around it; not, to be sure, in order to leave it
or to repudiate it, but in order to enfold it by indirection. Out of her
store of enormous practical wisdom she knows how to seduce with the
symbolism of Grace the gathering discontents and spiritual malnu-
tritions of the modern man. Her theology remains what for four hundred years it has been; but her theology is not the visible hand she holds
out to the world. What she does hold out is the mighty fascination of
her symbolical richness. She knows that logic follows being; and if entire areas of being can be meaningfully infused with overtones of Grace,
purpose, love, and salvation her theology will have ample time to add
the requisite calcium to the developing embryo.

Roman Christianity relates itself to the contemporary common life
by the thoroughly sophisticated and sinuous character of its practical re-
ligiousness. It has vast and varied provisions for the life of prayer and
praise, disciplined ways of meditation and adoration, so delicately at-
tuned to habitude. Sanctification, substantialized in discipline and sacrament, operates by a process of osmosis to permeate with churchly
meaning all extremes of man's life — the life of the faithful servant who
mops the marble tile before the altar rail and the life of the Monsignor
who exercises his pastoral office amid the glossy surroundings of a tele-

vision studio. Within the many-roomed and sprawling estate of Mother Church there is nothing that cannot find a bed for the night, a taper lit, and a square meal.

In my own vocation as a teacher of Christian theology, I have felt a deepening uneasiness about that tendency in biblical theology, generally known as neo-orthodoxy, whereby the promises, imperatives, and dynamics of the Gospel are declared in sharp and calculated disengagement from the stuff of earthly life. For it is, after all, asserted that "the spirit beareth witness *with* our spirit that we are the children of God" (Romans 8:16). This declaration, to be sure, dare not be understood merely as the Holy Spirit's seconding of the motion of the spirit of man. There are adequate denials of that interpretation throughout the Scriptures, particularly in the Fourth Gospel and in the very Epistle in which this statement occurs. But neither dare this activity of God's Spirit be interpreted as the Spirit bearing witness only *against* us, in total irrelevancy to our spirit. For there is a sort of *negative congruence* between the felt antinomies and ambiguities of man's spirit, and the ingressive activity of the Holy Spirit. The people that walk in darkness behold a great light. That light is not squeezed out of darkness by virtue of determination to transform darkness into light by the sheer alchemy of aspiration and felt need. But darkness *realized* is creative of a receptive theater for the drama of God's salvatory action in Christ; there is a *dynamics* of damnation, a process of perdition that may be used of the Spirit in such a way as to constitute of it a positive preparation for the Gospel.

> Brief glimpses have I had of Heaven
> Through the little holes in hell!

II

Alongside of this dis-ease with neo-orthodoxy's almost proud repudiation of the earth, and the feeling of some profound biblical promise distorted thereby, has gone another — a feeling that earth, fallen, cloven, and sinful — because given of God, capable in spite of all of becoming the cradle in which Christ is laid, is a transparency for the Holy. There is a meaning in the nonhuman world of nature: reason asserts it and all

24

great art bears it witness. When the artist Cézanne paints a barrel of apples, he shows it bathed with a light which is more like a luminous nimbus than even the softest light of autumn sun. And when Willy Loman in Arthur Miller's play, *Death of a Salesman,* digs and manures and cares for a pathetic patch of sooty earth beside the door of his house in the Bronx, he is seeking for some green and fertile token of meaning in stubborn nature — something that will speak back to the brittle and sterile perdition of his soul. When theology does not acknowledge and soberly come to terms with the covert significance of the natural, the world of nature is not silenced. "Nature is never spent," cries Gerard Manley Hopkins in a famous poem, "There lives the dearest freshness deep-down things."

> The world is charged with the grandeur of God
> It will flame out like shining from shook foil![2]

When Christian orthodoxy refuses to articulate a theology for earth, the clamant hurt of God's ancient creation is not thereby silenced. Earth's voices, recollective of her lost grace and her destined redemption, will speak through one or another form of naturalism. If the Church will not have a theology *for* nature, then irresponsible but sensitive men will act as midwives for nature's unsilenceable meaningfulness, and enunciate a theology of nature. For earth, not man's mother — which is a pagan notion — but, as St. Francis profoundly surmised, man's sister, sharer of his sorrow and scene and partial substance of his joys, unquenchably sings out her violated wholeness, and in groaning and travailing awaits with man the restoration of all things.

This theme — perilous if pursued outside Christian faith — when pursued within the context of the faith makes a man sensitive and restless under flashes of insight which have arisen within the uttered experience of our common life. While I cannot at the moment aspire to shape the systematic structure of Christian meaning out of these insights, I know that I shall as a son of earth know no rest until I have seen how

2. Gerard Manley Hopkins, "God's Grandeur," in *The Poems of Gerard Manley Hopkins,* ed. W. H. Gardner and N. H. Mackenzie, 4th edition (Oxford: Oxford University Press, 1967).

they too can be gathered up into a deeper and fuller understanding of my faith. For these earthly protestations of earth's broken but insistent meaning have about them the shine of the holy, and a certain "theological guilt" pursues the mind that impatiently rejects them.

The inner pattern of this theological guilt is suggested by analogy with the young English poet of the early nineteenth century. In passionate pursuit of a proper poetic idiom for the communication of the crowding and impetuous stuff of his perceptions and feelings, the young John Keats played experimentally on the massive organ of his mighty predecessor, John Milton. He tried desperately to shape the inflammable stuff of his abounding genius to the grave and solemn covalences of the older man. The opening lines of *Hyperion* are an instance of how successfully he actually did contrive to make his muse speak Miltonically. But the poem is unfinished because Keats came gradually to know that what was natural to Milton was false to Keats! — that the sonorous measures of the elder poet were alien to the incandescent lyricism of his own inspiration. His moment of liberation and return is marked by the line, "The poetry of earth is never dead. . . ."[3]

A second analogy will serve not only to suggest again the claim of earth upon our Christian thought, but will provide a transition to what I want finally to suggest. In his *Goethe's Faust* Professor Harold Jantz, discussing the Easter-Walk passage in the drama, declares of Faust as follows:

He has neglected the tangible and attainable of this earth for the intangible and unattainable. Had he pushed this tendency to the extreme he contemplated, with suicide on that critical night, his failure would have been complete, for the very reason that he failed with the Earth Spirit: he was attempting a direct approach without the necessary understanding which the full experience of life on earth would have given him. As he raises the cup to his lips to force the release of his heaven-tending soul from its earthly limitations so that it might soar up to its desired insights, he hears the first bells of Easter morning and the song, "Christ is risen." Christ's greatest tri-

3. John Keats, "On the Grasshopper," in *Poetical Works,* ed. H. W. Garrod (Oxford: Clarendon Press, 1958), p. 49.

umph comes with His resumption of His fleshly body; He will once more walk with it on earth and then ascend with it to heaven, thus completing his victory over eternal death. With Faust's childhood memories and his deep-seated, intuitive grasp of Christian symbol, he senses that a violent rejection of the earthly will not bring him the desired spiritual freedom. The Word itself was made flesh and dwelt among us. Man cannot fulfill his divine destiny on earth by a denial of the flesh. It is symbolical that Faust refrains from the folly of seeking to leave the material on the festival day of Christ's reunion with the material. He lowers the cup and says in simple, meaningful conclusion, "the earth has me again."[4]

III

There are, in the large, two ways by which man has sought to do justice to the realm of meaning in the natural world; two forms of relationship by which he has sought to come to terms with what he cannot silence.

First, nature can be subsumed under man. Materially, that is, she is reduced to a resource for his needs; spiritually she is envisioned as only an unreplying theater for his proud and pathetic life. Nature, that is to say, is divested of her own and proper life and is invested with the goods, the values, and the ends of man. Her life, infinite in richness and variety, is made a symbolic companion of man's life; and all the moods and shadows, the pride and the pathos, the ambiguity and the sudden delight of man's life is read in her mobile face.

Another effort exists alongside of this one and is its exact opposite: Man is subsumed under nature. This relationship gains in persuasiveness when man's spiritual powers, confused by their own perplexities, are conjoined with a fresh mastery of natural forces to serve his clamant lusts. In such a case man abdicates — and celebrates his shameful abdication by perverse delight in that which overcomes him.

Neither of these ways is adequate, and man knows it. For neither one does justice either to the amplitude and glory of man's spirit or to the

4. Harold Jantz, *Goethe's Faust as a Renaissance Man: Parallels and Prototypes* (Princeton: Princeton University Press, 1951), p. 109

felt meaningfulness of the world of nature. Christian theology, obedient to the biblical account of nature, has asserted a third possible relationship: that man ought properly stand alongside nature as her cherishing brother, for she too is God's creation and bears God's image.

When, for instance, one reads the 104th Psalm, one becomes conscious that this Psalm speaks of the relationship between man and nature in a quite new way. The poetical naiveté of the images must not blind us to the majestic assertions of the song. In this Psalm nothing in the world of man and nothing in the world of nature is either independent or capable of solitary significance. Every upward-arching phenomenon, every smallest thing, is derived from the fountain of life. Light is a garment the deity wears and the heavens a curtain for his dwelling. The heavy voice of the thunder is his rebuke; the springs are his largess to every beast of the field. The trees and the birds, the grass and the cattle, the plump vine and wine that gladdens the heart of man are all bound together in a bundle of grace.

Yet this mighty structure of process and vitality, this complex of given creatureliness in which "the sun knows its time for setting" — all hangs by a slender thread. Natural and mortal life are incandescent with meaning because of their mutual dependence upon the will of the ultimate and Holy one. The Psalm says,

> These all look to thee,
>> to give them their food in due season.
> When thou givest to them, they gather it up;
>> when thou openest thy hand, they are filled with good things.
> When thou hidest thy face, they are dismayed;
>> when thou takest away their breath, they die
>>> and return to their dust.
> When thou sendest forth thy Spirit, they are created;
>> and thou renewest the face of the ground.
>
> (verses 27-30)

Here is a holy naturalism, a matrix of grace in which all things derive significance from their origin, and all things find fulfillment in praise. Man and nature live out their distinct but related lives in a complex that recalls the divine intention as that intention is symbolically related on the first page of the Bible. Man is placed, you will recall, in the garden of earth. This garden he is to tend as God's other creation — not to use as a godless warehouse or to rape as a tyrant.

IV

Today, man is no longer related to nature in God's intended way. Nor can he from within himself find his way to the blasted garden of joy. That, fundamentally, is why he plunders what he ought to tend; why he finds in nature sardonic images of his own perversion, and at the same time cannot avert his eyes from his violated sister who is heard groaning "in pain and travail until now" (Romans 8:22).

"By the Word of the Lord," so we read, "the heavens were made" (Psalm 33:6). But this Word ignored is not thenceforth silent; this Word repudiated is not therefore quiescent. Is it possible that the Creator-Word, by whom all things were made, should be driven from his field by us? The central assertion of the Bible is that he has not been so driven, but rather drives, loves, and suffers his world toward restoration. It is of the heart of the Christian faith that this mighty, living, acting, restoring Word actually identified himself with his cloven and frustrated creation which groans in travail. "The Word became flesh and dwelt among us" (John 1:14). To what end? That the whole cosmos in its brokenness — man broken from man, man in solitude and loneliness broken from Holy Communion with his soul's fountain and social communion with his brother — might be restored to wholeness, joy, and lost love.

One finds nowhere in the Bible that strange assertion which one hears almost everywhere else — that God is concerned to save men's souls! How richly, rather, is restoration there presented in terms of men's material involvement in the world of nature. Real blindness is given sight, real hands of helplessness are restored, real death is overcome, real legs enable a paralytic to walk. God is the undeviating materialist. "He likes material; he invented it." I know no soul save an embodied soul, I have no body save this one born of other bodies, and there is no such thing as a man outside the created context of other men; therefore it is written that "God so loved the world" (John 3:16).

God — man — nature! These three are meant for each other, and restlessness will stalk our hearts and ambiguity our world until their cleavage is redeemed. What a holy depth of meaning lies waiting for our understanding in that moment portrayed on the last evening of Christ's life: "And he took bread, and when he had given thanks he broke it and gave to them, saying, 'This is my body.' . . . Likewise also the wine . . . 'this cup is the new covenant in my blood'" (Luke 22: 19-20; 1 Corinthians 11:23b-25).

Here in one huge symbol are God and man and nature together. Bread and wine, the common earthy stuff of our life when we have it, and of death when we've lost it. Both in the hands of the restoring God-man!

The problem of material is not a material problem, for man is in it, and he complicates every problem. The problem of enough to eat is not ultimately an economic problem. For as man confronts the marvelous richness of the earth he can use these riches or abuse them. Which of these he chooses is a matter not soluble by mere planning. For there will never be enough for both love and lust!

V

The largest, most insistent, and most delicate task awaiting Christian theology is to articulate such a theology for nature as shall do justice to the vitalities of earth and hence correct a current theological naturalism which succeeds in speaking meaningfully of earth only at the cost of repudiating specifically Christian categories. Christian theology cannot advance this work along the line of an orthodoxy — neo or old — which celebrates the love of heaven in complete separation from man's loves in earth, which abstracts commitment to Christ from relevancy to those loyalties of earth that are elemental to being. Any faith in God which shall be redemptive and regenerative in actuality dare not be alien to the felt ambiguities of earth or remain wordless in the resounding torments of history and culture. For the earth is not merely a negative illustration of the desirability of heaven!

Such positive theological work, it seems to me, must operate with the event of the Incarnation with a depth and amplitude at least as wide and far ranging and as grand as that of the New Testament. We may not be able to go beyond Ephesians, Colossians, and the eighth chapter of Romans; but we dare not stop short of the incomparable boldness of those utterances. For here heaven and earth are held together in the incarnate Christ; here the Scriptures sing both ends of the arc of the Christ-event in ontological footings.

The Incarnation has commonly received only that light which can be reflected backward upon it from Calvary. While to be sure, these events cannot be separated without the impoverishment of the majesty of the history of redemption, it is nevertheless proper to suggest that our theological tendency to declare them only in their concerted meaning *at the point of fusion* tends to disqualify us to listen to the ontological-revelational overtones of the Incarnation.

> We belong to our kind,
> Are judged as we judge, for all gestures of time
> And all species of space respond in our own
> Contradictory dialect, the double talk
> Of ambiguous bodies, born like us to that
> Natural neighborhood which denial itself
> Like a friend confirms; they reflect our status,
> Temporals pleading for eternal life with
> The infinite impetus of anxious spirits,
> Finite in fact yet refusing to be real,
> Wanting our own way, unwilling to say Yes
> To the Self-So which is the same at all times,
> That Always-Opposite which is the whole subject
> Of our not-knowing, yet from no necessity
> Condescended to exist and to suffer death
> And, scorned on a scaffold, ensconced in His life
> The human household.[5]

5. W. H. Auden, *The Age of Anxiety: A Baroque Eclogue* (New York: Random House, 1946), pp. 136-37.

Commencement Address

1 Corinthians 3:1-23

On this occasion the preacher has several alternatives. First, he may make his address a summary in which he seeks to discuss all that has been spoken about in the academic courses, or considered and learned in our Seminary. The speech may be, that is to say, a kind of reminding benediction and charge pronounced over the whole business. This summary conception of a Commencement Speech, it seems to me, is quite useless. If the task of the school has not been responsibly accomplished it's too late to talk about it now. Second, one may turn the head around and face the other way, that is, to let what one says be determined by the nature of the occasion as a commencement, as a sharp new beginning toward the fulfillment of our task as ministers.

I have elected the second way for this occasion, and for the following simply stated but not simple reason. The world is in a deep and a new kind of trouble. It is a deep trouble because the disorders that threaten us in every sphere, from the most private and personal to the most public and social, if not controlled and moved toward correction will certainly destroy us. And it's a fresh kind of trouble because the traditional resources which the preaching of the Gospel has been bringing to these troubles are more and more seen to be wan, or irrelevant, or not even understood. Many people call them escapist. It is to this trouble that Dietrich Bonhoeffer referred when he said, "The world has come of age."

The context of Bonhoeffer's statement makes perfectly clear what he meant. He meant to tell us that the old alliances upon which the Gospel could rely have been either repudiated or assessed as unnecessary. He is simply echoing the statement of Nietzsche many years ago when he said, "The housing problem has now arisen in the case of God." What Nietzsche meant, of course, is exactly what Bonhoeffer means, that other ways of viewing human life and other disciplines for the study and the ordering of it have taken over so much of the territory formerly occupied by a Christian view of life as to make that view of life unnecessary or irrelevant. For instance, the discipline of sociology now investigates and describes the dynamics of society in such a way, and points out the creativity resident within it with such clarity, that many people turn away from other alternatives as simply useless or sentimental. In the neighborhood in which I live, I find many of my neighbors, Jewish and pagan, turning to neighborhood and community problems with great vigor and resolution. They are doing this not on the presuppositions of a Christian or any other kind of faith, but in the confidence that by sociological know-how certain problems can be moved toward a solution.

There was once a time when the Christian faith was in close alliance with the philosophy of idealism. It was assumed, that is, that a certain understanding of human life and a certain assessment of the possibilities resident in human activity were alike in both the Christian message and in a philosophy of idealism. This alliance has completely broken down, and even the philosophy of idealism itself has no longer any certain confidence in its assertions. The alliance between theology and philosophy all along the line has, in fact, broken down. Contemporary philosophy is no longer concerned with matters of value or of truth, but rather in such an analysis of propositions as shall indicate what they intend to say.

This situation, and my vocation as a Church theologian within it, has made a certain New Testament text come alive with incandescent clarity. Its power is in both its mystery and its promise. It fascinates with the peculiar power of a statement that is clear enough to strike and attract the mind, and mad enough to trouble it. It is also close enough to experience to make sense; it transcends experience in such a way as to allure with the suspicion that it makes a wilder and holier sense than most of us have yet fathomed. "For all things are yours, whether Paul, or Apollos, or Cephas, or the world, or life, or death, or the present, or the future, all are yours; and ye are Christ's; and Christ is God's."

All things, says the apostle. And he means "all things." The scope of the catalog with which he gives content to his statement that "all things are yours" is simply stunning in its completeness. He talks of the world in its ultimate dimensions — the world spun between life and death, in its temporal scope including past, present, and the future. And all of this, says the apostle, to those who stand within the circle of the Gospel's promise and power, all these things are yours. Not as possessions, or simply as an inner pile of energy to be exploited. That is negative. Paul here is positive. The world is deprived, so he says, of its power to seduce or embitter or to subject man's life to its own life. Nothing in it can hurt a man anymore. And he is positive, too, in a joyful and creative sense. For he beholds the world not as a trap but as a theater, a place for joy and culture and creative ordering. Observe, too, that the apostle says that all things are ours because of *Christ.* When he speaks of Christ Paul does not mean an idea or a theory, or a formal principle; he indicates rather a Godly deed whose name and career was a man, Jesus Christ. Because the believer is now participating in the life of God's man, Christ, this believer is newly organized from the inside out. The great surpassing fact of this organization is that the world which killed him is also a world in which God raised that one from the dead. This means that over above the apparent victory of the world is the absolute victory of God. Therefore, Christ is God's.

But the apostle continues to say, "and ye are Christ's." Therefore nothing of the world has ultimacy. The Church of which you are shortly to be ordained ministers exists fundamentally to accept this, to declare this, to become a living community in which this fact is like a bubbling yeast in which all men are called to think through how life may be penetrated with the power of Christ. This text reminds us that the great issue for our time is simply a new and terrifying challenge to solve the oldest problem between the Christian message and the world — the problem of nature and grace. By nature I mean simply the creative world with all of its powers, potencies, and problems. In older days the term nature evoked the simple biblical image of "the cattle on a thousand hills." But a contemporary man knows that for millions of people that image is no longer one which points him to the place where he meets nature. Nature for the contemporary man is rather the technology in a thousand shops and laboratories, the teeming millions of men in a thousand cities, rockets and outer space, massive conflicts in a world power struggle equipped and controlled by manipulated nature. By nature we mean the potentialities of the earth transformed by the power of reason.

Nature thus beheld seems so far away from what the biblical images about nature refer to that we are forced to ask the question whether or not this kind of nature and man living within this kind of nature can really be addressed by the text. To that question the text makes two assertions: first, this managed nature is no less God's! A technician working with strains of virus or a metallurgist with alloys is, by virtue of that fact, no less close to God's nature than a farmer who goes forth to sow his field. And, second, more sophisticated knowledge of nature does not make men more evil; it only provides a bigger field for the evil. Perdition is now in orbit and damnation lurks under the sign of the mushroom. The arrow that flyeth by night is now in outer space.

By grace is meant all that God does to crack nature open to its God, to restore it to his love and to its intended destiny. This grace, according to the New Testament, is not simply a proposition *about* grace set over against a proposition about nature. This "grace and truth came by Jesus Christ" (John 1:17). The *fact* of this coming, and that it came into the theater of *nature,* means that it is the will of God that there should be a fusion of nature and grace. In him all nature, including human nature, is transparent to grace, is the invaded field of grace. In him all grace has nature for its field, its fellow, and its material purpose.

The incarnation of the son of God makes several alternatives not only impossible but traitorous. First, the Church, the realm of grace, dare not disclaim the world of nature. To be sure, the church seldom does this formally. She is always tempted, however, to understand herself actually so as to accomplish this end whether she makes such a formal announcement or not. She is tempted to become a cowering coterie of the devout, cultivating her interior life in a certain kind of fright and turning from the world as from a dirty place.

This text, in which we are told that we are Christ's and Christ is God's, drives us to tend the creation, to relate ourselves to nature in such a way that it may become an open and proper theater for the manifestation and the fulfillment of grace. Where but in the gospel of the incarnation of the son of God has there ever been a word adequate to the tyrannies of nature within which men are presently trapped? Our Church does sometimes look back nostalgically at the small town and country parishes which are set in a tranquil, pastoral situation, far removed from the noises and complexities of technology and the torments in human association which now beset our whole people. But the problems of the contemporary city if seen with sufficient imagination are just as exciting to the Christian mind, and as fair a field for the promises of God, as ever the rural situation was.

The other night I flew into Midway Airport from across Lake Michigan from the east. It was night, and as I looked down I saw the lights of the ships on the lake, carrying oil and grain and ore. I thought of the ports from which they came and the vast city whose people and work they serve, sparkling with its million lights, lights indicative of the million tasks and duties, responsibilities, and joys, and problems that beset this huddled people. And when I reflected that within this galaxy of lights there is organized a magnificent integration of responsibilities, hospitals that never close, forces of protection that are never off-guard, ways of maintaining health and sanitation that are fantastically complex and dependable, I became aware that one can love the city, too!

A great urban center presents a different quality of possibility than moves a farmer as he sows the small seed to become the stuff in the great barns. But the vision, though different, is equally challenging. The Church, the realm of grace, dare not so embrace the world of nature as to identify her resources simply with its older, simpler, less troubling possibilities.

God is not the same as the world — and grace is not the same as nature. But God came into the world and in Jesus Christ established a relationship which, once accomplished, can never be undone or ignored. When we try to dig back of the particular formulations with which our particular church celebrates the Reformation and get at the root differences between Reformation and Pre-Reformation Christianity, we begin to see that the sixteenth century represented the victory of grace over nature. And we are so placed before subsequent history as to know that the centuries that followed have represented the victory of nature over grace.

Our task, as I understand it, is to restore the right relationship of nature and grace — in obedience, in word and in thought. Steel is nature plus technology; but what is done with steel is a problem that involves the dimensions of nature and grace. White men are nature, and non-white men are nature, too. But for these to live together as men and not avoid, or simply suffer, or haughtily acquiesce in the presence of the other requires something that nature does not provide. Politics, in a sense, is nature; and it is necessary and good, for it exists for order and order is of God. But to envision public order as a field of grace has not sufficiently engaged our Christian mind.

This sermon has made no effort to speak of the task of the minister in relation to the Church, to the people of the parish. These are not unimportant matters, and on the occasions of your ordination and installation wise and kind words will be spoken about these things. Your faculty's duty has been to open and stimulate and furnish your minds. It is, therefore, our peculiar hope for you that in your solitary thought, in your preaching and teaching you remain aware that you are sent from the Church, through the Church — but *to* the world, God's tormented creation, that it may know all things natural to be transformable and redeemable by grace, and all things gracious restless and yearning until they find natural embodiment.

Called to Unity

He is the image of the invisible God, the firstborn of all creation;
for in him all things were created, in heaven and on earth, visible
and invisible, whether thrones or dominions or principalities or
authorities — all things were created through him and for him.
He is before all things, and in him all things hold together. He is
the head of the body, the church; he is the beginning, the firstborn
from the dead, that in everything he might be preeminent. For in
him all the fullness of God was pleased to dwell, and through
him to reconcile to himself all things, whether on earth or in
heaven, making peace by the blood of his cross.

COLOSSIANS 1:15-20 (RSV)

There are two reasons for placing these five verses from the Colossian letter at the beginning of what I wish to say about the unity of Christ's Church. (1) These verses say clearly *that* we are called to unity, and (2) they suggest *how* the gift of that unity may be waiting for our obedience.

These verses say that we are called to unity, that the One who calls us is God, that this relentless calling persists over and through all discouragements, false starts, and sometimes apparently fruitless efforts; it is

38

these verses that have engendered the ecumenical movement among the churches and steadily sustain them in it.

These verses sing out thir triumphant and alluring music between two huge and steady poles — "Christ," and "all things." Even the Ephesian letter, rich and large as it is in its vision of the church, moves not within so massive an orbit as this astounding statement of the purpose of God. For it is here declared that the sweep of God's restorative action in Christ is no smaller than the six-times repeated *ta panta*. Redemption is the name for this will, this action, and this concrete Man who is God with us and God for us — and all things are permeable to his cosmic redemption because all things subsist in him. He comes to all things, not as a stranger, for he is the firstborn of all creation, and in him all things were created. He is not only the matrix and *prius* of all things; he is the intention, the fullness, and the integrity of all things: for all things were created through him and for him. Nor are all things a tumbled multitude of facts in an unrelated mass, for in him all things hold together.

Why does St. Paul, in this letter, as in the letter to the Ephesians, expand his vocabulary so radically far beyond his usual terms? Why do the terms guilt, sin, the law, and the entire Judaic catalogue of demonic powers here suddenly become transposed into another vocabulary, general in its character, cosmic in its scope, so vastly referential as to fill with Christic energy and substance the farthest outreach of metaphysical speculation?

The apostle does that out of the same practical pastoral ardor as caused him, when he wrote to his Philippian community, to enclose a deceptive petty problem of human recalcitrance within the overwhelming therapy of grace. Just as selfishness and conceit in Philippi are drowned in the sea of the divine charity "found in human form . . . humbled himself and became obedient unto death, even the death of the cross," — so here. The Colossian error was to assume that there were "thrones, dominions, principalities and authorities" which have a life and power apart from Christ, that the real world was a dualism, one part of which (and that part ensconcing the power of evil) was not subject to the Lordship of the Creator in his Christ.

Against that error which, had it persisted, would have trapped Christ within terms of purely moral and spiritual power and hope, Paul sets off a kind of chain reaction from the central atom, and the staccato ring of *ta panta* is the sounding of its reverberations into the farthest reaches of human fact, event, and thought. All is claimed for God, and all is Christic. The fugue-like voices of the separate claims — of him, in him, through him, for him — are gathered up in the quiet coda — "For in him all the fullness of God was pleased to dwell."

We must not fail to see the nature and the size of the issue that Paul confronts and encloses in this vast Christology. In propositional form it is simply this: A doctrine of redemption is meaningful only when it swings within the larger orbit of a doctrine of creation. For God's creation of earth cannot be redeemed in any intelligible sense of the word apart from a doctrine of the cosmos which is his home, his definite place, the theater of his selfhood under God, in cooperation with his neighbor, and in caring relationship with nature, his sister.

> Unless one is prepared to accept a dualism which condemns the whole physical order as being not of God and interprets redemption simply as release from the physical order, then one is forced to raise the question of cosmic redemption, not in contrast with but as an implication of personal redemption. Physical nature cannot be treated as an indifferent factor — as the mere stage and setting of the drama of personal redemption. It must either be condemned as in itself evil, or else it must be brought within the scope of God's redemptive act.[1]

Unless the reference and the power of the redemptive act includes the whole of man's experience and environment, straight out to its farthest horizon, then the redemption is incomplete. There is and will always remain something of evil to be overcome. And more. The actual man in his existence will be tempted to reduce the redemption of man to what purgation, transformation, forgiveness, and blessedness is available by an "angelic" escape from the cosmos of natural and historical fact — and in that option accept some sort of dualism which is as offensive to biblical theology as it is beloved of all Gnosticism, then as now.

1. Allan D. Galloway, *The Cosmic Christ* (New York: Harper and Brothers, 1951), p. 205.

The Christic Vision of the Eastern Fathers

In our understanding of the vast Christic vision that informs the passage from Colossians it is Irenaeus, and not the western and vastly more influential Augustine, who must be our mentor. The problem forced upon us by the events of the present decade is not soluble by the covert dualism of nature and grace. At a certain period in Christian thought and practical life, this dualism worked itself out in the dualism of church and world, of spiritual and temporal. But the time when Christian theology and Christian life could operate with such a view of things is long past. The view was never appropriate to the organic character of biblical speech; in the present state of man's knowledge in all areas it has become unintelligible.

But before that cleavage occurred, and strong with the vitalities of a Christology as splendid as our case is desperate, a unitary Christology prevailed in the Church; Colossians and Ephesians are echoes of it. I recollect it here, and in connection with the theme Christ the Light of the World, because it is now excruciatingly clear that Christ cannot be a light that lighteth every man coming into the world, if he is not also the light that falls upon the world into which every man comes. He enlightens this darkling world because the world was made through him. He can be the light of men because men subsist in him. He can be interpretive power because he is the power of the Word in creation.

"Christ the light of the world" has not had a career in the Christianity of the west comparable to the rich career of this doctrine of eastern Christendom. Nor has this image been expanded to address with lordly power the multiple energies of other images of light as these live and shape spiritual life in the religions of millions of men in whose midst we now meet. God is light. Men have in nature the bent light of God. Therefore Christ the Lord, who in our confession is named "Light of Light," must not be reduced to Light against light.

The Church takes a large risk when she pulls into the center of her reflections the New Testament image of Christ as the Light of the world. For the holy meaning of light cannot be restricted to Christ, and cannot be separated from him. Creation is a work of God, who is light. And the light of the Creator-God falls upon and inheres within his creation. The world of nature can be the place of this light that "came" by Jesus Christ because, despite the world's hostility to that light, it was never without the light of God. Nature and grace are categories necessary to do justice to Christ the Savior of the world. But if they are absolute and contradictory categories they distort and reduce the doctrine of creation.

As we seek for a vision of Christ ample enough to draw us toward unity in his Church we would do well to turn back the pages of western theological reflection and attend to a Father in the Church whose understanding of Christ the Light was not able to settle for statements less majestic than the apostrophe to him in the first chapter of Colossians. From a recent and careful summary of the thought of Irenaeus, I quote the following paragraph:

> In Irenaeus . . . there are not two orders of goodness, but only one. All goodness, whether it belongs to this world or to the final consummation, is a manifestation of the grace of God. It is the same grace of God which sustains nature even in its fallen state and which confers salvation in Jesus Christ. The residual goodness in nature can even be regarded as an anticipation or foretaste of that salvation. The same . . . appears also in Irenaeus' attitude toward the sacraments as compared with that of the church of the Middle Ages. For Irenaeus the union of spiritual and material benefit in the Eucharist symbolizes the ultimate unity of nature and grace implied in Christian salvation. But for Aquinas that the sacraments are administered in a material element is merely God's gracious concession to man's regrettably sensuous nature (P.II. QI, A.8).

For Irenaeus, the Incarnation and saving work of Jesus Christ meant that the promise of grace was held out to the whole of nature, and that henceforth nothing could be called common or unclean. For the church of the Middle Ages, on the other hand, nature was essentially common, and, if not positively unclean, at least seriously deficient in that shining whiteness of the saints in the empyrean heaven, and essentially incapable of sharing in such glory.[2]

2. Galloway, *The Cosmic Christ,* pp. 128ff.

The Split Between Grace and Nature
in Western Thought

The doctrinal cleavage, particularly fateful in western Christendom, has been an element in the inability of the church to relate the powers of grace to the vitalities and processes of nature. At the very time, and in that very part of the world where men's minds were being deepeningly determined by their understanding and widened control of the powers of nature they were so identifying the realm of history and the moral as the sole realm of grace as to shrink to no effect the biblical Christology of nature. In the midst of vast changes in man's relation to nature the sovereignty and scope of grace was, indeed, attested and liberated by the Reformers. But post-Reformation consolidations of their teaching permitted their Christic recovery of all of nature as a realm of grace to slip back into a minor theme.

In the Enlightenment the process was completed. Rationalism, on the one hand, restricted redemption by grace to the moral soul, and Pietism, on the other hand, turned down the blaze of the Colossian vision so radically that its *ta panta* was effective only as a moral or mystical incandescence. Enlightenment man could move in on the realm of nature and virtually take it over because grace had either ignored or repudiated it. A bit of God died with each new natural conquest; the realm of grace retreated as more of the structure and process of nature was claimed by now autonomous man. The rood-screen in the Church, apart from its original meaning, has become a symbol of man's devout but frightened thought permitting to fall asunder what God joined together.

It is not necessary or proper on this occasion to specify more fully the factors that have caused that unhappy divorcement. It is sufficient only to affirm that it has occurred, and to listen to the voices that lament its effects and to some that, longing for a lost wholeness, celebrate the glimmerings of its recovery. A representative voice of the lament is Matthew Arnold:

The sea of faith
Was once, too, at the full, and round earth's shores
Lay like the folds of a bright girdle furl'd;

43

But now I only hear
Its melancholy, long, withdrawing roar
Retreating to the breath
Of the night-wind down the vast edges drear
And naked shingles of the world.[3]

And a seldom heard voice that celebrates the world as a God-haunted house is Gerard Manley Hopkins:

The world is charged with the grandeur of God.
    It will flame out, like shining from shook foil;
    It gathers to a greatness, like the ooze of oil
Crushed. Why do men then now not reck his rod?
Generations have trod, have trod, have trod;
    And all is seared with trade; bleared, smeared with toil;
    And wears man's smudge and shares man's smell: the soil
Is bare now, nor can foot feel, being shod.
And for all this, nature is never spent;
    There lives the dearest freshness deep down things;
And though the last lights off the black West went
    Oh, morning, at the brown brink eastward, springs —
Because the Holy Ghost over the bent
    World broods with warm breast and with ah! bright wings.[4]

Claiming Nature for Christ

Is it again possible to fashion a theology catholic enough to affirm redemption's force enfolding nature, as we have affirmed redemption's force enfolding history? That we should make that effort is, in my understanding, the commanding task of this moment in our common history. And by common history I refer to that which is common to all of

3. Matthew Arnold, "Dover Beach," in *The Poetical Works of Matthew Arnold,* ed. C. B. Tinker and H. F. Lowry (London: Oxford University Press, 1950), p. 211.

4. Gerard Manley Hopkins, "God's Grandeur," in *The Poems of Gerard Manley Hopkins,* ed. W. H. Gardner and N. H. Mackenzie, 4th edition (Oxford: Oxford University Press, 1967), p. 66.

the blessed obediences of the household of faith: Antioch and Aldersgate, Constantinople and Canterbury, Geneva and Augsburg, Westminster and Plymouth.

For the problem which first drove the Church, as our text reminds us, to utter a Christology of such amplitude is a problem that has persisted and presses upon us today with absolute urgency. We are being driven to claim the world of nature for God's Christ just as in the time of Augustine the Church was driven to claim the world of history as the city of God, for his Lordship and purpose. For fifteen centuries the Church has declared the power of grace to conquer egocentricity, to expose idolatry, to inform the drama of history with holy meaning. But in our time we have beheld the vision and promises of the Enlightenment come to strange and awesome maturity. The cleavage between grace and nature is complete. Man's identity has been shrunken to the dimensions of privatude within social determinism. The doctrine of the creation has been made a devout datum of past time. The mathematization of meaning in technology and its reduction to operational terms in philosophy has left no mental space wherein to declare that nature, as well as history, is the theater of grace and the scope of redemption.

When millions of the world's people, inside the church and outside of it, know that damnation now threatens nature as absolutely as it has always threatened men and societies in history, it is not likely that witness to a light that does not enfold and illumine the world-as-nature will be even comprehensible. For the root-pathos of our time is the struggle by the peoples of the world in many and various ways to find some principle, order, or power which shall be strong enough to contain the raging ". . . thrones, dominions, principalities" which restrict and ravage human life.

If, to this longing of all men everywhere we are to propose "Him of whom, and through whom, and in whom are all things," then that proposal must be made in redemptive terms that are forged in the furnace of man's crucial engagement with nature as both potential to blessedness and potential to hell.

The matter might be put another way: the address of Christian thought is most weak precisely where man's ache is most strong. We have had, and have, a Christology of the moral soul, a Christology of history, and, if not a Christology of the ontic, affirmations so huge as to fill the space marked out by ontological questions. But we do not have, at least not in such effective force as to have engaged the thought of the common life, a daring, penetrating, life-affirming Christology of nature. The theological magnificence of cosmic Christology lies, for the most part, still tightly folded in the Church's innermost heart and memory. Its power is nascent among us all in our several styles of preaching, teaching, worship; its waiting potency is available for release in kerygmatic theology, in moral theology, in liturgical theology, in sacramental theology. And the fact that our separate traditions incline us to one or another of these as central does not diminish either the fact, or our responsibility. For it is true of us all that the imperial vision of Christ as coherent in *ta panta* has not broken open the powers of grace to diagnose, judge, and heal the ways of men as they blasphemously strut about this hurt and threatened world as if they owned it. Our vocabulary of praise has become personal, pastoral, too purely spiritual, static. We have not affirmed as inherent in Christ — God's proper man for man's proper selfhood and society — the world political, the world economical, the world aesthetic, and all other commanded orderings of actuality which flow from the ancient summons to tend this garden of the Lord. When atoms are disposable to the ultimate hurt then the very atoms must be reclaimed for God and his will.

The Setting for the Study of Church Unity

If now we put together that threat to nature and a Christology whose scope is as endless as that threat is absolute, do we, perhaps, gain a fresh and urgent vision of the call of God to the unity of the Church, and some help toward its definition and obedience? Nothing that is affirmed here questions or slights the ways we have gone, or suggests that their continuation is not necessary and good. Incessant biblical study, penetrating theological analysis, the expansion of the scope and the deepening of our various traditions, and mutual acknowledgment in thanksgiving of the blessings God has bestowed upon us all in our several ways and works — all of this must go on.

Just as Faith and Order acknowledged at Lund that cooperative ecclesiological studies are a prolegomenon to unity but no guarantee of our willingness to receive it or even to continue to long for it — so we must here acknowledge the profound studies of Christ and the Church, while they show us clearly where our life and our center is, do not automatically furnish forth a common faith, or draw us toward a faithful ordering of the life of the church in history.

The alembic in which the dynamics of unity stir with life, fuse, give new forms to Godly vitalities, and have the power to generate new obediences amidst old recalcitrances — is history. That is why there is such a discipline as history of doctrine. For this study discloses that doctrinal statement and development is confession-thinking to the glory of God amidst historical denials or pretensions which would usurp the glory. It has always been within the clutch of a definite historical threat, or necessity, or a sheer intolerable malaise that the church has found her teaching voice. Doctrines are not born out of doctrines in an unchanging vacuum. Doctrines are evoked, clarified, refined, given force and precision within the challenge of exact circumstances. The facts of history are the exciters of insight; the nature of the moment's need engenders the doctrine to serve and bless it.

This dynamism that characterizes the church's stance and movement throughout history, this momentum and promise inherent in the church by the spirit, furnishes us with hope as we try to construct a fresh doctrinal counterpoint between the *ta panta* of the claims of Christ and the facts of nature's pathetic openness to glorious use or to brutal rapacity.

But how does doctrine, addressing the necessities of history with its own interpretive unfolding of the life of God in the life of the mind of the church, bear upon the calling of God to the unity of the Church? Just as the gracious gifts of God constitute and endow the Church and sustain her toward fulfillment in history, so right doctrine drives toward unity in two ways: it constantly clarifies in intellectual terms what it is that sustains the church, and it calls the church to celebrate in deed what it points to as alone adequate to the world's need. This is but to say that the *telos* of doctrine is action, the fulfillment of right teaching is not right teaching but decision and deed. Clarity without the love of the brother who is luminously before us as the brother is the clarity of damnation. "He that loveth his brother abideth in the light." The Church must think; but she cannot think herself into unity. The Church must seek order appropriate to her nature; but she cannot order herself into unity. But the unity of the Church may be given her when she thinks and when she worships, and when she reflects upon order — all in order to ethicality.

By ethicality is meant that actualization in the decisions of the common life of those commands, calls, gifts of God which are affirmed and celebrated in theology and in worship. Clarity, obedience, unity — that is the interior sequence of the light. The Church knows the light in deepening ethicality under the incandescence and guidance and judgment of that light. This it must do as a witness to the unity it now has and as the condition of the fuller unity it seeks.

It is the thesis of this address that our moment in history is heavy with the imperative that faith proposes for the madly malleable and grandly possible potencies of nature — that holiest, vastest, confession: that by him, for him, and through him all things subsist in God, and therefore are to be used in joy and sanity for his human family.

The Church is both thrust and lured towards unity. The thrust is from behind and within: it is grounded in God's will and promise. The lure is God's same will and promise operating upon the Church from the needs of history within which she lives her life. The thrust of the will and the promise is a steady force in the Church's memory: the lure is clamant in the convulsions that twist our times in the Church's present. The way forward is from Christology expanded to its cosmic dimensions, made passionate by the pathos of this threatened earth, and made ethical by the love and the wrath of God. For as it was said in the beginning that God beheld all things and declared them good, so it was uttered by an angel in the apocalypse of St. John, ". . . ascending from the east, having the seal of the living God: and he cried with a loud voice to the four angels, to whom it was given to hurt the earth and the sea, saying, Hurt not the earth neither the sea, nor the trees . . ." (Revelation 7:2-3, KJV). The care of the earth, the realm of nature as a theater of grace, the ordering of the thick, material procedures that make available to or deprive men of bread and peace — these are christological obediences before they are practical necessities.

We live in a *kairos* where Christ and chaos intersect, a moment in which the fullest Christology is marvelously congruent with man's power-founded anxiety and need. Contemporary man expresses his hurt in terms of his broken or uncertain relationship to society and nature.

We cannot, indeed, extrude from these the substance of his God-relationship. But it might be possible so to say to him that he entertain the possibility of its truth, that the problems that appear in this earthy and societal relationship are not soluble in terms of it. For created life is a triad of God, and man, and nature. If we meet him where he hurts, we may be given new ears and eyes for that triadic Word from which the Church lives in confessed acknowledgment, and under which all men live by creation.

The grace and truth which came by Jesus Christ, and which were celebrated in the Colossian hymn because ". . . it pleased the Father that in him should all fullness dwell . . ." is alone a source and power and interpretive principle for a meaning adequate to the longings and needs of this cloven and embittered world. There are perceptive men in the world who glimpse this, even outside the Christian confession, and in the dark language of nature's pathos as it groans and travails in pain they set it forth. From many voices I chose one. His utterance is called, "Advice to a Prophet." The poet speaks of man's nature as it is formed in nature's net; of how the deer, and the sky, and the sun, and the patient, mute life of the animals accompany and enrich us as we live out our days. And then, reflecting upon the possible event by which all of these should be stunned, silenced, or obliterated he cries of himself and his human fellows —

What should we be without
The dolphin's arc, the dove's return,

These things in which we have seen ourselves and spoken?
Ask us, prophet, how shall we call
Our natures forth when that live tongue is all
Dispelled, that glass obscured or broken

In which we have said the rose of our love and the clean
Horse of our courage, in which beheld
The singing locust of the soul unshelled,
And all we mean or wish to mean.

Ask us, ask us whether with the wordless rose
Our hearts shall fail us, come demanding

Whether there shall be lofty or long standing
When the bronze annals of the oak-tree close.[5]

The Church has found a melancholy number of ways to express her variety. She has found fewer ways to express her unity. But if we are indeed called to unity, and if we can obey that call in terms of a contemporary Christology expanded to the dimensions of the New Testament vision, we shall, perhaps, obey into fuller unity. For in such obedience we have the promise of the Divine blessing. This radioactive earth, so fecund and so fragile, is his creation, our sister, and the material place where we meet the brother in Christ's light. Ever since Hiroshima the very term *light* has had ghastly meanings. But ever since creation it has had meanings glorious; and ever since Bethlehem meanings concrete and beckoning.

5. Richard Wilbur, "Advice to a Prophet," in *New and Collected Poems* (New York: Harcourt, Brace, Jovanovich, 1988), pp. 182-83.

[1964]

The Care of the Earth

Scripture: Psalm 104

A sermon may move from idea to fulfillment in various and sometimes strange ways. It may be useful as an introduction to the theme of this sermon to say how that happened in the writing of it.

In April of last year I read a poem in the *New Yorker* magazine; the poet is Mr. Richard Wilbur. What the poet was saying struck and stuck for several obvious reasons. Beneath the quite clear apprehensions that float about just under the surface of our minds there is a root apprehension that churns deep down at the center. It is vague, but it is also relentless and undismissable. And the poet's words intersect this inarticulate anxiety, stop it cold, give it a "local habitation and a name." The substance of this anxiety is common to us all, and it is heavy. It is the peculiar function of the poet sometimes to say out loud and with resonant clarity what we all would wish to say had we the dark music and the language.

The substance is this: annihilating power is in nervous and passionate hands. The stuff is really there to incinerate the earth — and the certainty that it will not be used is not there.

Nor have we anodyne to hush it up or power to run away from it. We can go skiing with it, trot off to Bermuda with it, push it down under accelerated occupation with the daily round, pour bourbon over it, or say our prayers — each according to his tactic and disposition. But it goes along, survives, talks back.

Not in abstract proposition or dramatic warnings but in powerful, earthy images the poet makes his point. The point is single, simple, and absolute: man's selfhood hangs upon the persistence of the earth, *her* dear known and remembered factualness is the matrix of the self.

When you come, as you soon must, to the streets of our city,
Mad-eyed from stating the obvious,
Not proclaiming our fall but begging us
In God's name to have self-pity,

Spare us all word of the weapons, their force and range,
The long numbers that rocket the mind;
Our slow, unreckoning hearts will be left behind,
Unable to fear what is too strange.

Nor shall you scare us with talk of the death of the race.
How should we dream of this place without us —
The sun mere fire, the leaves untroubled about us,
A stone look on the stone's face?

Speak of the world's own change. Though we cannot conceive
Of an undreamt thing, we know to our cost
How the dreamt cloud crumbles, the vines are blackened by frost,
How the view alters. We could believe,

If you told us so, that the white-tailed deer will slip
Into perfect shade, grown perfectly shy,
The lark avoid the reaches of our eye,
The jack-pine loose its knuckled grip

On the cold ledge, and every torrent burn
As Xanthus once, its gliding trout
Stunned in a twinkling. What should we be without
The dolphin's arc, the dove's return,

These things in which we have seen ourselves and spoken?
Ask us, prophet, how we shall call

Our natures forth when that live tongue is all
Dispelled, that glass obscured or broken,

In which we have said the rose of our love and the clean
Horse of our courage, in which beheld
The singing locust of the soul unshelled,
And all we mean or wish to mean.

Ask us, ask us whether with the wordless rose
Our hearts shall fail us; come demanding
Whether there shall be lofty or long standing
When the bronze annals of the oak-tree close.[1]

By sheer force of these lines my mind was pushed back against the wall and forced to ask: Is there anything in our western religious tradition as diagnostically penetrating as that problem, as salvatory as that predicament?

Out of these back-to-wall reflections I therefore ask your attention to several statements that seem to me alone deep and strong enough to make adequate sense. These statements have in common this: they deal with the *enjoyment* of things and the *uses* of things. And together they add up to a proposition: delight is the basis of right use.

The first statement is the celebrated answer to the first question in the Westminster catechism. No one will question the velocity with which this answer gets to the point or that the point is worth getting at! The question is: What is the chief end of man? The answer: To glorify God and enjoy him forever!

The first verb, to glorify, is not primarily intellectual. It does not concern itself with the establishment of the existence of God, or with a description of his nature. The verb is not aesthetic either. It is not concerned to declare that God is good or beautiful, or propose that it is a fair thing to worship God. Nor is it hortatory, that is, it does not beat us over the head with admonitions about our duty to God.

The very "to glorify" is exclusively and utterly religious! The verb

---

1. Richard Wilbur, "Advice to a Prophet," in *Advice to a Prophet and Other Poems* (New York: Harcourt, Brace, and World, 1959), pp. 12-13.

comes from the substantive "glory": and that term designates what God is and has and wills within himself; it announces the priority, the ineffable majesty, the sovereign power and freedom of the holy. Glory, that is to say, is what God is and does out of himself; and when we use the term for what we do in response, that response is given and engendered by his glory.

The priority-in-God, and the proper work of this verb may be illustrated by its function in the sixth chapter of the book of Isaiah. The young prophet, rich and eager in his expectations of the new king, Uzziah, is stunned when the king dies. He goes into the temple, and then comes the vision of the glory of whose ineffable power the face of the king is but the reflection.

> In the year that King Uzziah died I saw the Lord sitting upon a throne, high and lifted up; and his train filled the temple. Above him stood the seraphim; each had six wings: with two he covered his face, and with two he covered his feet, and with two he flew. And one called to another and said: "Holy, holy, holy is the Lord of hosts: the whole earth is full of his glory."[2]

The glory is the light the holy gives off. The earth is a theater of the glory; it is rich with the ineffable glory because God, the holy one, has made it.

The holy is a numinous and absolute word. It is not contained within other categories; it is a category. The holy both evokes and demands thought, but it is a misunderstanding to assume that thoughts can contain the glory and the holy. The holy certainly has the effect that Professor Rudolph Otto in his great work, *The Idea of the Holy,* calls *mysterium tremendum et fascinosum* — but there is an unseizable plus to the term that eludes even the image-making genius of the Jews.[3]

The holy invites prayer, but rejects such an understanding of prayer as would make prayer a tool for working upon the holy, a device for making the holy disposable by man. The holy demands service, but no

2. Isaiah 6:1-3, RSV.

3. Rudolph Otto, *The Idea of the Holy,* trans. John Harvey (London: Oxford University Press, 1923).

service adds up to a responding equivalent — just as in our human love one serves the beloved but never affirms his service to be the measure of love.

The chief end of man is, then, to glorify God, to let God *be* God, to understand and accept his life in ways appropriate to the imperial, holy singularity of God. The meaning of this has, to be sure, ethical, psychological, even political implications. But the center is categorically religious.

But this statement about God and man, thus elevated, tough, and absolute, is conjoined in the catechism with a concluding phrase, "and enjoy him forever." The juxtaposition of commands to glorify and to enjoy is on several grounds startling to our generation. To enjoy is a strange thing, that is to say, to do about the holy God before whom even the seraphim do hide their faces. This joining of the *holy,* which is what God is, with *joy,* which designates what man is to have and do in him — this juxtaposition, in that it is startling to us, says a good deal about modern American understanding of the Christian faith. How it has come about that we are startled by what our fathers joined together without batting an eye is a matter we cannot now go into, but only observe it and ask after its significance. For we may have missed something. If the gravity of the glorification of the holy and the blithe humaneness of "enjoy him forever" seem strange, our churches in the very form of their buildings may be partly to blame. There is the clean, shadowless, and antiseptic colonial, the monumental melancholy of the Romanesque and Gothic adaptations — bereft of the color and ornament which in other lands are so devoutly joined in these forms. Our traditional churches affirm a heavy kind of solemnity that leaves us indeed with a lugubrious holy, but defenseless and aghast before the joy of, for instance, a Baroque church. Such a church is luxuriant, joy-breathing, positively Mozartean in its vivacity — replete with rosy angels tumbling in unabashed enjoyment among impossibly fleecy clouds against an incredible blue heaven.

We shall not draw conclusions from that — only observe it and let it hang — that the gravity of a life determined by God, lived to the glory of God, is not necessarily incongruent with abounding joy. It is interesting to recall that the most rollicking music old periwig Bach ever wrote is not dedicated to the joy of tobacco (although he did that) or coffee (and he praised that) or the inventiveness among his fellow musicians, nor dedicated to the levity of the Count of Brandenburg, but *In Dir ist Freude* ("In Thee is Joy")!

The second statement is ascribed to Thomas Aquinas, surely not the playful or superficial type. Thomas did not affirm Christianity as a consolatory escape hatch, or an unguent to the scratchy personality, or a morale builder to a threatened republic — all contemporary malformations. But he did say, "It is of the heart of sin that men use what they ought to enjoy, and enjoy what they ought to use." Apart from the claim that it is *sin* that men do that, and apart from the seriousness of the situation if that statement should turn out to be true, is the statement reportorially so?

Yes, it is so, for all of us, and in many ways. Thomas is simply condensing here the profound dialectic of use and enjoyment that distorts and impoverishes life when it is not acknowledged and obeyed. To use a thing is to make it instrumental to a purpose, and some things are to be so used. To enjoy a thing is to permit it to be what it is prior to and apart from any instrumental assessment of it, and some things are to be so enjoyed.

I adduce a small example: it may bloom in our minds into bigger ones. Wine is to be *enjoyed;* it is not to be *used.* Wine is old in human history. It is a symbol of nature in her smiling beneficence — "close bosom friend of the maturing sun." That is why it has virtually everywhere and always been the accompaniment of celebrative occasions, the sign of gladness of heart. It is to be enjoyed; it is not to be used to evoke illusions of magnificence, or stiffen timidity with the fleeting certainty that one is indeed a sterling lad. Where it is enjoyed it adds grace to a truth; where it is used it induces and anesthetizes a lie.

Observe in Psalm 104 how the Old Testament man who sought to glorify God and enjoy him forever stood in the midst of nature. "He . . . gives wine to gladden the heart of man, and oil to make his face shine." "This is the day which the Lord has made;" he exults, "let us rejoice and be glad in it." Why? Not primarily for what he can turn the day's hours into, but rather on the primal ground that there *are days* — unaccountable in their gift-character, just there. And here he is — permeable by all he is sensitive to: texture, light, form, and movement, the cattle on a thousand hills. Thou sendest forth thy Spirit and they are! Let us rejoice and be glad in it!

i thank You God for most this amazing
day: for the leaping greenly spirits of trees
and a blue true dream of sky; and for everything
which is natural which is infinite which is yes[4]

It is of the heart of sin that man uses what he ought to enjoy.

It is also, says Thomas, of the heart of sin that man is content to enjoy what he ought to use. Charity, for instance. Charity is the comprehensive term to designate how God regards man. That regard is to be used by man for man. That is why our Lord moves always in his speech from the source of joy, that man is loved by the holy, to the theater of joy, that man must serve the need of the neighbor. "Lord, where did we behold thee? I was in prison, hungry, cold, naked" — you enjoyed a charity that God gives for use.

If the creation, including our fellow creatures, is impiously used apart from a gracious primeval joy in it, the very richness of the creation becomes a judgment. This has a cleansing and orderly meaning for everything in the world of nature, from the sewage we dump into our streams to the cosmic sewage we dump into the fallout.

Abuse is use without grace; it is always a failure in the counterpoint of use and enjoyment. When things are not used in ways determined by joy in the things themselves, this violated potentiality of joy (timid as all things holy, but relentless and blunt in its reprisals) withdraws and leaves us, not perhaps with immediate positive damnations but with something much worse — the wan, ghastly, negative damnations of use without joy, stuff without grace, a busy, fabricating world with the shine gone off, personal relations for the nature of which we have invented the eloquent term "contacts," staring without beholding, even fornication without finding.

God is useful. But not if he is sought for use. Ivan, in *The Brothers Karamazov,* saw that, and Dostoevski meant it as a witness to the holy and joy-begetting God whom he saw turned into an ecclesiastical club to frighten impoverished peasants with, when he had his character say, "I deny God for God's sake!"

---

4. E. E. Cummings, "i thank You God," from *Poems 1923-1954* (New York: Harcourt, Brace, and Co., 1954).

All of this has, I think, something to say to us as teachers and students to whom this university is ever freshly available for enjoyment and use. For consider this: the basis of discovery is curiosity, and what is curiosity but the peculiar joy of the mind in its own given nature? Sheer curiosity, without immediate anticipation of ends and uses, has done most to envision new ends and fresh uses. But curiosity does this in virtue of a strange counterpoint of use and enjoyment. Bacon declared that "studies are for delight," the secular counterpart of "glorify God and enjoy him forever." The Creator who is the fountain of joy, and the creation which is the material of university study, are here brought together in an ultimate way. It is significant that the university, the institutional solidification of the fact that studies are for delight, is an idea and a creation of a culture that once affirmed that men should glorify God and enjoy him forever.

Use is blessed when enjoyment is honored. Piety is deepest practicality, for it properly relates use and enjoyment. And a world sacramentally received in joy is a world sanely used. There is an economics of use only; it moves toward the destruction of both use and joy. And there is an economics of joy; it moves toward the intelligence of use and the enhancement of joy. That this vision involves a radical new understanding of the clean and fruitful earth is certainly so. But this vision, deeply religious in its genesis, is not so very absurd now that natural damnation is in orbit, and man's befouling of his ancient home has spread his death and dirt among the stars.

The Role of the Spirit in
Creating the Future Environment

M y inquiry into this topic will proceed along three lines and in three logical steps. First, a survey of the several meanings of the term *spirit,* combined with an effort to specify what aspects of that enormous referential complex suggest themselves as most useful to advance the purposes of this conference. Second, an effort to relate the term thus more precisely specified to those operations of the critical intelligence which are presupposed by the three parallel studies, i.e., the roles of science, technology, and art. And, third, an effort to suggest how the critical intelligence, thus enriched and deepened, must confront the promise and perils of the next fifty years.

The term *spirit* is a primordial symbol in every language of which we have knowledge. The universality of its occurrence is matched by the difficulty of specification. The sheer referential richness, and the many and various functions of the term in usage, is attested by the twelve packed columns in the Oxford English Dictionary. And while I shall necessarily restrict our consideration to the English term, it is proper to note that into the pool of our use of the term flow all the streams of all the meanings of the term in all the languages. The Semitic *ruach* is breath, animating and creating power; and it is by the *ruach* of the Creator that things are, and that they are the things they are. The Greek *pneuma* is both the fountain of that ardor with which Odysseus embarks upon and is sustained in his adventures and in Greek philosophy the power by which the mind of man participates in the Eternal forms of things. The Latin *spiritus*, with the verb *spirare*, to breathe, suggests what I have called the primordial level of the term's intention. In the German language the term *geist* has all the meanings of Semitic *ruach*, Latin *spiritus*, and French *esprit*; but so richly is the German term combined with others that it has become a central term in cultural and intellectual history. Not only does the term, thus combined, reach after the grandest conceptualizations — as in *Zeitgeist* and *Weltgeist*, but a fundamental division in all intellectual disciplines is proposed by the large categories of *Naturwissenschaften* and *Geisteswissenschaften*.

It is perhaps in the use of the term spirit in the French language that one is driven closest to panic! The familiar Holy Spirit of the Christian Trinity is clear — *L'Esprit Saint*. But one can perhaps be forgiven this preliminary survey of the scope of the term when *Le Figaro* solemnly reports, "In the showing yesterday by Balenciaga the handling of the neckline was reminiscent of the characteristic spirit of that house"!

The legitimacy, indeed the necessity, of what I proposed in this first is now, I think, quite clear — to make an effort to specify what aspects of an enormous referential complex suggest themselves as useful to the purposes of this conference. And while I have no confidence that the several meanings I shall suggest are sufficiently precise or exhaustive, they will serve to articulate how the term spirit is understood by the common mind of our society.

As we look at several popular usages of the term, we do that not in the confidence that such usages are helpful but only to demonstrate that along this way lies no hope at all. For the term *spirit* as commonly used is a kind of huge verbal scoop for all sorts of things persons want to say, but, lacking the energy or competence for precision, designate with this term. This most general habit must be recognized and illustrated in order to be set aside as of no help in our present effort.

We say *spirit,* for instance, when we mean morale. When a group enterprise has clear purpose, general and enthusiastic support, a program of action, and engenders a feeling of camaraderie among the members, we speak of *morale,* e.g., the morale of the student body. Or when the disposition of a person or a group is characterized by a brisk and lively manner, joyous, eager, youthful — we speak of *élan.* Or the term spirit, as in the instance of the aforementioned neckline, may be used to designate what were better called *flair* or *style*. *Style* is the mark of a highly in-dividual manner in the doing or fashioning or performance of some-thing; it is the exterior and formal mark of an imaginative particularity. The term *mood,* a term unhappily dominated by its negative adjectival use as *moody* — is a precise term with which to indicate that cast of mind and grave concern with proper methods and procedures that marks, for instance, the staff of a hospital or the disposition of a team of scholars to-ward each other and their common purpose. When an important com-mon concern is conjoined with commonly developed and trusted proce-dures, and when all engaged are agreed about the intention and confident in the procedures, there emerges a *mood.* The mood lacks the evident bounce of *élan,* what we have called *morale* is taken for granted, and *flair* and *style,* while not obliterated, have a less manifest field of ex-ercise. But most of the world's work is done within the quiet matrix of intra-individual expectation, responsibility, and confidence, which is the mood of man's most general operations with his fellows.

It may appear that by all of this nimble dancing about meanings of the term that will *not* do, we are not moving toward the necessary preci-sion and clarity. But we are indeed in motion; and the first large step has already been taken and has only to be seen in its positive usefulness. For informing all the imprecise uses of the term *spirit* is a verbal embarrass-ment that points absolutely to the heart of the matter. It is quite clear that spirit is a reality that does not exist as an item in the sum of a bun-dle of components but is at home and diffused among, in, with, under the entire structure. While, to be sure, we must presently move beyond this insistence we shall not do so with any truth or force if we do not ac-knowledge and reflect at some depth upon this basic fact — that a real-ity is no less there and crucial for all the difficulty of its specification and definition. Charm is a reality. Charm is not located in data although it has by data its theater and voice. Charm is not a resultant of look and manner and figure and style and gesture and a certain immaculate par-ticularity of mind and emotional quality. These are the annunciatory actualizations of charm, the visibilities of our encounter with it. But charm is an ensemble of fullest total presence and being.

Some things are isolatable, concrete, specifiable in terms of structure and process. And some things not only resist so clean a method but by their resistance to it amplify their reality in the very recalcitrance they display. The first are brought to effectual knowledge by analysis operating mathematically; the second are brought to effective knowledge by analysis operating humanistically and historically. And for the clarification of the latter it is by illustration that one gathers up in language the actual force and presence of what he seeks better to know.

I proceed therefore to an illustration. This one is a justly celebrated utterance from the romantic period of English poetry. And because no adjective is more often used to damn into annihilation any effort to pierce the recalcitrance we have alluded to, I hasten to suggest that if every image used in these lines to unfold and further the poet's intention were rejected as premodern (as indeed they all are), the *reality* that is announced and deployed in its pervasiveness would be left untouched to stop and trouble us. The lines are from Wordsworth. But modern literature is drenched and heavy with the same effort to catch in the net of language the ductile reality of spirit.

> A presence that disturbs me with the joy
> Of elevated thoughts; a sense sublime
> Of something far more deeply interfused,
> Whose dwelling is the light of setting suns,
> And the round ocean and the living air,
> And the blue sky, and, in the mind of man;
> A motion and a spirit, that impels
> All thinking things, all objects of all thoughts
> And rolls through all things.[1]

The concept of spirit is there put with an intellectual clarity that uses images for immediacy and force. But if what is hypothesized were wrenched free of the prescientific nature-response characteristic of the period and translated into contemporary data, the allure and the passion that lives in the mind's longing to know wholeness and depth would be unchanged and unreduced. For the phrase "something far more deeply interfused" points to the glow and the power, the passion and the prom-

1. William Wordsworth, "Lines Composed a Few Miles Above Tintern Abbey," in *Wordsworth: Poetical Works,* ed. Thomas Hutchinson and revised by Ernest de Selincourt (London: Oxford University Press, 1950), p. 164.

ise of the human enterprise as such. This vitality is not confined to the interior of "thinking things" but is postulated of "all *objects* of all thoughts"; the deepest intentionality of social and behavioral thought. Something of the intention of natural science, historical study, philosophical reflection is here specified at a level primordial to the methodological modalities of these inquiries as distinct disciplines.

A second illustration may address some to whom the highly imagist manner of the poet is not congenial. The illustration is drawn from my own discipline but is not by that fact restricted in its applicability. Some years ago there appeared a book by Professor Louis Bouyer, *The Spirit and Forms of Protestantism*.[2] Unlike the works of many Roman Catholic scholars in pre-ecumenical days, this work was neither pejorative nor merely dogmatically comparative. Its originative insight was simply that the plurality and substance of forms is disclosive of an integral, organic, structured morphology of the religious life, that a basic stance begets intentionality of a consistent structure and that phenomena of practice unfold to knowledge a profound coherence. And for the specification of this unitive if outwardly baffling disclosure Professor Bouyer used the term *spirit*.

Now it is precisely this understanding of spirit as a principle of coherence-seeking-wholeness, resident within the data and operating in the conceptualizing intelligence, that must be acknowledged and liberated for effective force. To such acknowledgment and liberation there are, to my mind, two barriers — and both of them exist most powerfully *within* the very community that the spirit, as I have spoken of it, seeks to penetrate, enliven, deepen. If the spirit as a positive power operating within actual intelligence — which I shall presently defend as not only possible but crucial — is to play a role in the next fifty years appropriate to the assumptions that list it as a force along with science, art, and technology, then two very common judgments and evaluations of spirit have to be corrected. In the two paragraphs that follow I shall make two affirmations about spirit. Neither of them is generally acknowledged as true in the American intellectual community in our day, and the movements of mind, in theory and in practice-as-judgment, daily deepen the hostil-

2. Louis Bouyer, *The Spirit and Forms of Protestantism*, trans. A. V. Littledale (London: Harvill Press, 1956).

ity with which they are greeted by that community. But unless these affirmations are postulated one would be wholly justified in questioning the usefulness of introducing this notion of spirit into our discussions at all.

1. The term spirit, in the context of the concern of this conference, designates a conceptualizing power having its own role in the work of the mind. While, to be sure, that affirmation must be given substance by analysis to follow, let us be content at the moment to specify understandings of spirit that are excluded by it. I have the impression, based upon considerable evidence, that the term spirit is admitted to occasions of intellectual reflection by motivations identical with those that urge a university to maintain a chapel from which a vague reality generally called spiritual is assumed to insufflate the accredited disciplines of university study. The spiritual, thus located and isolated, has an additional advantage: a kind of prestigious container is both provided and applauded. Not, to be sure, by the faculty, who are mostly indifferent or pityingly tolerant, but by the public relations office. But the disciplines, decisions, special schools stand to gain, also. So commodious is this container and by tradition so hallowed, that into it may be tossed many facts of history, aspects of social and personal reality, issues having to do with means and ends, the relation of facts to purposes. The very notion of spirit may become an administrative dispose-all; indeed it has become that. Counter to that, and lest the description of the situation may have lost the point of affirmation, let us again state it: the spirit, in the context of this conference, designates a conceptualizing power having its own role in the work of the mind.

2. The integrity of this power and the right exercise of this role must be protected against misappropriation. By misappropriation I mean the too uncritical taking over of a body of data by disciplines whose methods have been refined by data which suggest models of truth and which models both define an orbit of competence and establish a perspective. Methodology both sharpens and delimits competence; perspective influences interpretation. Demonstrable effectiveness may invite tyranny, and field success may blunt sensitivity and breed incaution.

A single illustration must suffice for the general peril to understanding that I have called misappropriation of data. Each of us can, according to his special area of research, extend the illustration. Of particular significance to the field of history of religions has been the refinement of a way of observation and interpretation that is known as phenomenology. Indeed none of the disciplines within the category of the *Geisteswissenschaften* has escaped deep penetration by the ideas and methods of Edmund Husserl, Ernst Cassirer, Merleau-Ponty. In the specific field of the history of religions, the work of many contemporaries, notably Mircea Eliade and Paul Ricoeur, have flooded obscure data with light by their insistence upon the intellectual impropriety and the actual futility of data-misappropriation. They insist that negative pre-judgments are the enemy to understanding: that an initial validity must be granted to religious rites, forms, language. Truth is not served by *reduction* to categories proper to science, anthropology, reason, or by such translations as diminish or distort past experience to the modes of contemporary experience, or by a lineal disposition of mind that is impatient with the primordial. Rather, and constructively, this discipline is learning that "the symbol is capable of revealing perspective in which diverse realities can be fitted together or even integrated into a system."[3]

Completely consonant with the extensive and magisterial work of Professor Levi-Strauss is a statement of Professor Eliade which is a virtual summary of this second peril: "One cannot sufficiently insist on this point: that the examination of symbolic structures is not the work of reduction but of integration."[4]

In trying to argue that the category of *spirit* presents itself to the mind with authentic credentials and with the promise of contributions to knowledge in virtue of its specific modes of seeing and evaluating, it has been necessary to set aside the most common connotations of the term. It has also been acknowledged that this setting aside is not generally welcome in intellectual discourse, for it supposes that the term means somewhat more and somewhat other than a gaseous ambiance, desirable as a territory into which to send questions generated by the procedures of the various disciplines but not answerable in their terms.

The capital task now confronts us — and in undertaking it we make

3. Mircea Eliade, *Mephistopheles and the Androgyne: Studies in Religious Myth and Symbol* (New York: Sheed and Ward, 1965), p. 203.
4. Eliade, *Mephistopheles and the Androgyne*, p. 201.

the second step: In what concrete way does spirit enhance the sensitivity, deepen and correct the operations of the critical intelligence, and so increase knowledge as to commend itself to the unprejudiced mind?

In the explication of this second step it will be necessary to speak historically, attend to events that are historical rather than natural, walk at some length around a huge question that confronts us in terms of our common history rather than trust to the quality of the understanding thus illumined to authenticate the category of spirit.

This conference is called "The Nation's Consultation on the Future Environment of a Democracy." That statement appeals for concreteness. We are not summoned to undertake analysis and fashion proposals as if we were doing our thinking in infinite space or in endless time. The moment's need and the terms of our summons discourage supratemporal cerebrations that float with elegant finish in the ocean of the general. We are asking after the peril, promise, and possibility of our own future as a nation in American space and American time; and we cannot do that intelligently unless we are aware that our reflections are weighted and freighted with the actuality of our national experience-in-time in this specific American-space. The past does not indeed determine the shape of the future; but past is an unsilenceable reality that has a substance, a momentum, and a structure that must be attended to if our analysis is to be adequate and our designs rational.

If the spirit operating analytically in historical reflection can disclose dynamics of formative profundity, the concreteness we need and the integrity I have affirmed to reside in spirit as a category will be manifested.

In October 1954, Professor Sidney Mead published an essay entitled "The American People: Their Space, Time and Religion."[5] Dr. Mead's essay moved its analysis forward to certain judgments about American religion. In what follows I shall ignore those conclusions and recall for our use in our present effort only the general argument. And this can be properly done; for the general analysis is in no part determined by the special data of the church historian. The purpose of the essay is stated in the first paragraph, "to suggest that, in the shaping of the American

5. Sidney Mead, "The American People: Their Space, Time and Religion," *The Journal of Religion* 34 (October 1954): 244-55.

mind and spirit, space has thus far overshadowed time in formative significance and to suggest some of the implications of this insight. . . ."
The essay begins with the recollection of de Crèvecoeur who in 1782
asked the question that has not ceased to trouble all thoughtful men in
this place. "What then is the American, the new man?" (It is a tribute to
the virtue of perspective that some of the most discerning reflections
upon American spirit and institutions have been achieved by Europeans
— Crèvecoeur, Tocqueville, James Bryce, George Santayana.)
Crèvecoeur not only saw that the American man was a "new man"; he
saw that what was new about him was not separable from the startling
experience of space as this penetrated the immigrants from the closed
and tight spaces of the old world.[6]

The formative power of the vast seemingly illimitable space that had
been available to the American man during the formative years of his nation's life can only be rightly felt when this existence-in-space is seen
over against the existence-in-time which was the old life-setting of those
who came to these shores. They had been, without exception, "a people
hemmed in, confined within the spatial boundaries set by geography
and by the closely related boundaries set by tradition and custom.
Within such boundaries, and impressed by the regular passing of one
generation after another within the confines of familiar places, they
tended to find what freedom they could for the human mind and spirit
within the context of time — time as duration, as the endless flow and
flux of events. . . ."[7]

In the new world the power of the twin forces of space and time was
reversed; here it was space that constituted the field of pragmatic operations, the matrix of personal and familial and vocational decisions, the
very particular American voluntary organization for practical ends — so
necessary for a few in the hostile and lonely environment of the frontier.
The "new birth of freedom" that a later American president was to celebrate was not a "concept"; it was a reality arising out of the condition of
life in open space meeting personal material needs. The "unconfined
movement in space — while concurrently the time ties were tattered or
broken by the breaking of the continuity of the regular passing of one

6. Mead, "The American People," pp. 244-45.
7. Mead, "The American People," p. 247.

generation after another in one place" — is the fundamental motif of that entire strain in American literature which is most authentically indigenous.

From Dr. Mead's abundant documentation of this time-space reversal as formative of the American mind and spirit, we can select only a little. Particularly telling is the doublet from Stephen Vincent Benet's *Western Star.* The poet imagines the piled-up occasions of crisis, the unrelenting struggle of the little communities on the edge between the forest and the sea, the pathos of death as it struck the very young and the very old, and he puts into language something of the men who were forbidden reflection in the perilous present by the hurtling exigencies of physical fact.

There is no time to grieve now, there is no time —
There is only time for labor in the cold.[8]

The essay also tells us of the cultivated man from New England, Francis Parkman, who, in order to study the Indians, undertook the terrifying privations of the Oregon Trail. Dr. Mead adjudges an entry in Parkman's *Journal* (on a day when, hunting for food, he shot an antelope) to be a statement of positive parable-like significance.

When I stood by his side the antelope turned his expiring eye upward. It was like a beautiful woman's dark and light. "Fortunate that I am in a hurry," thought I; "I might be troubled by remorse, if I had time for it."[9]

The American man has always been short of time! And not time only in the sense of hours to do things in, but rather as the mordant awareness of passingness, of the somber music of man's enormous journey in historical time, of time as that absolute matrix of mutability in which the common events of birth, unfolding, accomplishment, and death were, for our devout fathers, in some sense both ennobled and made meaningful by the sonorities of the old Psalm.

8. Mead, "The American People," p. 246.
9. Mead, "The American People," p. 246.

Lord, Thou hast been our dwelling place in all generations. Thou
turnest man to destruction; and sayest, Return, ye children of men.
For a thousand years in thy sight are but as yesterday when it is past,
and as a watch in the night. (Psalm 90:1, 3-4 KJV)

But this man, short on time, has been long on space! And whoever
would understand America's past in order to deepen his wisdom as he
envisions her future must measure the consequences of this — that space
has overshadowed time in the formation of all the ideals most cherished
by the American mind and spirit.

In a moment I want to suggest what I think some of these consequences are, and justify their power sufficiently to deserve my judgment
that they are indeed crucial for our future vision and decision as I have
claimed. But first an effort to give more vivid substance to the role of
space in the formation of American character.

It is now thirty-one years since my first extended period of study in
Europe. Those months were spent mostly in Germany. At Heidelberg,
in the year 1936, there were very few American students, and these few
were eagerly invited into the closest relations with the German students.
University courses in American literature and cultures were not then, as
they have since become, a common feature of continental universities.
The absence of such formal studies did not, however, inhibit the eager-
ness with which thousands of central European students were devouring
and discussing American literature. Invited to participate in one of several such informal groups at Heidelberg, I was asked each night we met
to read aloud from American novels certain passages with which the students were fascinated. All read English but very few could speak the language well, and none with sufficient ease to realize the resonance and
movement of it.

What American life in open space has meant for us, in contrast with
European life realized in given space — this became completely clear to
me when I reflected upon the particular items from American literature
I was asked to read aloud. Melville, his periods rising and falling like the
ocean swell beneath which swam Moby Dick, that huge symbol of freedom both benevolent and malicious; Walt Whitman, the intoxicating,
line-loosened spaciousness of his rushing verse. And finally, and in the
1930s, Thomas Wolfe, whose paragraphs about the vastness of the

American land under the enormous sky at night, and the great trains plunging through the scattered villages whose few lights rushed past the cars roaring into darkness — the headlong prose itself a realization of the difference between the yearning of life for satisfying order as this is sought in the numbered possibilities of an established pattern and as this is sought in the numberless and frightening boundlessness of open space.

I am arguing that the special character of a place gives measure to experience and imparts a tacit understanding of events whereby the intelligence is disposed toward all judgments and selections among possibilities, and that the term spirit is the name for this operation of the mind. Having promised a moment ago to illustrate with a concrete instance that quite formal claim, I suggest that we reflect upon the very concept of freedom as this concept has been articulated in America and among other peoples.

The matter has been discussed in these terms: "American experience has profoundly qualified the European intellectual tradition brought to this land and produced a spirit and mind, which is peculiar to this country."

The American feeling for freedom, which is in a sense the American soul of life, must be understood as an expression of American experience. Its peculiarly American quality arises from work together, and the public and private well-being which have come out of it. The quest for freedom in the context of an organized society is one thing; the exercise of freedom in work together is another. Freedom from restraint in a social order is one thing; freedom of response in a social venture is another. The former tends to be sought by way of imprudence and even unreason. The latter tends to be reasonable and even calculating. Freedom in an institution is a matter of status and power, and the quest for it is egoistic. Freedom in trans-action goes with a rational accommodation to others in an undertaking in which all parties expect to prosper. It is the fruit, not of rebellion and repudiation, but of thoughtfulness and cooperation. It requires sensitivity as well as self-love, and is the practice of mutuality. Indeed American feeling for freedom goes with the individual's self-love but self-love itself is exercised in the context of work and enjoyment together. In short, the sheer opposition of lust for freedom to prudent behavior in an established and sovereign social order is replaced in American experience with an exercise of freedom which is inseparable from the use of intelligence in trans-action.[10]

The same specification of the spirit of American understanding of freedom is explicated with somewhat more objective reference in the essay by Professor Mead to which I earlier alluded.

This concept [freedom] has always had for Americans a primary dimension of space. The pioneer felt "free" so long as he felt that he could move on when he could see the smoke from a neighbor's cabin or hear the sound of his neighbor's rifle — just as his descendant, the modern city dweller, feels "free" so long as he feels that he can move away from the undesirable location or neighbors to the suburbs, to the country home in "Connecticut." The trailer-house hitched to an automobile is as fitting a symbol of the Americans' concept of freedom today as once were the saddlebags, the rifle, and the ax. The Civil War, the center of American history, can be seen as an attempt to exercise this freedom of flight from an undesirable alliance that had almost as much appeal in the North as in the South. And one evidence of the genius of the gaunt, brooding man in the White House was his seeing that, in the long run, this was an inadequate conception of freedom, and his reminder that the mystic chords of memory that bound the Union of these people together could not be stifled by the simple expedient of dividing themselves along a geographical line.[11]

Of the authenticity of the insight represented in the preceding description of the powerful effect upon the American nation of its physical setting for now almost three hundred and fifty years and of the importance of that insight for our common future, there can, I think, be no doubt. The final and crucial task of this paper is to ask after the suffi-

10. Joseph Haroutunian, "Theology and American Experience," *Dialog* 4 (Summer, 1965): 172-73.
11. Mead, "The American People," p. 251.

ciency of such a way of feeling, thinking, planning, acting for the future of our society. The terms of the issue are quite clear; they might be stated in this way: Can a mentality and spirit nurtured upon the availability of open space even envision, much less attack, the tasks that now confront us? Can the indubitable spiritual energies called forth and shaped by frontier circumstance be informed, disciplined, reformed, and released for a future whose setting is a radically different one? Operations in new space make appropriate and effective a manner of public order that is pragmatic; can operations in a closely woven, ecologically integrated and delicate structure be rightly guided by the same cast of mind? Is the institutionalization of pragmatism an adequate public philosophy for circumstances, which in a thousand large and small particulars are new? Can the spirit that won a continent sustain a national society?

The answer, in my judgment, is clearly no. But the structure of spirit which in the new situation must, in St. Paul's phrase, constitute the "spirit of our minds" (Ephesians 4:23) must now be explicated as over against that structure of the spirit which has until now been most determinative of our nation. To that we address ourselves in these last pages.

Man lives in space and time. These dimensions of his actual existence are profound spiritual symbols, and reflection upon them as they penetrate and fructify the critical intelligence bestows both cognitive sensibility and power. Spirit, as this paper has used the term, points to that. And just as life in space is educative for the achievement of right order, so too the reality of life in time is educative to right order. The maturation of societies in space may, at a certain phase of unfolding, be so dramatic a fact that the society can ignore, set aside, or in the exuberance of its expansion repudiate the lurking and ultimately unavoidable requirements placed upon man by that other dimension of historical reality, life in time. Space offers options that may be realized by moving; time stands as a symbol for that historical accomplishment of order which is achieved by decisions made where one is. Space may operate to confront issues by flight; time is the symbol of that boundedness within the less dramatic, tougher, but ultimately more human society which is attempted by the discipline of the spirit, the perception of human values along with the operating decisions proper to such values. Time in history stands for maturity, order, discipline, choice. The spirit of the man who looks out upon the future in space, and the spirit of the man who looks inward upon the issues of right order for human life in space and time — this difference is too eloquent for abstraction. In two bits of American verse the difference is sung. In the nineteenth century, Walt Whitman got into the language the scope, the opulence, the space-intoxication of the American place and person:

> Land of coal and iron! land of gold! land of cotton, sugar, rice!
> Land of wheat, beef, pork! land of wool and hemp!
>   land of the apple and the grape!
> Land of the pastoral plains, the grass fields of the world!
>   land of those sweet-air'd interminable plateaus![12]

And a half century later George Santayana, a Boston intellectual wise in the pathos of the human problem and dedicated to the liberation of the human spirit to meet time's immemorial issues, looked out upon Cape Cod, so rich in its images of long habitation, so heavy with the signs of our human plight and promise, and wrote the lines through which thrust up the unquenchable questions. These are man's questions as spirit — and a nation becomes a human society only when it seeks an order in which its people can live and draw man open to his human size.

> The low sandy beach and the thin scrub pine,
> The wide reach of bay and the long sky line —
>   O, I am far from home.
> The salt, salt smell of the thick sea air,
> And the smooth round stones that the ebb tides wear —
>   When will the good ship come?
> The wretched stumps all charred and burned
> And the deep soft rut where the cart wheel turned —
>   Why is the world so old?
> The lapping wave, and the brood grey sky,
> Where the cawing crows and the slow gulls fly —
>   Where are the dead untold?

12. Walt Whitman, "Starting from Paumanok," in *Leaves of Grass* (New York: Aventine Press, 1931), p. 23.

And among the dark pines, and along the dark shores,
O the wind, and the wind forevermore —
    What will become of Man?[13]

The American epic has come to a turning point in the spirit of our
minds. We have, while solving some problems, ignored others. We have
fashioned a society and an industrial order at a cost, and the bill is due
and payable. The magnificence of our endowment has been cleverly used
and appallingly abused. The accumulated garbage of the achievement
has befouled the air, polluted the water, scarred the land, besmirched the
beautiful, clogged and confused our living space, so managed all human
placement and means of movement as to convenience us as consumers
and insult us as persons.

This essay began with a reminder of the many meanings, in dictionary
and in usage, of the word spirit. The meaning of the term is both holy and
human; its reference is to the divine and to the human, and in the Jewish
and the Christian traditions, these two always together. As early as the
Jewish and Christian Scriptures this difference and relation is made clear
in the difference between the *pneuma tou theou* (the spirit of God) and
pneuma tou anthropou (the spirit of man). But the reality, knowledge, and
right exercise of this spirit is affirmed to occur *in the relation.* In the creation story in the Bible this difference realized in relation, this enfolding
of Creator, Cosmos, and man the Creature in spirit, is put in literal language that contains an inexhaustible symbolism. The spirit "was moving
over the face of" the abyss (Genesis 1:2 RSV) as yet unorganized, yet un-
called into creation. The spirit was "breathed into" the creature so that he
became a living being. And in the New Testament it is affirmed that when
men in the power of the spirit envision, seek, long for fulfillment of every
lurking and restless good — it is the spirit that troubles all stasis, fatness,
despair, and engenders hope and joy. One puts it this way: "When we cry
'Abba! Father!' it is the spirit himself bearing witness *with our* spirit that
we are the children of God" (Romans 8:15-16 RSV).

I am not here as a theologian speaking to a religious community but
as a citizen of this republic, inhabitant of contemporary America, a hu-

---

13. George Santayana, "Cape Cod," in *Poems* (New York: Charles Scribner's Sons,
1923), p. 91.

man being distressed by data that witness to a failure of critical intelligence in the forms of public order in these form-shattering times. And precisely in that role I apotheosize the term spirit as that alluring pattern of wholeness, that power at once delicate and tough, whereby the possible in human terms both drives and draws the actual.

When this grace — for that is the lovely name for the presence and work of the spirit in both Jewish and Christian communities — seems to have departed from the secular city as neither affirmed, sought, nor desired, or when God is dead — that departure and that death is but the fateful report that realities that belong together have come apart. For this spirit-grace is a bestowal for, to, and within space, time, and matter. The right realm of its realization is in man's dealing with the fellowman in his hurt and promise, with science in its truth and power and possibility, with technology in its service to man beheld in the full compass of his humanity and fulfilling his manhood in the massive ecological matrix which is as penultimate as clear air and as ultimate as eternal meaning.

[1970]

Ecological Commitment as Theological Responsibility

There are two reasons why this will not be a long speech. First, I understand that I am here to excite a discussion, not to preempt one. Second, consideration of so large a matter in so short a time requires that we be very precise about theology and ecology. I intend to make an effort in that direction.

Dr. Wald's address has made it unnecessary for me to review any of the polluted facts of the case. If we can neither read nor listen, we can all see and smell. From Dr. Wald's remarks, even the offhand ones, it is clear that there is an economics of ecology. There obviously is emerging a politics of ecology. There is already a well-developed statistics of ecology. There is an aesthetics of ecology and a history of it. And there is also a biology and a botany and a chemistry of ecology.

I have been asked to speak about a theology of ecology or a theology for ecology, and I want to make a distinction. A theology *for* ecology is obviously demanded by the facts of the case. But it is rather a theology *of* ecology that I want to talk about. For if we start talking about a theology *for* ecology, we will try to manufacture out of uncriticized theological categories consequent moralistic efforts stretched to enclose new and crucial facts. Such an effort will not really be a redoing of theology in view of ecology but only an extension of traditional ethics in the presence of crisis. If that should happen, and if uncriticized fundamental categories are simply reassessed and extended, we will get ecology in the textbooks on systematic theology probably as one part of eschatology! I can already envision the busy Jehovah's Witnesses adding to the *eschaton,* which they so gleefully anticipate, the ecological disintegration as the divine mechanism of catastrophe!

A theological analysis can therefore omit further talk about the facts because *Life* magazine can outphotograph the theologians, *Look* magazine has recently demonstrated that it can certainly outdramatize them, *Time* magazine can outinterview and propagandize the theologians, and the scientists certainly outsearch and outproduce empirical data about this matter. And that is their proper business.

My task is to suggest a series of propositions, which I trust are derived from catholic, Christian, and biblical theology, and so put these before you as to help excite discussion and focus it, to open the mind to old and perhaps forgotten, or in some cases forcibly suppressed, aspects of the venerable classic theology of the church. To open the mind toward these aspects which now stand before us with terrible necessity calls for fresh theological reflection as we behold and think and feel the world. Observe, I do not say behold and think *about* the world, but behold and think and feel the world! And that helps introduce my first point, which is to state the theological position from which I think this subject can be most fruitfully approached.

The notion of God which was presupposed in Dr. Wald's reference to the "tribal God of Israel" is not the one we operate with. It is not the one the Bible operates with very long, either. The God of prophet, psalmist, Our Lord Jesus Christ, and Saint Paul and Saint John, is conceptually a considerable distance beyond the notion of the tribal God. The notion of God, which most adequately, comprehensively, and dynamically gathers up the vast biblical witness, is very close to John Calvin's statement, "The God who is the Fountain of all livingness." It has never occurred to me that my understanding of God could be threatened by galaxies or by light years. A new precision about the structure of the physical universe is not in fact disintegrative of a biblical understanding of God, but rather tends to be illustrative of it. I have never been able to entertain a God-idea which was not integrally related to the fact of chipmunks, squirrels, hippopotamuses, galaxies, and light years! All of this came forcibly to my attention sometime ago when a student in one of my classes interrupted a lecture to say, "But look, how can *anything* mean if *everything* doesn't?" which I regard as a fundamental theological question.

It seems to me that we are pretty much in the same situation, culturally and theologically, as the world of the West in the fourth century. Some of you know Charles Norris Cochrane's *Christianity and Classical Culture* (the subtitle is *A Study of Thought and Action from Augustus to Augustine*).[1] He says that the world of the fourth century required a new *arche*, a new *principium*. The fundamental notion of *Romanitas* which held the world of antiquity together had virtually been drained of integrity, of force, and of any sealing and adhering content. And therefore, as Cochrane puts it, the massive achievement of Saint Augustine was so to interpret the doctrine of the Holy Trinity that the whole of creation, the drama of redemption, and the residency of God's spirit within mankind were made understandable again as a reality to men of his time. And it lasted for one thousand years.

We are, it seems to me, in some such situation as we confront this problem. No surface tinkering with theological categories or no ever-so-petulant or patient tugging with ethical categories will really do. We are confronted with a task, as Philip Hefner has put it, of "relocating the God-question"[2] in such a way that the relocation is undertaken within the ecological situation including, of course, anthropological and historical self-understanding. But such relocation as puts the question at the point where the student asks, "How can anything mean if everything doesn't?" will demand such a fresh proposal of God-meaning as matches the size of the question.

Fresh Proposals on the Questions of Reality

So the first proposal I want to make is that the question of reality is itself an ecological question! Because the question is ecological, reality itself must be spoken of ecologically. Reality is known only in relations. This

1. Charles Norris Cochrane, *Christianity and Classical Culture: A Study of Thought and Action from Augustus to Augustine* (Oxford: Oxford University Press, 1944).

2. Philip Hefner, "The Relocation of the God-Question," *Lutheran Quarterly* 21 (1969): 329-41; a revised version appears in *Zygon* 5 (1970): 5-17.

statement conflicts with the very structure of a good deal of post-Enlightenment thought in the Western world. I mean by such a statement that we must think it possible that there is no ontology of isolated entities, or instances, of forms, of processes, whether we are reflecting about God or man or society or the cosmos. The only adequate ontological structure we may utilize for thinking things Christianly is an ontology of community, communion, ecology — and all three words point conceptually to thought of a common kind. "Being itself" may be a relation, not an entitative thing.

This notion, carried that far, is really not, I think, discontinuous with the biblical story of Creation, of the speech about God, or man, or the cosmos, or of the drama of redemption. It belongs to the "story character" of the biblical mode of expression that things are what they are declared to be only in relation to other things. There is no definition of God in the Bible. Calvin's statement responsibly reflects this: "He is the fountain of all livingness." God is the name for that one from whom all things flow. Man is what he is because he is related to that one. The fundamental term *imago Dei* is not a term that points to a substance, an attribute, or a specifiable quality, but one which specifies a relation. The fundamental terms of the Scripture — God, man, love, sin, hate, grace, covenant — are all relational words. The same fountain of life brings into being, we are told, all that is. That is, man has what being he has among things, and with things, and in a particular sense among his fellowmen. He is an ecological entity in relation. If one goes through, then, the words with which the Scripture talks about man and God and life and the world and history, he finds these relational terms the central disclosive and operational terms: restoration, redemption, salvation, faith, hope. Each of these is a term that points to the establishment of a relationship, or the breaking of a relationship, or the perversion of a relationship; and each one points to the promise of blessedness as the reestablishment of a relationship. So much for the first suggestion.

Second, reality-as-relation demands a beholding of actuality which is appropriate to the structures of reality thus beheld. I use the word "beholding" with some calculation. The new dictionaries, which play so fast and loose with old distinctions, play extraordinarily fast with this one. They say, "to behold," that is, "to see, to look." One can only lament this obtuseness! When the New Testament, for instance, reports Jesus as saying, "Behold the lilies of the field" (Matthew 6:28), one is precisely *not* saying, "Look at those lilies!" The word "behold" lies upon that which is beheld with a kind of tenderness which suggests that things in themselves have their own wondrous authenticity and integrity. I am called upon in such a saying not simply to "look" at a nonself but to "regard" things with a kind of spiritual honoring of the immaculate integrity of things which are not myself. "To behold" means to stand among things with a kind of reverence for life which does not walk through the world of the nonself with one's arrogant hat on. Therefore, to "behold" actuality from the standpoint of reality understood as relational is not just a quip of language; it is rather a rhetorical acknowledgment of a fundamental ecological understanding of man whose father is God but whose sibling is the whole Creation. To stand beholding means that one stands within the Creation with an intrinsically theological stance.

This way of regarding things is an issue that the religious community has got to attend to before it gets to the more obvious moral, much less the procedural and pedagogical, problems. For we must somehow bring under question the notion that man in his historical entity, his individual selfhood, is so set apart from the rest of God's Creation that he can deal with it with Olympian arrogance as if it had no selfhood of its own by virtue of the Creation. Unless somehow we recover and fashion anew a religious consciousness which disintegrates this, we shall only accomplish a sufficient cleaning up of industrial procedures to secure profits and a reasonably comfortable life for one generation or so, and fail to penetrate the heart of the problem.

This penetration of what Saint Paul calls the "spirit of our minds" is the fundamental task of the religious and theological responsibility in the ecological issue. And this applies all the way to such issues as the way we regard water (that it may be clean), air (that it may be pure), and things (that they be allowed to live and be their unperverted and undistorted existence). G. K. Chesterton somewhere affirms that there is something primitive in man which ought to enjoy the *thingliness* of things — "the sheer steeliness of steel, and the unutterable muddiness of mud!"

Let us look at this matter from another angle. There is a given integrity built into the variety that issues forth from the fountain of life. And all integrity in man can only be kept uncorrupted when and insofar as he honors the integrity in the thingliness of the thing itself. I have some hope this is a growing acknowledgment; and I locate that hope not so much in the homiletical or theological community as in the artistic community. One of the contributions of Picasso to my generation has been that he held starkly, interestingly, and fascinatedly before us what Chesterton called the thingliness of things. Why are people so fascinated with Picasso's mandolins? Because he paints a mandolin in such a way that, with visible simultaneity, one sees it all sides at once, inside, outside, topside, bottomside. The very thingly "mandolinness" of mandolins is what he wants to announce, a visual statement that is continuous with Gertrude Stein's effort when she says that "a thing is a thing is a thing," "a rose is a rose is a rose." Both the painting and the statement are a kind of artistic homage to the variety and the integrity of the creator. It is an appeal to permit color to be what it is, texture what it is, and let things celebrate their thingliness. Mies van der Rohe said about architecture that we should let steel celebrate the particular quality of steel by not making it do what wood ought to do, or glass ought to do, or some other thing ought to do. This is reverence for the creation by an act of intelligence and craftsmanship.

Third, an ontology of relations begets a beholding in relations, and this begets a thinking in relations. In this matter some reconstruction, it seems to me, and some demolition, too, have got to take place in the spirit of our minds. Why is it so hard for the Christian, and to some degree also the Jewish community, to get through their theological heads the idea that because one has a God relationship whose nature is called "spiritual" this category has so little to do with the category "natural"? I think I see one reason: Christianity proudly presents itself as a historical religion. The episodes that mark its emergence, the stories which convey its tradition, the stories and episodes whereby the constitutive community reports itself to us in the earliest documents — these are all historical data. The Christian believer is liable, therefore, to make an *opposition*, not just a distinction, between man-as-nature and man-as-history. This is the fateful separation which marks the post-Enlightenment community particularly. We suppose that redemption is a historical drama which leaves untouched and has no meaning for and cannot be celebrated in terms of the care of the Creation. This is a fundamental misunderstanding. Put it another way. A negative assessment of the world and man-as-nature and a solidification of this negation beget complete freedom of action toward the world of the Creation. And this freedom of action, unrestrained by any care for the Creation, can even be sanctified theologically as man's proper service of God — to be eager, busy, in his work with the world.

Integration of Theological Categories

This separation inspires some embarrassing reminders. First of all, it no longer makes any sense to make this absolute distinction, much less separation, between man-as-history and man-as-nature. The behavioral sciences and the life sciences eliminate such a separation on the first page of any responsible textbook.

The second embarrassment occurs when we turn to the Scriptures. The basic terms of *hesed, tsedeq, charis* are words whose fundamental referent is the *cosmos* that God loves — primarily the human community to be sure, but not in isolation from the rest of Creation. Creation is, as it were, an ecological event. Even the legend of the Creation in the first book of our Bible is presented in ecological context: God, and man, and the neighbor, and the whole earth as the garden for the exercise of both joy and labor! Salvation is an ecological word in the sense that it is the restoration of a right relation which has been corrupted. And observe, this drama of redemption is never satisfied with purely historical categories. We are embarrassed today because purely historical categories are no longer capable of operating sociologically or in the life sciences or in any other kind of descriptive science. And why? They have come to this incapacity because our generation has witnessed the drawing of the life and the vitality and the potentialities of *nature* into the realm of *history*. The life of nature is now pathetically open to the decisional life that man lives as a historical being. For the first time man has added to his natural curiosity and creativity a perverse aggressiveness whereby nature is absolutely suppliant before him in such a way that she lives by his sufferance and can die by his decision.

This possibility has actually never existed until our generation. That means that theological categories may no longer be only historical categories. They have got to deal with man as history and as nature; and therefore, categories of creation, redemption, and sanctification have got to operate with the same scope as the fundamental categories of man and God. And this requires not only that Christian and Jewish *morality* shall be offended by pollution but that *theology* must do more; it must be reconceived, under the shock of filth, into fresh scope and profundity.

For your further reflection, I offer two texts which might give you concrete material to reflect upon. I suggest that you read Psalm 104. That song is an ecological doxology. Beginning with the air, the sky, the little and then the great animals, the work that man does upon the earth and the delight that he takes in it, the doxological hymn unfolds to celebrate both the mysterious fecundity that evermore flows from the fountain of all livingness, up to the great coda of the psalm in which the phrase occurs — "These all hang upon Thee." The word "hang" is an English translation of a word that literally means to "depend," to receive existence and life from another. These all *hang together* because they all hang upon Thee. "You give them their life, You send forth Your breath, they live." Here is teaching of the divine redemption within the primal context of the divine Creation. Unless we fashion a relational doctrine of creation — which doctrine can rightly live with evolutionary theory — then we shall end up with a reduction, a perversion, and ultimately an irrelevance as regards the doctrine of redemption.

The world is not God, but it is God's. Or to put the issue another way, nature and grace belong together. The old theology made a distinction that some of you grew up on — the distinction between created grace and uncreated grace. By created grace is meant the ecological matrix Psalm 104 talks about. When the psalm sings a doxology by and out of a man of the earth, there is a celebration of the grace which comes to man in virtue of the Creation and precisely because of man's placement in it. This man is not singing a doxology because he is a gaseous spirit with no relation to chipmunks and corn and wine and oil; these gifts are rather the matrix and occasion whereby he knows the joy out of which he now praises God as creature. Created grace is exactly the grace that inheres in the world by virtue of a gracious God.

Uncreated grace points to that specification, incandescence, concentration, humanization, and incarnation of grace which comes not as a naked nonhistorical or nonnatural word but precisely as a historical man born of the Virgin Mary. The accent, in order to make *that* point, belongs not upon Mary but *born* of a woman. That is, of our common lot.

The second text that I think invites our reflection (and such reflections may lead us into that subbasement of theological formulations where these profound openings toward the future may take place) is the difficult eighth chapter of Romans — "The whole creation waits with eager longing for the revealing of the sons of God" (Romans 8:19). Does this not suggest that the Creation, in its suppliant and open way, waits for such human operation by men of faith as shall challenge them to be what they are called to be — sons of God — and not simply operators within the resources of the world?

One is not falling into words only in sentiment or poetic fancy but extrapolating from a clear theological position when he makes the affirmation that *Christianly* Lake Michigan must be regarded as "groaning in travail, waiting to be set free from its bondage of decay."

What strikes one, if he has worked for some years trying to call attention to this virtual demise of a vigorous doctrine of Creation, is that it is difficult but possible to get men to understand that pollution is biologically disastrous, aesthetically offensive, equally obviously economically self-destructive, and socially reductive of the quality of human life. But it is a very difficult job to get even Christians to see that so to deal with the Creation is *Christianly* blasphemous. A proper doctrine of creation and redemption would make it perfectly clear that from a Christian point of view the ecological crisis presents us not simply with moral tasks but requires of us a freshly renovated and fundamental theology of the first article whereby the Christian faith defines whence the Creation was formed, and why, and by whom, and to what end. The word essential to such renovation is not the social, aesthetic, economic, or even scientific word, but the Christian word — blasphemy!

When a contemporary theologian argues that one must think in relation, and proposes an ontology of communion as more appropriate to our time than an ontology of entities, he is liable to be called at best eccentric, or in the middle range, a Teilhardian, or at worst a sentimental Franciscan. But I would recall with you that it was not Karl Rahner or De Lubac or Schillebeeckx or Charles Davis or Metz or any of the other theologians to whom this extraordinary college was host four years ago, but it was rather Saint Thomas who said, "Gratia non tollet naturam, sed perficit." Grace does not destroy nature but perfects it! So that if any of you is frightened lest he get hold of the wrong theological handle

84

whereby to exercise this point, I give you an indubitably legitimate one. And if any of you feels left out, both Luther and Calvin quote Thomas with great approval on this point. Now, my last point.

An Ecological Understanding of Grace

I would suggest that ecology, that is, the actuality of the relational as constitutive of all that lives, is the only theater vast enough for a modern playing out of the doctrine of grace. If we are to ask which of the comprehensive Christian doctrines is the one large enough and ready enough and interiorly most capable of articulating a theological relationship between theology and ecology, I would suggest that the doctrine of grace is the one. For grace, in our understanding of it, has to be reassessed over against the scope of the biblical use of the term. And reassessed, too, by a critical restudy of the formulations about grace in the history of Christian doctrine. Augustinian individualism may not be a sufficient schema for current proclamation to contemporary man, and puritan moralization of grace may come under equally critical scrutiny. The human reality in its contemporary operations with nature, when really deeply pondered, opens up new ways of understanding grace.

As we confront the black problem, for instance, we are somewhat surprised and a bit taken aback when we observe that our extension of gracious acceptance to the black man is often not met by him with what we regard a mutuality in grace or in goodwill. And I have often wondered why that is. I think it is because he properly reads us, knows that what we intend as we go out toward him is often in obedience to the moral doctrine that all men are our brothers; in which doctrine we acquiesce, under which necessary obedience we bow as with the granting of a gift, bestowing upon him, as if it were *ours,* our acceptance. And this is understood by him as a sanctified form of insult. That we by "Christian obedience" now invest him with that which we take as our "own" endowment and do this as an act of "grace" on our part creates an even greater distance between us. But if grace is understood ecologically as built into the whole constitution of the world of nature, society, and the life of man with fellowman, if grace is explicated from the standpoint of the doctrine of the creation as bringing forth life-giving *variety,* then a quite new way of beholding the world and our fellowmen comes into possibility. I then affirm not that *I* bestow grace or *I* invest with grace but that grace comes in black and white and yellow and red! Grace comes in colors. That is a quite different understanding of grace, for it is bound up with the unthinkable variety of God the Creator who loves all colors, textures, forms, nuances, and modes of life. It is grace as the joyful acknowledgment of the variety that God loves, the variety he has made. This is quite a different theological understanding from the moral conclusion that simply commands you to obey the commands of God, and one of these is that you deal with your brother as man!

Now I conclude, as those who have been my students know I never can manage to conclude, with two lines from Gerard Manley Hopkins. The sonnet is called "Spring." The poet cries:

And what is all this juice and all this joy?
A stain of earth's sweet being in the beginning in Eden garden.[3]

Which means that the doctrine of the juice and the joy of this fountain of livingness not only is a grace that waits upon the incarnation in Jesus Christ and then is explicated under a doctrine of redemption, but is also given with the ecological situation: prehuman, human, and in all other relations.

3. Gerard Manley Hopkins, *The Poems of Gerard Manley Hopkins,* ed. W. H. Gardner and N. H. Mackenzie, 4th edition (Oxford: Oxford University Press, 1967), p. 67.

[1972]

Excerpts from
Essays on Nature and Grace

Introduction

This book is an effort to relate the ancient doctrine of the grace of God to the experience of man in the world of nature. The classical formulations of that doctrine were made long before man's understanding of nature and his manipulation of its elements and forces achieved the crucial role in his life that they presently have. What centuries of Christian reflection have felt and thought about God's grace is not to be repudiated. But the doctrine must be relocated for our time and a fresh way must be found to propose the reality of grace to men who understand the cosmos as a closed system.

The old theological rubric of "Nature and Grace" did not have to attend to Copernicus, Newton, Darwin, Marx, Freud, or to the world- and self-understanding which has been engendered by the knowledge and insight these names represent. As late as Luther and Calvin, that rubric could still put the problem and deal with it according to the fundamental terms of the catholic centuries. The question Luther and Calvin asked was no different from that raised by their fathers all the way from St. Paul to St. Thomas Aquinas. The natural-world matrix of the issue was the same, and they asked: How does the disposition and power of a gracious God impact upon, penetrate, change, and redeem sinful man?

Man is a sinner, and he lives in a world. But his life in that world has become literally a new kind of life. Where is grace in this world that has been experimentally taken apart by empirical science, its laws disclosed, its structure and process translated into statistical terms, and the knowledge of which, even if fragmentary, is sufficient to secure predictability and enable fantastically complicated manipulation of its forces and processes? Is it possible to reconceptualize, expand, experience, and bear witness to the grace of God within a world that is beheld and practically dealt with as a closed system? That is the issue to which these chapters are addressed.

The ecological issue is introduced, not because that issue solves the problem, but because it forces the problem upon the mind's attention. Reflection upon grace does not depend upon viewing the world as an ecosystem; the world as an ecosystem provides the fateful occasion for such fresh reflection. When, therefore, in the pages to follow the ecological facts of life are alluded to, such allusions are not introduced as arguments for the reality of grace; they are rather descriptions of the *field* of grace, expositions of the actuality of man's life and placement within the web of nature. The life of man so placed, related, and embedded constitutes a factual precondition to the kind of speech about grace which has the possibility really to address him.

The title, *Essays on Nature and Grace,* is a way of saying to the reader something about procedure and style. The word "essays" announces that no single starting point is fixed, that a variety of perspectives are employed, that whatever force the argument has is cumulative and symbiotic. Style of presentation, while a kind of obedience to differences in data, is more than that. For what is necessary is to reenact in representation in language the order or disorder, the logic or accidental sequence by which facts, events, and relations invite new reflections on previously solidified themes.

Alfred North Whitehead once remarked that ". . . style is the morality of the mind." He was saying that style is not a formal addition to the operation of sensibility and mind but is of the very substance and lively nature of their working in a man. If, in the pages to follow, there is a certain looseness, a seeming leap from one kind of data to another, an unusual putting together of facts and reflections that seem on the surface to be far apart, a symbiosis of insights that are biblical, historical, poetical, practical — in short, if the style of these chapters seems out of step with prevailing mores in theological exposition, I can only say that these peculiarities are a way of being "moral." For in writing about a theme in a way that shall reenact in diction and vocabulary the living process by which that theme emerged, unfolded, intersected, became enforced and modified by others, one owes to honesty the effort to expound what comes out of his mind in a style appropriate to the fundamental unsystematic of the way it entered his mind. The matter, that is to say, not only controls the manner; it is dependent upon it for right release.

The perils of this stylistic path are clearly known to me; I live my life among articulate colleagues and students who forcibly remind me of them. I choose to disobey with my eyes open. A model professor professes and practices his competence around a well-defined item within an enormous web. He is most clear about the item if he ignores the web! But to have a mind that honors that way of working and at the same time retains a sense of humor about that way's adequacy to the kind of Christian theme he wants to express and about the receiving equipment of the community to which the address is made, is to be forced to open up theological speech according to the requirements of the theme itself.

The "web" apart from which I cannot think, or think about thinking, is the ecological structure of the human reality. The term "ecology" has a transphysical meaning. It points with undismissable stubbornness to the *context* of all things; it insists that no thing exists apart from all things. All orders have uncertain edges, all categories leak, all propositions conceal a presupposition, or an aware or unaware limitation within which alone they are accurate or represent truth.

The recognition that one is in deepest nature vehemently ecological is a recognition that cannot without betrayal be distorted by style or denied. It is to that danger that Whitehead points in his aphorism that ". . . style is the morality of the mind." Something of the same ecological embeddedness of thought informs George Santayana's statement in the introduction to a little volume of his work. He was speaking of the formal conventionality of his poems, and explained, "If their prosody is warm and traditional, like a liturgy, it is because they represent the initiation of a mind into a world older and larger than itself; not the chance experiences of an individual, but his submission to what is not his chance experience, to the truth of nature, and to the moral heritage of

89

mankind."[1] Santayana's poems, that is to say, are not episodic expostulations; they are "like a liturgy" — having a language and a quiet rhythm that honors the life and experience of men long dead and the immemorial continuities that persist through change.

About a hundred years ago William James, in a Harvard College lecture, declared that:

> The real world as it is given objectively at this moment is the sum total of all its being and events now. But can we think of such a sum? Can we realize for an instant what a cross-section of all existence at a definite point of time would be? While I talk and the flies buzz, a sea gull catches a fish at the mouth of the Amazon, a tree falls in the Adirondack wilderness, a man sneezes in Germany, a horse dies in Tartary, and twins are born in France. What does that mean? Does the contemporaneity of these events with one another, and with a million others as disjointed, form a rational bond between them, and unite them into anything that means for us a world? Yet just such a collateral contemporaneity, and nothing else, is the real order of the world. It is an order with which we have nothing to do but to get away from it as fast as possible. As I said, we break it: we break it into histories, and we break it into arts, and we break it into sciences; and then we begin to feel at home.[2]

All my life I have sought a form of theological discourse which should be obedient in style to James's *dictum,* especially "collateral contemporaneity." And when one seeks, as I presently do, to articulate the immediacy of grace, to interiorize the objective reality of the dogma so that it shall become forceful for our time's need to stand *within* the creation as we receive redemption, the difficulty becomes enormous. For theological exposition itself is ordered, sequential discourse, but the gifts of grace whereby grace is apprehended, acknowledged, and allowed to focus sensibility and excite reflection — these are not ordered or sequential. The life-liveliness of a thing-becoming is not the same as the

---

1. George Santayana, *Poems* (New York: Charles Scribner's Sons, 1923), p. 2.
2. William James, "Reflex Action and Theism," in *The Limits of Language,* ed. Walker Gibson (New York: Hill and Wang, 1962), pp. 8-9.

static status of a thing-become. And a way must be found to reenact in the style of the report the wild unsystematic of the occurrence.

One must, to be sure, seek order. The election of a discursive rather than a logical sequence does not deny this necessity. But the order imposed must be appropriate to the end sought. The reality of disorder in the "collateral contemporaneity" must not be repudiated or forgotten. It is this effort to make the style of utterance appropriate to contemporary sensibility that characterizes the "disordered-order" one finds in modern poetry, the short story, the novel, current nonconsecutive humor, and drama. Language has to be sprung open to the fact, the chaos, the novelty of experience. The serene diction of Jane Austen would not serve to represent in language the life-pace and shocks of our time. All uses of language are an imposition of order. And all language comes short of what it would communicate. In even its most ample and precise exercise language is a verbal groping for sufficiency, a grammar stalking elusive relations, flung loops of sentences tightening around the undulant and the evanescent.

I should like, then, to set down the bundle of components that have determined a central theme. It is sometimes the case that one's reflections upon problems, crises, and experiences are troubled by a persistent suspicion that they are all related, that facts and relations lack definition and move so slowly toward conceptual resolution because the reality in which they have their unity has not declared itself.

In virtue of what gift, love, understanding, and appropriate behavior can man live with the world-as-nature so as rightly to enjoy and use it? That is the problem. It is the thesis of these chapters that nothing short of a radical relocation and reconceptualization of the reality and the doctrine of grace is an adequate answer to that problem.

CHAPTER 2

Grace in the Scriptures

When one sets out to describe the meanings and energies designated by the term "grace" he confronts a simple but powerful impediment. Most Christians first heard the word in preaching or in catechism or some other adolescent or earlier situation. And when the Old Testament is directly read we commonly come at it via the New Testament. What is said in the Gospels and Epistles about the grace of God so fills the term that pre–New Testament statements about God and his grace are either not attended to (because the term "grace" is not an Old Testament term) or are subsumed under the grace-Christ rubric so firmly as to invite the mind to suppose that before Christ, and without Christ, grace does not exist.

This "location" of the term continues to operate reductively at more sophisticated levels. Trinitarian formulations have begotten a triadic sequence of creation, redemption, sanctification. Appropriate and useful as this triad may be for Christian theology, the application of it to the experience of Israel — and the more unconscious the more obscuring — pulls into wrong proportions the Old Testament way of understanding God, the power and scope of the goodness of God, and the implications of faith in him for the formal ethics of Israel and for her mode of life in its various cultic manifestations. In the Old Testament the magnetic and dominating central term is "redemption." That term draws about itself the meaning, presence and promise of God to Israel which, in her own understanding was disclosed to her in creation, in historical covenant, and in the interpretation of historical events whereby the fidelity of God to his people was known and celebrated.

The fundamental meaning of grace is the goodness and loving-kindness of God and the activity of this goodness in and toward his creation. Israel knew God in that way, but this knowledge is never specified in the sense of being identified with a term, or a concept, or a single action having an absolute primacy. The uncovenanted, precovenanted will and disposition that does what it does from within itself (and then "covenants" to secure the reality of the doing), has as its most common names the terms *chen* and *chesed. Chen* is God's initiating grace; *chesed* is faithfulness or loyalty in all covenants and relationships based on *chen.* The content of these terms shines through such passages as Exodus 33:17-19 and 34:6-7.

A feeling for the form and function of such statements, integral as they are to Israel's understanding of God, of how he manifests, rules, blesses, and intends for his people, indicates that later large categories under which life was divided into life-as-nature and life-as-history are useless for grasping the structure of Israel's faith. It must rather be seen that God is "the Holy One," that all that is is given, and all that happens as event and process is to be related to his faithfulness in mercy and in judgment. This fidelity and presence is manifested in "the glory" and nothing that is or happens is intrinsically incapable of refracting this glory. The "glory of thy people Israel" is the lens in the eye of faith through which all things — natural, personal, social, historical — are beheld. Nebuchadnezzar can be the strange agent of this glory; the glory which "thou hast set *above* the heavens" is also declared *by* the heavens. Nature is not an entity or a process set alongside God and having its own autonomy, its own "insides," its "laws." It is, rather, continuous with the reality of God as Creator. This is not to say that for the man of the Old Testament God is knowable by *Naturwissenschaft,* just as God is not knowable by *Geisteswissenschaft.* God is made known to man in the matrix of space, time, and matter, which are the substance of that mortal theater in which God deals with his people in their historical actuality.

These comments about Israel are intended as a background whereby what shall presently be said about the movement of New Testament testimony to Christ and the scope of his grace may be understood both in its Christ-concentration, and in its extent. For if the doctrine of the divine redemption there centered upon Christ is not assessed as moving toward the same spatial largeness as characterized the Old Testament celebration of the "space of the glory" such a movement will continue to be ignored in Christian theology, or rejected, or regarded as marginal or esoteric.

If grace, as witnessed to in the New Testament, is to be proposed in fresh ways of address as actually the will and power of God in Jesus Christ for the redemption of men, and if the actuality of contemporary man's formation-as-man in virtue of his life-conditions and transactions with nature is to be taken seriously, then Christian theology must explicate a doctrine of grace in continuity with the Scripture and in such bold and new reformulations as the reality of grace and its salvatory power demands.

To undertake that task of obedience is a large order placed upon the desk of the theologian, and the task falls with both particular urgency and promise upon all who stand within the Protestant tradition. The urgency does not require much amplification. When a tradition announces that its peculiar contribution to catholic Christendom is its clear and permeating witness to the freedom of God in his grace, and organizes its theological systematic around that proclamation, the urgency is in the tradition itself. And the promise lies in the evangelical insight that made it central there.

But even so tentative an essay as this must specify some practical embarrassments as the task is undertaken. The chief one is this: the same confessional tradition which has been relentlessly acute and productive in biblical studies hesitates (particularly in such theological statements as emanate from its self-conscious confessional assemblies) to introduce the results of such studies into its theological schematizations and formulations. The same church whose scholars have contributed so richly to the clarification of the conditions within which the New Testament was written, the variety of its focus and terms of witness, the startling fecundity of its faith-responding speech and the vast reach of its vision and reference, has permitted highly stylized accents and motifs in the Scripture to control its present as, in quite a different era in biblical scholarship, they controlled its past.

With no diminishment in gratitude for the past, and in the conviction that centeredness upon grace is indeed proper and obedient, we must reacknowledge with our fathers that formulations must follow the energies of realities, and that theology has a transbiblical obligation to be exercised in that creative reflection to which reference has been made. And if such reflection is to be creative, some responsible risks have to be taken, some realities and meanings have to be proposed for faith within, but not derived from, the ever-changing formation of man within the convolutions and creativities of culture.

There is within the New Testament no single or simple way of speaking of God and man and grace and history and the natural world. Indeed, the New Testament witness to God and to Christ discloses a process, with the Scriptures of Israel back of it and a variety of world situations around and in front of it, which can be characterized as a process of fusion, transformation, and clarification.

Fusion means that elements disclosed in separated episodes are put together in fresh combinations. Transformation means that the resultant motif is more than and different from the sum of the components. Clarification means that what was partial, opalescent, and potential in components thus fused becomes more full, transparent, and concentrated. That such fusion, transformation, and clarification characterizes the New Testament is here argued; it is not the point at the moment to evaluate that happening.

The community that produced the New Testament did not undertake its task of witness to Christ with a full heart and an empty head. Nor did it fashion its statements with minds that were innocent of the substance, texture, referential opulence, or historical solidity of the terms, images, and symbols of the people of the old covenant. They bore witness to Christ as the center and intention of all these; but the Christ to whom they bore witness was in continuity with the God of Abraham, Isaac, and Jacob. That this witnessing Christocentrism was intended as a modification of the theocentrism of the faith of Israel is a notion that would have been regarded by the writers of the New Testament as both incredible and blasphemous. When the community spoke of Christ's doing they were speaking of God's doing; when they cherished and transmitted Christ's speaking they were reporting what they believed to be an address to them and through them of the reality of God. This faith, this continuity, and this intention was, indeed, generative of a community that knew itself to be constituted by an event that was nothing less than a new form of the God-relationship; but the articulation of that new form at the same time testifies to the old in the very substance of its reportorial and testimonial language.

Form-critical methods in New Testament study have in our time so powerfully intersected with the evaporation of transcendent categories as to produce the current hermeneutical impasse. For the purpose of this discussion it is not necessary to come down with a decision for or against any of the many parties and positions of that effort to forge an ample and correct method of interpretation. I have in another place[3] stated my conviction that the radical either-or's of the academicians are excessively rigid, and achieve their apparent total demolition of opponents by a strange humorlessness about the richness of the modalities of historical life. Kerygma without narrative leaves unaccounted for the very substance which made kerygma effective; and narrative without kerygmatic proclamation leaves unaccounted for the very evaluation that preserved and cherished the narratives. But there is happy evidence that the more doctrinaire proponents of various positions in this debate are beginning to be embarrassed by their departure from sober attention to the multiphasic force and form of the Gospel proposal as this proposal was made to both Jew and Gentile.

> The key to our problem taken as a whole is not the question of the historical Jesus as such and in isolation over against the kerygma, but the kerygmatic reversion to the narrative form *after* enthusiasm, mythological representations and dogmatic reflection had already carried the day to the extent illustrated by the primitive Christian hymns. Correspondingly, in the case of the mysterious Cosmocrator, a dazzling light is reflected back upon him who traverses Palestine as a rabbi. How could they revert from glorifying him who was the object of preaching to telling the story of him who was himself the preacher — and within the framework of the kergyma at that? This question is of pre-eminent significance, both historically and theologically — but Bultmann has not put it. Obviously, he hardly sees it.[4]

Generations of scholarship have noted and specified the huge variety of the New Testament witness to Christ. And dogmatic response to that variety has very often been an imposition upon it of an order dictated by concerns foreign to the data, but creative of a hierarchy of importance by which the wilderness of the data could be given the neatness and sequence so satisfying to system. But the vitality of the variety continues

3. Joseph Sittler, *The Anguish of Preaching* (Philadelphia: Fortress, 1966), ch. 2.
4. Ernst Käsemann, *New Testament Questions of Today* (Philadelphia: Fortress, 1969), p. 62.

to trouble the seeming solidity of the system. One tradition begins with the prophetic announcement in dramatic terms that the time of the kingly rule of God is imminent; another tradition sets the incomparable evaluation of the event of Christ within the birth stories; another sets the events it employs for the construction of its pattern within the vast matrix of "In the beginning was the Word." It thus organically relates the redemptive grace which is the burden of its new message with the uncovenanted and covenanted grace of God in creation and in Israel's history.

Nor is this variety, including the conceptual magnificence of the Fourth Gospel, an aspect of the testimony to Christ that comes to us only in those literary forms that we know as the Gospels. In the Pauline and other voices of the first century there is a language of testimony, an articulation of vitalities and relations into concatenated forms that reach back historically into Israel's past, grope forward into the future, and impart an eschatological cruciality to the present eon.

Is it possible to speak of this variety in such a way as, on the one hand, to honor the warning against dogmatic "arrangement," and, on the other, to acknowledge that there is movement in this witness, that the referential amplitude is vastly wider in some voices than in others, that the vision of the meaning sweeps in some an arc whose circumference enfolds things near and clear and in others an arc whose axis is "before the foundation of the world" and whose outriding reaches are ". . . the mystery of his will — a plan for the fullness of time, to unite all things in him, things in heaven and things on earth"?

It is possible not only to remark these differences but also to behold them as differences-in-motion. That motion is clearly not chronological; and efforts to make "high Christology" late and "low Christology" early in the community's recorded experience are clearly illegitimate. If, then, that "motion" was not chronological, how may its nature and direction be designated? It is here proposed that christological momentum may be the most accurate term for what the literature of the New Testament discloses. Differences in the size of the circles of range and reference are clearly in the material, and the types of the rhetoric of celebration which these employ can be noted.

The phrase "rhetoric of celebration" is calculated to break discussion loose from the grip of such language-analysis as would bestow intelligi-

97

bility and "truth-claim-possibility" upon only such statements as can be shorn of their force-constituting images and reduced to verifiable components. For when theological discourse consents to divest itself of speech appropriate to the modalities appropriate to the historical, and acquiesces in the lust for clarity, intent, purport, and meaning as these take their model from ahistorical operations of the mind, Christian theological discussion will have bowed itself out of the company of significant disciplines.

As biblical and theological scholarship moves toward a more inclusive and precise formulation of the hermeneutical problem, more serious attention is being given to what theological implications inhere in style of speech and forms of rhetoric as these come to us from the earliest Christian communities. The phrase "style of life," common among contemporary ethicists, is a reminder that there is an organic and integral *gestalt* which is back of, down under, and formative of lived-experience and response, and is a force that escapes overly systematic efforts to specify and contain it. When, then, appeal is made to "style" or "type of rhetoric" the intention is not to evade or give a low estimation of such painstaking textual analysis as grounds theological insight. The appeal is rather that we consider whether problems disclosed by analysis and not soluble in terms of analysis alone might be illuminated by such ways of listening as are denoted by the words "style" and "rhetoric." For there is an undilutable momentum, a "blooming" of the language of Christ-testimony, in the New Testament. There is a way of praise and glorification that probes for a largeness of language appropriate to its ultimacy. This intention describes widening circles of meaning; it is a living illustration of that embarrassment of purely designative language in the presence of overwhelming encounters and freshly given possibilities. Is it possible to formulate a typology of rhetoric that might both discern and to some degree illustrate patterns in this process? The following is a tentative proposal.

Rhetoric of Recollection

In this type, the testimony to Christ has its ground in, receives its force from, and takes its direction from the rich and various vocabulary for the hope of Israel. The promises of God are the hope of Israel. These promises, the hope engendered and sustained by them, and the designations in specific terms of how this hope had become incandescent in Jesus Christ constitute a major strand in the New Testament. The terms and images of these promises and of this hope are recollected, used in fresh continuations with recorded teachings and deeds, fused with one another and welded to present events, transformed in many and sometimes strange, sometimes strained ways.

The list of such promise-transmitting and hope-carrying terms is a long one: Son of God, servant of God, royal king, David's son, Priest, suffering witness to the covenant, sorrowing man of the remnant, Lamb of God, Shepherd of Israel, the Word and Wisdom of God, the "glory" of Israel manifest in the "light" to the Gentiles, etc.

This way of testifying-forward by recollecting-backward characterizes many of the words of Jesus. It was a way of opening the mind, shocked by the marvelous deed or the astounding word, to the promise and power already known and attested by Israel. Its momentum toward the cruciality of the moment and the indeterminate possibility of the future is fused within and kerygmatically uncoiled from the inheritance already known — "you know neither the Scriptures nor the power of God!"

The way in which this rhetoric of recollection was worked out is, to be sure, different in the various documents. It is quite clearly the organizing principle of the first chapter of St. Luke's Gospel: the management of the birth narratives is a superb quasi-liturgical prolegomenon to the record about to be entered. The continuation of the testimony in the Acts of the Apostles fashions entire sermons that disclose the same intention.

The Fourth Gospel grounds its particular christological momentum farther back and deep under the historical manifestations in Israel's life, in that beginning which was "the Word." The writer asserts that the Word has always shone in a darkness that has not overcome it, leaps to "a man sent from God," and from the Baptist to the enfleshed Word who is focused presence in humanity of "the glory."

The prologue to the Fourth Gospel is an instance of something that has very often happened in the history of exegesis and in the development of doctrine: a term, or a pericope dominated by a term, may be so closely identified with a particular theological issue that consideration of it apart from that issue becomes difficult. The power of association determines the interpretation.

Writing in 1951, Allan D. Galloway said:

It is unfortunate that modern theology has always regarded the Logos doctrine primarily as a doctrine of the person of Christ rather than a part of the doctrine of the work of Christ. The two can never be completely separated, of course. And the Logos doctrine is manifestly a doctrine of the person of Christ. But if we interpret it against its background in Paul, we shall see that it is a doctrine of the person of Christ which arose in answer to the problems of interpreting the *work* of Christ to the gentile world. Therefore, in the long run, it is primarily as an assertion of the cosmic significance of the *work* of Christ that we should see it.[5]

It is a responsibility, and a pleasure, to record here my debt to Dr. Galloway's work. While I had, before reading *The Cosmic Christ,* come some distance along the road marked out by the argument of these essays, Dr. Galloway's work was instructive, stimulating, and supportive.

A formal analysis of the structure of St. Paul's proposal of Christ discloses a steady if sometimes allegorical and strained use of the same rhetoric of recollection. One has only to reflect upon the regularity in St. Paul's letters of such connective terms as "Well then," "therefore," "If then," "for this cause." So absolutely is this recollective "connective-tissue" the substance of the point of the address in any section of Paul's letters that responsible preaching about anything the apostle says requires that the verse or pericope be thrust into the entire argument. This process requires nothing less than the recollection of everything he says as the sufficient context for anything he says.

Rhetoric of Participation and Reenactment

The "model" of this type, if one may substitute a modern way of speaking for an ancient one, is not so much the carrying forward of the past

5. Allan Galloway, *The Cosmic Christ* (London: Nisbet and Co., Ltd., 1951), p. 54.

into remembrance in order to interpret the present, as it is an organic process whereby redemption is given in and by participation in that One who is in himself the culmination of a process. If in these days, as one testimony has it, God has spoken to us in the enpersonalized Word, then participation in and vital reenactment of that Word in its earthly career is the model of redemption.

This type of rhetoric proposed that in the actual life, obedience, suffering, death, and resurrection of Jesus Christ is concentrated both the reality of alienation and its conquest by the grace of God. The morphology of this divine-human microcosm is the reality and model of redemption; nothing short of a responding reenactment of the dynamics of it, as these are illuminated and empowered by the Spirit, is the reality of the Christian life.

The morphology of grace "repeats" itself within the morphology of the life called into new being by grace. Professor Amos Wilder puts the matter as follows:

> . . . the gospel is not a history so much as a ritual re-enactment or *mimesis.* The believer did not hear it as a record of the past. With the brotherhood he found himself in the middle of the world-changing transaction of conflict, death and glory. We have here a new speech-form in the profound sense of a new communication of meaning, by which men could live.[6]

The speech of Jesus about the vine and the branches roots this model firmly in the recollected tradition; but in the pastoral counsels recorded in the Epistles this way of redemption is fully and variously filled out. The eloquence and immediacy of this rhetoric of participation and reenactment gains in force when one recognizes that its introduction into apostolic discourse is suggested not by pedagogical-doctrinal concerns but by concrete pastoral situations. The doctrinally crucial statements are evoked by the necessity for the apostle to ground his pastoral counsel; and when, as in the passages we are about to note, the biographical detail is inserted, that insertion is not an end

6. Amos Wilder, *The Language of the Gospel* (New York: Harper and Row, 1964), p. 37.

in itself, but en route to an elaboration of the morphology of preve-
nient grace in Christ.

The significance of this pastoral occasion for the formulation of the
doctrine lies not only in the sufficiency of the doctrine to address the situation confronted, but — and this is more important — in the complete
naturalness with which, to adduce an instance from Paul, the apostle
forges a vast christological statement as alone sufficient to deal with
concrete problems in the Philippian community. The last verses of the
first chapter report the apostle's concern over the threats to unity and
courage among his fellow believers at Philippi. The great christological
song in 2:5-11 is but a doxology in Christ whereby the apostle places
the moment's trouble in the context of Incarnation, ablation, and exalta-
tion. We are to "have this mind" because this mind *is* ours for the having
in the man Jesus. "Have this mind — which you have!" The interchange
is a product of that grace whose model is participation and reenactment.

In the third chapter of the same epistle occurs an even more dramatic
instance of the same type. The community is to "Beware of those dogs,"
"the evil-workers," "those who insist upon circumcision." Between the
warning and the responding counsel are seven verses of biographical detail about Paul himself. But the point of that detail is only to witness
and certify out of the intimate experience of the writer that he has been
and continues to be formed in grace by an obedience repetitive of the divine grace. What God does in Christ has a shape; it is an entering into
human life, a suffering, a dying, a resurrection from the dead. This
lived-out structure of the Christ-deed of grace is identical with the
lived-out interior drama of the life of the believer. Faith is participation,
and participation is reenactment, and the stages of reenactment are the
same as the stages of the Act. "To know him" is not a matter of cognition at a distance or an obedience by affirmation. Knowledge is a gift
given to giving one's self over to that renewal of the self which is nothing less than a "resurrection from the dead." Suffering and death, the reality of Christ's life, are actual reenactments within the life of faith.

This grace-from-above, in its power to deal in and by grace with
things within and around, is disclosed and illustrated in the final chapter of the Philippian letter. This chapter is a veritable Christology for
secularity. The grace of God whereby "Christ Jesus has made me his
own" establishes the center. But the center is not the circumference; the

circumference of the grace which is redemption is not smaller than that theater of life and awareness which is the creation. The grace that *came* in enpersonalized Incarnation in Jesus Christ is no other than the grace of God who is Creator, Sustainer, and Lawgiver. From the pinnacle of this grace of God, given in the desolation and victory of Christ's immolated life, all things are to be seen, evaluated, used, enjoyed, and made the field of grace. *Therefore* — "whatever is true, whatever is honorable, whatever is just, whatever is pure, whatever is lovely, whatever is gracious, if there is any excellence, if there is anything worthy of praise, think about these things. What you have learned and received and heard and seen in me, do; and the God of peace will be with you" (Philippians 4:8-9 RSV).

In Romans 6:1-11 the pattern is almost exactly repeated. The dynamics of sin and grace are presented with the same rhetorical type of discourse. The actuality wrought out by a man in one place becomes the morphology of grace for every man in every place, and the transmission of power is by way of participation-as-reenactment: baptism-burial-raised from the dead. The language of reenactment here takes on a fierce literalness — "For if we have become incorporate with him in a death like his we shall also be one with him in a resurrection like his. If we thus died with Christ we believe that we shall also come to life with him."

When we extend illustration of this type of Christ-grace testimony to the Epistles we find that every centrally operational term of that rich vocabulary receives added relations and meanings. The concept of faith as participating membership "in the body" is so constant and crucial that one is led to hope that the currents of post-Reformation theology and devotion, in the course of which the doctrine of the mystical body was virtually excised from Protestant reflection, might be reconsidered. For any effort to reduce the organic structure of the New Testament language about grace to terms which ignore life in the body of Christ as participation, reenactment, and interchange is so radical an excision as to constitute a mutilation.

Rhetoric of Cosmic Extension

While our attention in this section will be centered in that strand of testimony that we have called "cosmic extension," it is necessary to refer, however briefly, to that understanding of the scope of the power of God and images appropriate to it which were ready at hand to the Jewish Christians of the first century of the Christian era. The material was there and capable of christological extension because it could not be avoided; it belonged to the substance of God-understanding and nature-understanding in Israel. In his *Inspiration and Revelation in the Old Testament,* H. W. Robinson has the following paragraph:

> The Hebrew vocabulary includes no word equivalent to our term "Nature." This is not surprising if by "Nature" we mean "The creative and regulative physical power which is conceived of as operating in the physical world and as the immediate cause of all its phenomena." The only way to render this idea into Hebrew would be to say simply "God." We should have to describe a particular physical activity through anthropomorphic phrases such as the "voice" of God, heard in the thunder; the "hand" of God, felt in the pestilence; the "breath" of God, animating the body of man; the "wisdom" of God, ultimately conceived as His agent in creation.[7]

Our modern view of nature as by definition not having anything to do with the divine is in complete hiatus with the Old Testament view. There, nature comes from God, cannot be apart from God, and is capable of bearing the "glory" of God.[8]

Such a view of God and nature makes completely clear why the redemption of God is celebrated in proleptic visions of a restored nature. For the realm of redemption cannot be conceived as having a lesser magnitude than the realm of creation. The creation as "fallen" is never per-

7. H. Wheeler Robinson, *Inspiration and Revelation in the Old Testament* (Oxford: Clarendon Press, 1946), p. 1.

8. Cf. the relevant sections in Gerhard von Rad, *Theology of the Old Testament* (New York: Harper and Row, 1965), and the article "Ktisis," in Gerhard Kittel, ed., *Theological Dictionary of the New Testament,* trans. and ed. Geoffrey W. Bromiley, vol. 3 (Grand Rapids: Eerdmans, 1965), pp. 1000-1035.

mitted to exempt its form and creatures and destinies from the great salvation. Professor Allan D. Galloway has written:

> But the Synoptic Gospels do not merely repeat the earlier Jewish insight. Apart from any other considerations, there is this great difference that for the New Testament writers the great redeeming event was no longer a distant future hope, but had already occurred. It had not come fully or finally, but only partially and ambiguously: yet it had become sufficiently actual to transfer their eschatological hopes from the realm of dreaming fantasy to that of present reality. The Messiah had come and already the eyes of the blind were opened and the ears of the deaf unstopped. The lame man leaped as an hart and the dumb sang, and the multitudes were fed on miraculous bread. Whatever the events which lay behind these stories in the early tradition of the church they were sufficiently powerful in their significance to convince the first Christians that the new age had actually come, and only its final fulfillment was still lacking. Already in the Anointed One the things of heaven and the things of earth were joined together.
>
> Something physical, as well as spiritual, had happened in the work of Christ. Indeed these two concepts are not held in the same kind of contrast as they would be now in the twentieth century. Our Lord made a sharp distinction between outward forms and personal faith: but this is a different thing from the contrast between spirit and matter.[9]

As we turn to the Epistles for a type of christological ascription which swings out to cosmic dimensions, we are aware that we are dealing with statements which, in Western Christology at least, have remained marginal, if admitted at all, to the most influential treatises. In the section to follow, we shall indicate the eccentric character of this development and propose some speculations to account for it. But a preliminary task is to face and put into proper perspective two common objections to such attention as shall be given to sections in the letters to the Colossians and the Ephesians where the cosmic type receives fullest statement.

9. Galloway, *The Cosmic Christ,* pp. 34-35.

The first objection is the still unsettled problem of authorship of both epistles, and, in the instance of the Colossians, the literary integrity. This objection is legitimate but not crucial. It has greatest weight for those scholars whose purely textual work has alienated them, or kept them from even having been interested in that entire process whereby documents achieve status in a tradition, or in the theological and historical importance of the fact that such status has never been withheld from these letters. The theologian cannot, to be sure, formulate serious statements by scooping up fragments from whatever he finds interesting in the milieu of the early church. But he is also forbidden to permit open questions of a technical nature to dash from his hand sources which have indubitable standing in the tradition, which have from the earliest times been accepted as having apostolic authority, and whose substance is not severable from powerful strands of patristic teaching, preaching, and catechesis.

As systematic theological reflection moves through historical time, it must not only discard biblical literalism (and that battle is far behind us); it must also discard a subtle form of literalistic thinking which persists in what might be called "quantitative literalism." By that I mean a higher or lower regard for the power and implications of a theme according to the frequency of its presentation in the Scripture. The Christian reality is not separable from the Scripture, and it is not identical with or limited to the Scripture. Theological reflection is in continuity with themes, records, episodes, teachings, etc., as these meet us in Scripture, and has in these its engendering and controlling norm. But hearing the Word and doing theology is an exercise in faithful reflection which, if it is to be intelligible, must partake of the dynamism of all historical, cultural, and experiential life. In the evolution of man's biological form and capabilities across the millennia of time, nature probed in an infinite virtuosity of effort the possibility for higher forms — some abortive, some rich with phyla that led to higher forms. As from one strand among the very many, and that one not in its earlier stages notably different from others, nature fashioned the progenitors of man. So the Christologies that emerged in the first several centuries, while certainly not "wrong," do not in their number or structure actualize all the potentialities that lie resident within the magnificent doxological witness of the community to Christ.

Theology always, to transform a statement of Goethe, in the need of the moment seizes that which shall serve and bless it. Such a strand of early witness to Christ is here alluded to under the phrase "cosmic extension." That this theme is in the New Testament a tentative, probing theme, some expressions of which seem to have been evoked by the gnostic, or another, heresy, that the theme has not been worked out with the systematic fullness that characterizes clearer and more amply attested christological images and ascriptions — all of this must be acknowledged. But it must also be insisted that the theme is a legitimate accent in the rhetoric of the earliest community, that its referential roots in the Scripture are deep, that confessional or other solid continuities dare not impose impediments to its scrutiny. The contours of need and interest in the long life of the people of God have time after time found contours of disclosure in the Scripture. St. Augustine's treatise on the Holy Trinity is no less admirable because we know the cultural crises that evoked it and gave to it the particular analogical form it has.

The implications that are resident within the preceding paragraph are most likely to be seized upon by New Testament scholars whose hermeneutical principles (a) are unchanged by the exposure of the community-forming and preaching character of the New Testament documents and, (b) would restrict theological development to changing forms of statement believed identical with the "intention" of the writer and the text.

The development of the science and art of interpretation has, however, moved through several stages, and has now come to a way of hearing and understanding a text which provides not only a fresh encounter with the old discipline of biblical theology but also a creative way to move from biblical theology to the ever-new tasks of systematic theology.

The several stages through which hermeneutical inquiry has moved are most generally designated as a hermeneutics of symbolical language, a hermeneutics of existential phenomenology, and a hermeneutics of structure. This last model relies mainly on the affirmation that language, before being a process or an event, is a system, and that this system is not established at the level of the speaker's consciousness, but at a lower level, that of the structural unconscious.

This third phase actually stops all legitimate efforts to use biblical texts for constructive theological efforts. For the

. . . idea that language is a closed system of signs within which each element merely refers to other elements of the system, excludes the claim of hermeneutics to reach beyond the "sense" — as the immanent content of the text — to its "reference," i.e., to what it says *about* the world. For structuralism, language does not refer to anything outside of itself, it constitutes a world for itself. Not only the reference of the text to an external world, but also its connections to an author who *intended* it and to a reader who *interprets* it are excluded by structuralism.[10]

The business of hermeneutics is presently in a vigorous shambles. This is so largely because of the adamant and humorless way in which each position has pounded itself into meaningless pulp by its own narrowness. In the same essay to which reference has been made (in note above), Professor Ricoeur feels his way toward a method of interpretation of texts which seems to me most fully appropriate to the way the community of faith bore witness in the words of Scripture, most rich in that potential for hearing and obedience which has in fact been the force of biblical speech for centuries, and most congruent with that "living Word" to which the church gives proper praise.

The kind of hermeneutics which I now favor starts from the recognition of the objective meaning of the text as distinct from the subjective intention of the author. This objective meaning is not something hidden behind the text. Rather it is a requirement addressed to the reader. The interpretation accordingly is a kind of obedience in this injunction starting from the text. The concept of "hermeneutical circle" is not ruled out by this shift within hermeneutics. Instead it is formulated in new terms. It does not proceed so much from an intersubjective relation linking the subjectivity of the author and the subjectivity of the reader as from a connection between two discourses, the discourse of the text and the discourse of the interpretation. This connection means that what has to be interpreted in a text is what it says and what it speaks about, i.e., the

10. Paul Ricoeur, "From Existentialism to the Philosophy of Language," *Criterion* 10, no. 3 (Spring 1971): 16.

kind of world which it opens up or discloses; and the final act of "appropriation" is less the projection of one's own prejudices into the text than the "fusion of horizons" — to speak like Hans-Georg Gadamer — which occurs when the world of the reader and the world of the text merge into one another.

This shift within hermeneutics from a "romanticist" trend to a more "objectivist" trend is the result of this long travel through structuralism. At the same time, I had to depart from my previous definition of hermeneutics as the interpretation of symbolic language. Now I should tend to relate hermeneutics to the specific problems raised by the translation of the objective meaning of written language into the personal act of speaking which a moment ago I called appropriation. In that way the broader question, What is it to interpret a text? tends to replace the initial question, What is it to interpret symbolic language? The connection between my first definition and the new emerging definition remains an unsolved problem for me. . . .[11]

The foregoing provides a way of replying to any who would stop all current reflection about the reality of the cosmos in the determination of God by saying of, for instance, my statements about the "cosmic" Christology of Colossians 1, that "this is not what the writer intended!"

It is not, I think, what the writer "intended"; for the writer did not look out upon a world as an organism, as an evolutionary ecosystem. The writer was not an enthusiastic proleptic Teilhard de Chardin, or a Darwin, or a Niels Bohr. But the writer does, from a faith that affirms the grace of God the Creator and the incarnated grace of God the Redeemer and the present working of God the Sanctifier, enfold within his vision of the new evolution a "horizon" of meaning and hope that cannot stop short of "all things." "Intention" is no adequate guide for biblical hermeneutics; to *see the world* as the text speaks of it is a constructive theological enterprise that must not be dismissed out of hand by the too easy demonstration that meanings in an ancient context are not identical with meanings in a present context.

The second objection to extensive theological reflection based upon

11. Ricoeur, "From Existentialism to the Philosophy of Language," p. 16.

the rhetoric of cosmic extension arises most commonly from those scholars who are aware of the gnostic influence against which the "cosmical"
passages from the Colossians are likely directed, and who, while admitting the scanty state of accurate knowledge of gnosticism, feel that these
verses should be regarded as marginal to any theological employment.
While the caution urged by such a position must be attended to, other
facts have balancing weight. There is, first of all, the fact that the
christological scope of these verses is not esoteric within the body of the
Epistles. The organic nature of the language and of the concepts is continuous with, although bold extensions of, central and repeated celebra-
tions of the role and rule and scope of Christ's presence and power. Sec-
ondly, the occasion for the statements — and this regardless of how clear
or how problematical the gnostic incitement of that may be assessed —
has really little to do with the substance of the argument. Occasions may
explain why something is said as it is said to those to whom it is said.
But clarity about occasions does not validate or invalidate substance.

If then it is granted that the gnostic heresy was probably the occasion
for raising the issue of the scope of Christ's redemptive reign, and if our
knowledge about the peculiar vocabulary of gnosticism provides the
clue to the language of some parts of the epistles to the Colossians and
the Ephesians, some kind of systematic reply was required, and these
epistles supply it. The reply is clear, unambiguous, and has a magnitude
that matches the size of the issue. Galloway has a summary of the reply:

> The implications of this teaching [gnosticism] places a limit on the
> work of Christ. It says in effect: Christ has redeemed us from Satan
> and the spirits of the lower air. But we are still subject to the ele-
> mental powers beyond that. In other words, some doubt had arisen
> whether Christ's work really was cosmic in its scope. [Note the im-
> plication of this heresy: That if it was thus limited, then something
> further was required for our complete redemption.][12]

The essence of the answer is the assertion that the work of Christ is
universally effective for all creation. The demonic powers in all parts of
the universe have been "disarmed" by him (Colossians 2:15):

12. Galloway, *The Cosmic Christ*, p. 48.

The argument runs as follows: Christ is eternally preexistent (Col. 1:17), therefore he has power over eternal spheres. He is the image of the Father (Col. 1:15), and this insures his supremacy over all angels and powers. He was actually the divine agent in the creation of all these things (Col. 1:15-16). Therefore, his redeeming work which has been declared ἐν πάσῃ κτίσει τῇ ὑπὸ τὸν οὐρανόν is unlimited in its efficacy. In him God "reconciles all things to himself, whether on earth or in heaven, through him alone" (Col. 1:20).[13]

To appreciate what has been called a type of christological teaching that employs a "rhetoric of cosmic extension" we should have the entire pericope before us:

He rescued us from the domain of darkness and brought us away into the kingdom of his dear Son, in whom our release is secured and our sins forgiven. He is the image of the invisible God; his is the primacy over all created things. In him everything in heaven and on earth was created, not only things visible but also the invisible orders of thrones, sovereignties, authorities, and powers: the whole universe has been created through him and for him. And he exists before everything, and all things are held together in him. He is, moreover, the head of the body, the church. He is its origin, the first to return from the dead, to be in all things alone supreme. For in him the complete being of God, by God's own choice, came to dwell. Through him God chose to reconcile the whole universe to himself, making peace through the shedding of his blood upon the cross — to reconcile all things, whether on earth or in heaven through him alone. (Colossians 1:13-20 NEB)

How the scope of this claim and its language of absolute inclusiveness bears upon the issues of grace and nature, grace and history, grace and the problematic of the modern self is to be the matter for later discussion. What is required here is that we permit this christological affirmation to question, profoundly modify, and open to fresh dimensions of interpretation types of christological thought which have a less broad

13. Galloway, *The Cosmic Christ*, p. 49.

reference. For the range and interior resonance of this doxological theology is astounding. Nothing less than the vast orbits of natural structure and of historical process and mystery constitute the far-circling of it. Even in these times, when events have tightened human thought around the tormented center of the meaning of personal existence, and when, consequently, the church's Christology has focused about a radically existentialist interpretation of Christ the Redeemer, this polyphonic hymn to the scope and energy of the divine redemption sounds to haunt the church's mind.

When in the doxology that marks the long and tortuous argument in the letter to the Romans, St. Paul gathers up the elements that enter into his reflections about the destiny of Israel under the fresh manifestation of God in the gospel of Christ, the apostle does not really solve the problem. The continuing history of this argument in the career of the church attests that. He thrusts the insoluble into the indisputable. The recalcitrant historical fact is that ". . . God has consigned all men to disobedience, that he may have mercy upon all." The doxology that follows is the language of startled praise, a rhetoric of wonder before God's mercy and the puzzle of history, which has the same magnificence as characterizes the Colossians rhetoric about grace and nature.

O depth of wealth, wisdom, and knowledge in God! How unsearchable his judgments, how untraceable his ways! Who knows the mind of the Lord? Who has been his counsellor? Who has ever made a gift to him, to receive a gift in return? Source, Guide, and Goal of all that is — to him be glory for ever! Amen. (Romans 11:33-36 NEB)

The eighth chapter of Romans is another occasion in which we see the conceptually insoluble gathered into a doxological affirmation in which elements that are resistant to logical penetration are fused together. The statement in verse 28 that the spirit ". . . pleads for God's people in God's own way — and cooperates for good with those who love God" is not a logical outcome of the mighty themes of the chapter. It is rather a remembering at the end of the insoluble that only the unmerited fact that he who "did not spare his own Son" is One who in that action is to be trusted to "lavish upon us all he has to give." Then follows, not a fresh attack upon the issue, but a doxological celebration of the God who having done the central action will not ultimately have his love either frustrated or bounded by whatever meaninglessness persists in natural structures, or historical mysteries.

> . . . and yet, in spite of all, overwhelming victory is ours through him who loved us. For I am convinced that there is nothing in death or life, in the realm of spirits or superhuman powers, in the world as it is or the world as it shall be, in the forces of the universe, in heights or depths — nothing in all creation that can separate us from the love of God in Christ Jesus our Lord. (Romans 8:37-39 NEB)

These instances from the Pauline manner and speech are not proposed as supportive of the substance of the Colossians hymn in 1:15-20, but as evidences that the scope of the passage shall not be thought marginal either to the apostle's thought and range or to the imperial christological momentum of which he is in other contexts capable. The entire axis from the "invisible God" to the repeated "all things" is unbroken. The reality of that Godly action, Christ, is declared present in, the agent of, and the goal and meaning of literally all that is. The relational prepositions "in" him, "through" him, "for" him are here constitutive of a christological claim that stretches out endlessly in time, space, and effectual force. The reality of Christ as the focal point for world and life meaning is sunk back into the "invisible God," is that energy whereby "all things hold together," and is proposed forward into the yet uncut pages of historical life as God's purpose and power "to reconcile to himself all things."

The "systematic" of this energy as it may be proposed as conceptually apposite to our time with its radically new understanding of nature and its excruciatingly acute historical consciousness, is a task that must be taken up in following pages. But in order that the clarity of the claim shall not rest upon too narrow a formulation in the New Testament witness, the language of another document must be heard.

The salutation to the letter to the Ephesians, as in every Pauline or probable Pauline epistle, fuses into a unity what older dogmatic treatises differentiated by the terms "created" and "uncreated" grace. But grace is single. Its source is "God the Father," its historical agent and embodiment is "the Lord Jesus Christ," and its gift and work is "grace to you and peace" (in 2 Timothy, "grace, mercy, and peace").

To relate style of speech to the task of understanding is an often neglected component of exegesis. Verses 2-14 in the first chapter of Ephesians is a passage whose very structure demands that this component be considered as somewhat more than an idiosyncrasy of interpretation favored by those peculiar persons who attend to rhetoric as an art. The sheer fecundity of the reality of grace in these verses creates a syntax and a diction to serve its abundance, and a rhetoric to resonate to its richness in unity. The concatenation of phrases, as each within the ordering mind of the writer begets clauses to amplify its reference, is astounding even for one accustomed to and sometimes impatient with the Pauline style. The English translations commonly break up the rushing momentum of the Greek text, but such a convenience does little to check the felt unfolding of the single massive fact of grace as it multiplies celebrative clauses to adore and proclaim the mystery.

> Grace to you and peace from God our Father and the Lord Jesus Christ. Praise be to God and Father of our Lord Jesus Christ, who has bestowed on us in Christ every spiritual blessing in the heavenly realm. In Christ he chose us before the world was founded, to be dedicated, to be without blemish in his sight, to be full of love: and he destined us — such was his will and pleasure — to be accepted as his sons through Jesus Christ, in order that the glory of his gracious gift, so graciously bestowed on us in his Beloved, might redound to his praise. For in Christ our release is secured and our sins are forgiven through the shedding of his blood. Therein lies the richness of God's free grace lavished upon us, imparting full wisdom and insight. He has made known to us his hidden purpose — such was his will and pleasure determined beforehand in Christ — to be put into effect when the time was ripe: namely, that the universe, all in heaven and on earth, might be brought into a unity in Christ. . . . In Christ indeed we have been given our share in the heritage, as we decreed in his design whose purpose is everywhere at work. For it was his will that we, who were the first to set our hope on Christ, should cause his glory to be praised. And you, too, when you had heard the

message of the truth, the good news of your salvation, and had believed it, because incorporate in Christ, and received the seal of the
promised Holy Spirit; and that Spirit is the pledge that we shall enter upon our heritage, when God has redeemed what is his own, to
his praise and glory. (Ephesians 1:2-14 NEB)

The subject of the pericope is God. The substance of the affirmations
is the work of Christ. The intention of that work is to the "purpose" and
"counsel" of God's "will" and "pleasure." The theater of the action is
"when the time was ripe." The *telos* is "that the universe, all in heaven
and on earth, might be brought into a unity in Christ." And the leitmo-
tif of the passage, which twice gathers all together upon a plateau of
praise, breaks loose again to magnify and clarify the action in fresh ascription, and comes to its target and summation in the third repetition
— "to the praise of his glory."

The manner and the matter are one. The graciousness of the structured strophes seems to form their sonorous rhythms from the awesome
grace they declare. If the phrase "praise of his glory" seems to modern
ears too vaporous to control the great song, that fault lies in us and not
in the phrase. If the clear, powerful, absolute meaning of "the glory"
strikes no comprehending fire there may be some relation between that
failure and the apostle's later word in the fourth chapter where we read:

This then is my word to you, and I urge it upon you in the Lord's
name. Give up living like pagans with their good-for-nothing notions. Their wits are beclouded, they are strangers to the life that is
in God, because ignorance prevails among them and their minds
have grown hard as stone. (Ephesians 4:17-19 NEB)

The implicit Christology of this hymn to grace goes in unbroken sequence from the purpose of God "who has bestowed on us in Christ every spiritual blessing in the heavenly realms" to those communities in
concrete historical places where men by the Holy Spirit have "heard the
word of truth" and by faith live on acknowledging life "in all insight
and mystery." This acknowledging community is the body of Christ
who is its head. When, later, a conceptualization of the scope of grace
was compelled to give dogmatic precision to these organic images of the

energy of grace operating in so wide a range, nothing short of the dogma of the Holy Trinity was adequate to set it forth.

We began this section with the assertion that there are within the New Testament types of rhetoric which can be specified, and that such a specification is useful for correction in view of a dogmatic tradition that has not always attended with equal gravity to each of them. It is now necessary to look at several "moments" in the development of the doctrine of grace and see something of the persistence and proportion of these types in that long career.

In the following chapter I shall describe and emphasize a particular strand of the developing doctrine of grace. The intention is to restore a proportion, not to establish a dominance. Such reflection upon the rich and various elements, movements, leading motifs, and receding interests is a constant task of historians of dogma. Indeed, the greatest contribution of this discipline to constructive theology may be that it engages in such reflection, over and over again, pondering the long story from the perspective of each moment in the church's life. Such reflection discloses how intimately related are the thoughts in men's minds and the circumstances of their bodies. Out of this plenitude of possibility a time draws forward now this, now that. It thrusts one aspect of a manifold theme aggressively forward and permits other aspects, equally venerable and well attested, to fall into the background.

Every historian of doctrine has observed that the development of Christian thought is not of equal force and creativity along an entire front. Thought does not move like a wave at full crest. Its movement is rather like that of a slow incoming tide that reaches forward along an uneven beach, pushing forward into low places with long probing fingers. These low-lying or mounded contours are what they are by the working of historical forces which it is the task of research to isolate and describe. The political involvements of a particular people at a particular time in a particular place, the emergence of a single strong person to a position of leadership, a theological position stressed into dominance by a chance congruity of that doctrine with a regnant political position — these and a hundred other influences have a part in the shaping of the undulating life of doctrinal development.

Although, to be sure, there are those who resist the admission of such fortuitous forces as an embarrassing modification of the presidency of the

Holy Spirit over the thoughts and practice of the church, such resistance must finally give way before the facts. Nor is this acknowledgment of historical force an abandonment of the integrity of Christian doctrine in its development, or a dismissal of the working of the Spirit. It is rather the coming to effective maturity in historical consciousness of what it really means to say that God discloses his will in history, that the Word really becomes flesh, that the Word of God and the word, and works, and always mixed intentions and protestations of men, exist in a mortal relationship.

If in the pages to follow we shall be selectively attentive to a few figures in the history of doctrine, or stress a single theme as it sounds in concert or even dissonance with others, the intention of the essay must be the defense of the practice. If, quietly present but available within the story of Christian thought there is a christological pattern that has very special power for the life of both faith and culture in this moment, it is both right and good to draw it forth and propose it for reflection.

CHAPTER 3

Some Crucial Moments in Ecumenical Christology

Between the material to which we have thus far been attending and the constructive sections to follow, the present chapter has a clear and urgent task: to recognize that the traditional scope of christological understanding is under pressure to achieve vaster amplitude in virtue of contemporary man's apprehension of the world-as-nature, and further, to inquire if the doctrine of grace does not also require a way of proclamation which shall be correlative with new self- and world-understanding. In order to give sequence and concreteness to my reflections on these matters I shall recapitulate the theological course whereby I came to entertain them. After some years of participation in Faith and Order dialogue one's mind becomes aware of a triple process at work: confidence in the comprehensiveness of all theological formulations is relativized; motivation toward fresh forms of theological discourse, in recognition of powerful cultural changes, is energized; and conviction about the enduring and incomparable realities of the Christian faith is solidified.

In such a situation one learns to be wary of sentences which begin, "There is only one way . . . ," or "The central and persisting teaching of the church (on this or that topic) is clear . . . ," or "From the earliest times Jesus has been regarded as . . . ," etc. The christological ascriptions in both New Testament and theological reflection resist report under any general statement that can claim ecumenical plenitude or common authority.

The East — The Pantocrator

It was the heightened participation of Orthodoxy in the conversations of Faith and Order which first turned my attention to aspects of New Testament language about the grace and the Lordship of Christ which, muted or ignored in entire ranges of Western Christology, have been enormously formative of both theological position and piety in the churches of the East.

If one would analyze to its roots the theological excitement and embarrassment that has occurred within ecumenical encounters because of Orthodox participation one must be careful not to stop at surface factors. Almost a thousand years of theological, ecclesiastical, even personal alienations have begotten a strangeness that proclaims itself in personal bearing, liturgical forms, ceremonial mores, exegetical style, etc. But underneath and absolutely pervasive of the two styles, Eastern and Western, is a different way of speaking about the work of Christ. In the West that work is centered upon redemption from sin; in the East it is centered upon the divinization of man. In the West the doctrine central to that work is atonement; in the East the central doctrine is participation, illumination, reenactment, and transformation. In the West the work of Christ is spoken of chiefly as restoration; in the East the work is reunification. The Western *Savior* is the Eastern *Pantocrator*. The Western *corpus* is the Eastern *Christus Rex*. The Western representation of Christ is Dürer, Grünewald, Rembrandt, Rouault, and a thousand others who center upon the oblation in the passion of Christ. These are matched in the East by the iconography in mosaic, in fresco, and in panel-icon by the known and unknown artists — Byzantine, Russian, and other — in which the serene and cosmos-ruling Christ is acknowledged in the heroism of the figures of the saints. The reality of this heroism is not different in the two, but the style and visage and mien of the figures is almost totally different. In the West these figures speak of a rescue from particular forms of lostness — sin and aberration. In the East this rescue is ontologically total; the realization of restored being bestowed by the transformation of grace is manifest in the strong docility, the passionless visage of absolute serenity. Since Harnack, who understood this "stillness" as death, this docility as debility, and this serenity as a defect in personal identity, the West has not known how to understand energy in any form or attitude save motion and activity.

Two paragraphs, the first elaborating the Johannine life-mingling participation in Christ, the second elaborating the theme of cosmic harmony in virtue of the whole creation as brought within the effectual compass of redemption, are here selected. Both are from St. Gregory of Nyssa, and both illuminate the differences in East and West to which we have alluded.

> Let no one accuse us of seeing two Christs or two Lords in the one Savior. But God the Son, who is God by nature, Lord of the universe, King of all creation, the Maker of all that exists and the Restorer of what has fallen, has not only not deprived our fallen nature of communion with Him, but in His great bounty He has deigned even to receive it again into life. But He is Life. Therefore, at the end of centuries, when our wickedness had reached its height, then in order that the remedy might be applied to all that was diseased, He united (literally, "mingled") Himself with our lowly human nature, He assumed man in Himself and Himself became man. He explains this to His disciples: "Ye in Me, and I in you" (John 14:20). By this union He made man what He Himself was. He was the Most High; lowly man was now elevated. For He who was the Most High had not need of being elevated. The Word was already Christ and Lord.[14]

> Since He is in all, He takes into Himself all who are united with Him by the participation of His body; He makes them all members of His

14. Emile Mersch, *The Whole Christ* (London: Denis Dobson, 1938), p. 315.

body, in such wise that the many members are but one body. Having thus united us with Himself and Himself with us, and having become one with us in all things, He makes His own all that is ours. But the greatest of all our goods is submission to God, which brings all creation into harmony. Then every knee shall bend in heaven, on earth. and under the earth, and every tongue shall confess that Jesus Christ is Lord (Philippians 2:10). Thus all creation becomes one body, all are grafted one upon the other, and Christ speaks of the submission of His body to the Father as His own submission.[15]

What is remarkable in that paragraph, so characteristic of Orthodoxy, is the way in which the confession that *Jesus Christ is the Lord* gathers about itself images of the divine energy. This gathering, incohering divine energy is testified in the strongly active verbs — he *takes into himself,* he *makes them members,* he *makes his own all that is ours.* The starting point of this theology, as had been remarked and carefully worked out by Professor Charles Moeller, is the efficacious and divinizing presence of Christ in the world and in the church. The classic aphorism in Greek patristic theology asserts:

Whoever is not assumed is not saved. . . . This doctrine, absolutely common to the whole Christian Church has taken a particular form in the theology of Gregory Palamas, who has had great prominence in the Orthodox tradition since the XV Century. His distinction between the essence and the divine created energies is probably unfamiliar to us. . . . What interests us here is the meaning this distinction takes on in the theology of grace. The choice of terms "uncreated energies" stresses that God reveals himself by acting, which excludes all "passion" from God; but as the energies are "uncreated" there can be no question of making them the fruit of man's merit in any way at all.[16]

Gregory Palamas (1296-1359), bishop and saint in the Orthodox Church, was initiator and expounder of the famous distinction between

15. Mersch, *The Whole Christ,* p. 319.
16. Charles Moeller, *Lumen Vitae,* vol. 19 (Brussels, 1964), p. 721.

God's being and his energy or operation. He rejected the Western explanations based on the idea of grace as created and supernatural.[17] Energy,
fusion, concorporeal presence — such notions, so common in Orthodoxy, can be understood in their operational force only when we listen to
them in an extended passage from Palamas.

> Since the Son of God, through his inconceivable love for man has not
> only united his divine hypostasis to our nature, and taking a living
> body and a soul endowed with intelligence, appeared upon earth and
> lived among men, but even, O wondrous miracle, unites himself to
> human hypostases, and fusing himself with each believer by com-
> munion of his sacred Body, becomes concorporeal with us and makes
> us a temple of the whole divinity, for the plenitude of the divinity
> dwells corporally in Him (Colossians 2:9), how does He not en-
> lighten, by surrounding them with light of those who participate in
> it worthily, as He enlightened even the body of the disciples on Ta-
> bor? Then, indeed, this Body possessing the source of the light of
> grace was not yet fused with our bodies; He enlightened from with-
> out those who approached worthily and sent light into their souls
> through their bodily eyes. But today He is fused with us, He lives
> within us, and naturally enlightens our soul from within. . . . Only
> one can see God . . . Christ. We must be united to Christ — and
> with what an intimate union! — in order to see God.[18]

The foregoing excursion into what is to Western ears an archaic style
of christological speech, and the confidence that it will sound exotic to
Western ears, is a deliberate tactic. The risk, of course, is great: such a
vocabulary for man's gracious God-relation through Christ will likely
turn off as many readers as it turns on. But the risk must be taken. For a
Christology of the total cosmos with the force and the scope necessary to
constitute Christian illumination of Western man's absurd and suicidal
operations with nature is not a prominent or even popularly accepted
strand within the churches of the West. If one recalls that catholic tradi-

---

17. Cf. J. Meyendorff, *A Study of Gregory Palamas,* trans. G. Laurence (London,
1964); and V. Lossky, *The Vision of God,* trans. A. Moorhead (London, 1963).

18. Cited by Moeller, *Lumen Vitae,* p. 723.

tion does indeed include such a possibility, and if his own attachment to it is to escape the charge of idiosyncrasy, then he cannot do other than specify, explicate, and defend. To that end let us listen to a church father in whom the tradition to which we are appealing is strong and clear.[19]

Irenaeus (c. 130-202) relates God and man and grace and nature in a lively way. His explication of the faith is like a complex circuit in a radio receiving set: the wires are all there, all in order, and every connection firmly soldered. But this maze becomes functional for faith, glows with life and clarity, only when plugged in, i.e., admitted to thought via participation! In the Cathedral of the Holy Trinity at Zagorsk, Russia, during the Feast of the Dormition, standing for hours amidst the prayers of the faithful before the iconostasis with its Anton Rubleff icons — literal presences of the "mighty cloud of witnesses" — I came to understand a mode of Christ's reality that shattered assumptions about Western christological comprehensiveness and beckoned toward partly forgotten dimensions of catholic Christology.

Irenaeus is chosen for detailed discussion for three reasons: (a) of all the early theologians he most fully worked out a systematic, biblically derived exposition of God's grace and man's experience of the world-as-nature; (b) because his christological images were fashioned in opposition to gnostic dualism and because ever-renewed forms of that heresy have been a steady accompaniment to the course of catholic Christology, Irenaeus's "model" has a startling potential for our time; (c) the doctrine

---

19. The following discussion of Irenaeus is based principally upon two documents: *The Demonstrations of the Apostolic Preaching,* trans. T. Armitage Robinson (New York: Macmillan, 1920); and *Against Heresies,* trans. E. R. Hardy, Library of Christian Classics, vol. 1 (Philadelphia: Westminster, 1953). But access to the spirit of the Christian East is by no means supplied only by documents! Transdocumentary experience in the worship of the Orthodox churches, whose living piety, practice, and preaching still resonates with an understanding of grace first set forth systematically by Irenaeus — this is the right door to understanding. Lest this devout encounter in worship be too easily dismissed I would call attention to the old aphorism, *Lex orandi, lex credendi!* And further, if one acknowledges the force of the claim that one does not "hear" Shakespeare save in the lively realization of his words as spoken by voices of living men in an actual theater, it should not be thought strange that the meaning and truth of Irenaeus's teaching about faith's "reenactment" within the believer's life in the web of the created world, and never severed from it, requires the living theater of the church's worship as the place and precondition for understanding.

of grace as elaborated by Irenaeus invites the mind to stand within a rich and neglected mode of thought, and from that position conceive afresh how the reality of God's grace may be discerned and celebrated within a desacralized culture.

Let us start with Irenaeus and gnosticism.

The gnostics, pondering the problem of the role of Christ in the riddle of the universe, found the Christian faith in its apostolic form too simple. They undertook to give a more complex and subtle analysis of how the grace of God could be related to the "graceless space" between the realms of creation and redemption. This reply, in most general categories, took two forms.

The first form, usually ascribed to Valentinus, postulated a hierarchy of beings who in their totality constitute the Fullness, or Pleroma, of the deity. Those of the lowest order had departed from the bright world above and brought into being the material universe. And from this universe gnosticism assumed, in continuity with a Plotinian extension of Platonic notions, that it is the goal of true wisdom *(gnosis)* to escape.

The second form of gnostic teaching is in the form of a dualism which explains the ambiguities of mortal existence by telling of a conflict between two independent powers, good and evil, or perhaps merely perfect and imperfect. This is Marcionite gnosticism. The proposed way of escape is not merely contemplative; it requires moral athleticism. The world has to be repudiated, despised. This despisal could take the form of ascetical denigration of the physical, or a kind of contemptuousness toward and indulgence of the body. In either case the point was clear: only the higher order mattered; the body was not redeemable. Not even a lesser deity could enter into human nature.

Thus, catholic Christology was repudiated. Gnosticism was an occult form of religion within which nature and grace could not be spoken of together. They mutually excluded each other. While the Irenaean refutation has profoundly intellectual and biblical argument as its support, the style of it, because Irenaeus was a bishop and responsible for saving men from the seductions of a vastly appealing esoteric religion, is pastoral and homiletical. This argument may be detailed as follows:[20]

20. For a full treatment of Irenaeus's theology, cf. Gustav Wingren, *Man and the Incarnation* (Philadelphia: Fortress, 1959).

There is *one* creation, not two; there is one source of all things, not many. The "hands" of God in creation are the *Law* and the *Spirit.* They are uncreated: they belong to the Creator and are active in all creation. God and his creating "hands" are inseparable; it is impossible to penetrate into this "mystery" and find the point of their creation.

The Son is revealed in Jesus Christ but does not originate in Jesus Christ. Therefore it is not correct to argue that belief in him could only come with the Incarnation, "The Word was in the beginning with God." He is (for us) in the Incarnation; there we see him. But he is before the creation of the world.

When man was created he was created through the Son and in the Son and is to reach his destiny in the Son. By this insistence, which characterized early Christian thought, creation and redemption, nature and grace, are formally kept together in a way which when broken, leads to literally endless theological confusion.

Irenaeus, on the contrary, holds that everything is created in the Son, and thus secures a theological way to hold nature and grace together. The Word in which all is created is the same *Verbum* which became flesh in Christ. This makes it possible to go from the revelation of God in the Son to a corollary and further revelation of the Father in nature. This is not a "natural theology" in the sense that God is disclosed in nature without the revelation in the Son; but it is a *theology for* nature in the inevitable sense that the hand of God the Creator, which is the hand of the Son, should be seen, following the Incarnation, also in nature.

Just as it is the characteristic of God to create, it is characteristic of man that he is created. He is made, he not simply *is*. His ontology is a resultant of a decisive action: and his "isness" is not a static ontological being but a becoming. He increases. These two, that he is and that he grows, are one reality seen from two different aspects.

Irenaeus regards all life — man's life in solitude and fellowship, in history, and in the life of nature — as in the hands of God. Death is a lost connection with God. By this refusal to adopt a matter-spirit dualism, by keeping together in God all aspects of the creation, Irenaeus held together in his understanding natural life and the Spirit, creation and the sacraments, man's body and his communion with God.

Adam, Irenaeus says, was created by God in God's *imago and similitudo,* and was put into God's creation by the same God who sent

Christ into the world. Like Paul, Irenaeus plays out the strong contrast between Adam and Christ. But whereas in the Western theology prevailing after Irenaeus the fall of Adam was stressed almost exclusively, Irenaeus fastens attention upon what Adam was created *for,* which is to live, body and soul, in accordance with God's will. By virtue of this accent upon the possible divine intention for man, what is stressed between Adam and Christ is not their separation but their connection.

Christ was the pattern upon which God created man. Christ is the man about to be — the *Homo futurus.* While all things were being formed Christ was in the mind of God, and all things have within themselves this intention: "For this reason the Son also appeared in the fullness of time to show how the copy resembles him."

Adam as a child is the dramatic figure Irenaeus uses to give concreteness to his interpretation. For man, to be unsaved means to remain undeveloped: salvation is maturation and fulfillment. Christ is called and is man's Savior because in him man is shown what maturation is, is called to be nurtured into it, and to grow up into the form of the Son. The healthy, newborn child, says Irenaeus, while unable to talk, possesses every likelihood of becoming able to do so. An injury, to be sure, may prevent the development. And this is the situation of Adam in the world. He is a child, created in the image of God. That he lacks something is not due to sin. No injury has yet happened to the child. Uninjured, he is yet a child, he does not realize what he is yet to be. All the while, however, there is already in creation one who is the full image of God, the Son.

A second influential focus in the teaching of Irenaeus is the large place he gives to the New Testament notion of *anakephalaiosis* (recapitulation), and the quite systematic extension it receives in his hands. In this treatment, the parallel, contrast, and connection of the two Adams is central; but a way of thinking about the relation of God, the grace of God, and man's condition as a part of the natural world does not remain confined within the terms of the image. What begins as a "process-soteriology" originated by grace and fulfilled in recapitulation, participation, and reenactment unfolds into something approaching a Christian ontology.

Father E. Mersch describes Irenaeus's use of the term *anakephalaiosis* as follows:

By the word recapitulation as applied to Christ Irenaeus means a sort of recommencement in the opposite direction by which God, reversing, as it were, the process whereby sin infected the earth, gathers together and reunites all creation, including matter, but especially man, in a new economy of salvation. He gathers up His entire work from the beginning, to purify and sanctify it in His Incarnate Son, who in turn becomes for us a second stock and a second Adam. In Him, the first Adam and all his posterity are healed; the evil effects of disobedience are destroyed and as it were reversed by their contraries. Man recovers the holiness which was his at the beginning and he is divinized by union with the God from whom he came. As we see, the term presents many meanings: a resume, a taking up of all since the beginning, a recommencement, a return to the source, restoration, reorganization and incorporation under one Head. But these meanings are all related; in spite of their diversity they fit into one another, and even when expressed singly each one suggests all the others.[21]

What is remarkable in this teaching is the way Christ and Adam are so related as to do justice to both difference and bond, to what is wrong and to what is right. Irenaeus clearly foresees what later Trinitarian formulations had to work out in detail: God is over all things as the Word; God is in all things as the spirit who cries "Abba, Father" and forms man in the image of God.

It is instructive to observe that some insights, muffled or forgotten in formal theology, may persist in the liturgies of the church. Irenaeus's "recapitulation" image is a case in point. Still today the powerful image of Christ's active recapitulation of Adam's fateful choice survives in the Lenten Preface to the Holy Communion. "It is truly meet, right, and salutary, that we should at all times and in all places, give thanks unto Thee, O Lord, Holy Father, Almighty, Everlasting God: Who on the tree of the cross didst give salvation unto mankind, that whence death arose, thence life also might rise again; and that he (Satan) who by a tree once overcame (the tree in Eden), might likewise by a Tree (the cross) be overcome. . . ."[22]

21. Mersch, *The Whole Christ,* p. 230.

22. *Service Book and Hymnal* (Philadelphia: The Board of Publication, The Lutheran Church in America, 1958), p. 30.

While, to be sure, the constant claim of Irenaeus that the orbit of the salvatory work of Christ is universal in scope was a claim which was probably evoked from him by the universalist speculations of gnosticism, the warrant for the teaching is clearly rooted in the New Testament. The disposition of some historians of doctrine to regard Irenaeus as idiosyncratic is manifestly a Western prejudice. It is significant that the more deeply the contemporary church searches her tradition for a christological understanding appropriate in formal and substantial largeness to contemporary nature-knowledge and its resultant technology, the more concentrated is her attention to this father. A study of the investigations into patristic theology which have attended the efforts of the Roman Church during Vatican Council II, and the deepening efforts of Faith and Order studies to relate Christ, church, and world supplies clear evidence of such reawakened attention.[23]

Near the beginning of the treatise *Against the Heretics* is a long passage that is quoted here because it illustrates how the idea of a "recapitulation" operates as a kind of hub from which the spokes of a very full confession of faith extend. These elaborations are bound together by the encircling rim, and describe a pattern which is later spoken of in Roman theology as the Mystical Body, and in non-Roman terms as the community of believers:

> The Church, spread over the whole world even to the confines of the
> earth, has received from the Apostles and from their disciples faith in
> one God, the Father Almighty, who created heaven and earth and the
> sea and all that is in them; and in one Christ Jesus, the Son of God,

23. The contemporary theological scene is a veritable convulsion induced by a large number of studies advocating "religionless Christianity," "worldly faith," a faith for man in "The Secular City," and, under the unverifiable proposition that "God is Dead," offering varieties of options. If upon reading these books one has the uneasy feeling that the theme, despite its modern phenomenological data, has been heard before, that feeling might with profit be investigated! And particularly by a generation of theological students who are inclined to suppose that before Schleiermacher the issue of Christian faith and total world-meaning had never been entertained. For when one threads back into apostolic doctrine he finds that the Fathers, too, dared to affirm that if Christ is to be sufficient meaning for anything he must be affirmed in faith as the meaning of everything. The issue was no smaller than that for Irenaeus and, compared with the specious novelty of some who are frantically splashing in the perturbed puddle of secularity, his massive Christology is a masterful feat of navigation.

who became incarnate for our salvation; and in the Holy Spirit, Who by the prophets announced the dispositions and the comings and the virgin birth, the passion, the resurrection from the dead, and the ascension into heaven in the flesh, of the beloved Christ Jesus our Lord, and His coming from the heavens in the glory of the Father to recapitulate all things and to raise up all human flesh, in order that to Christ Jesus our Lord and God and Saviour and King, every knee may bend, according to the good pleasure of the unseen Father.[24]

In *Demonstrations of the Apostolic Preaching,* Irenaeus argues that by the Word of God (and by that Irenaeus always means the acted-out nature, will, and power of God) everything is under the sign of the economy of redemption, and the Son of God was crucified for all and for everything precisely to restore the entire human and material creation in himself. In this understanding the whole of nature is associated with the destiny of man, for man enfolds it and conditions its state. The central sentence reads:

> . . . it is the Word of God, the Son of God, Jesus Christ our Lord, who appeared to the prophets in the form described in their oracles and according to the special disposition of the Father; [the Word] by whom all things were made; and who, in the fullness of time, to recapitulate and contain all things, became man, in order to destroy death, to manifest life and to restore union between God and man.[25]

Perhaps because Irenaeus was a bishop, pastor, preacher, but more certainly because the concreteness of his theological formulations were forged out of the vivid episodic speech of the Scriptures, his writing has an earthy and dramatic character. Force impacts against force, direction is violently reversed by a power turning it, images clash in surprising juxtaposition. The Adam of the Garden of Eden is recapitulated by the second Adam of the garden of Gethsemane; a garden-rebellion is reenacted to redemption by a garden-obedience. The first Eve who stood straight in autonomy is recapitulated by the second — the bowed and rapt theonomous Eve of the Magnificat. A summary sentence is:

24. Mersch, *The Whole Christ,* p. 231.
25. Mersch, *The Whole Christ,* p. 232.

He recapitulated in Himself the long history of men, summing up and giving us salvation, in order that we might receive again in Christ Jesus what we had lost in Adam, that is, the image and likeness of God.[26]

Father Mersch, commenting upon the scope of the recapitulation theme in Irenaeus, writes:

He possesses most intimate relationships with all. Thus, according to a view that is peculiar to our Saint, Christ passed through all the ages of a man's life in order to sanctify them all in Himself; thus, too, the events of His mortal life have a perpetual influence upon our justification. In Him, we have all been obedient unto death; in His Passion, we have all been roused from sleep, and when He ascended into heaven, we ascended with Him.

His work is one of solidarity and of unity. In dying, He traced the sign of the Cross upon all things, and, in the beautiful words uttered by one of the early Christians and recorded by Irenaeus, His two crucified arms, wide outstretched, were an appeal to union addressed to every nation.[27]

Professor Hugo Rahner chooses as his most summarizing paragraph from Irenaeus the following:

The true Creator of the World is the Logos of God who is our Lord and who in these latter days became man. Although he is in the world, his power invisibly embraces all created things, and his mark has been set upon the whole of creation since he is the Word of God, who guides and orders all things. And that is why he came in visible form to that which was his own and became flesh and hung upon the wood, so that he might recapitulate the universe in himself.[28]

26. Mersch, *The Whole Christ,* p. 233.
27. Mersch, *The Whole Christ,* p. 234.
28. Hugo Rahner, *Greek Myths and Christian Mystery* (New York: Harper and Row, 1963), p. 51.

The "cosmic" Christology of Irenaeus cannot be dismissed by the too easy argument that its contours are determined by conflict with the gnostics. Specification of occasion does not dissolve consideration of substance. Other Fathers, their thought not shaped by gnostic claims, speak of God and Christ and grace and nature in the same organic way. The idea that the Incarnate Word is in himself the unity and harmony not only of men, but also of the entire material universe, was a theme that runs throughout virtually the whole of the writings of many influential Fathers. What differs in their treatments of the theme is the conceptualization of the notion of recapitulation, the particular language by which the image is expounded.

As the thought of the church came to center more and more upon the meaning of Incarnation rather than upon polemical defenses against gnosticism, the necessity to elaborate the force and scope of Incarnation determines ideas, language, and use of scripture. When, for instance, between 318 and 320 St. Athanasius was writing his tracts *Against the Pagans* and *On the Incarnation,* the occasion for the elaboration of a cosmic Christology is clearly not the gnostic heresy. Philosophical atomism seems to be the position against which Athanasius directs his words:

> The Greek philosophers say that the world is a great body. And in this they are right. For we see that the world and its parts are sensible things. If, then, the word of God resides in this world which is a body; if He is present in each and every thing, is there anything strange or absurd in our claim that the Word is present in man?
>
> Like a musician who has attuned his lyre, and by the artistic blending of low and high and medium tones produces a single melody, so the Wisdom of God, holding the universe like a lyre, adapting things heavenly to things earthly, and earthly things to heavenly, harmonizes them all, and, leading them by His will, makes one world and one world order in beauty and harmony.[29]

In that citation our point is clearly made. Irenaeus was confronting a cosmic demonology or angelology, and he threw against it a cosmic Christology. Athanasius was confronting in Arianism a cosmic religious

29. Mersch, *The Whole Christ,* p. 264.

psychology, and he threw against it an equally cosmic Christology of the divinization of all things in and by grace.

Grace, for Athanasius, was both a comprehensive term for the created goodness of all reality, and a term wherewith to specify the incarnated presence and historical focus of that Light which is God. The following paragraph by Jaroslav Pelikan is summary:

One of the most persistent themes of Athanasian apologetics was this defense of the intrinsic goodness of reality against its detractors. And a frequent image for this defense was the metaphor of the light. If one accepted the proposition that the Logos of God was present throughout the universe, one would likewise have to grant that the entire universe was both illumined and moved by the Logos, from whom there came the light and movement and life of all things. Again, it was the Logos that granted light and life to the universe; and because the Logos had illumined all things, visible and invisible, it was the holy Logos of the Father that held them all together. This goodness of all reality was built into the very structure of being by the Logos, who was the principle of life, light, and movement. Committed as he was to the defense of the salvation wrought by Christ, Athanasius did not, like Tertullian and some later theologians, find it necessary to denigrate nature in order to glorify grace. On the contrary, he took his stand as the defender of the goodness of nature against its detractors; for this defense of the goodness in all of reality was at the same time an act of praise for the God of grace. There was not only revelation in the creation; there was even grace in the creation.[30]

The words in the title of this chapter, "Some Crucial Moments," suggest the limits of it. No effort will be made to discuss the persistence of the theme of the relation of Christ and nature in patristic theology as a whole. For such a task I have not the competence, and the task has been performed in works that are easily available.[31] The intention is to say

30. Jaroslav Pelikan, *The Light of the World* (New York: Harper and Row, 1962), pp. 44-45.

31. P. Evdokimov, *L'Orthodoxie* (Neuchâtel: Delachaux et Niestle, 1959); John Meyendorff, *L'Eglise Orthodoxe hier et aujourd'hui* (Paris: Editions du Seuil, 1969); Timo-

only enough to invite the reader to suspect that Christian tradition about this theme is richer, fuller, more broadly attested than is indicated in the manuals for history of doctrine most commonly used in the schools.

The West — The Light
That Lighteth Every Man

So we turn now to another and later "moment" and choose St. Augustine, for two reasons. First, in his understanding of the grace of God in and with the creation, Augustine stands with catholic tradition; indeed he deepens and expands this tradition by the exquisite and probing analysis whereby he locates the operation of grace within the "natural" dynamics of man's loves, man's search for knowledge, and the solidification of man's will. But, second, aspects of Augustine's thought which, disengaged from his total theology, have been most influential in later doctrines of grace as popularly declared have worked to reduce that fuller understanding of grace to which he so richly contributed, and which is in continuity with the thought and spirit of Irenaeus.

How did so strange an outcome occur?

Students of intellectual history have often remarked how ideas of great generality and force may by circumstances be reduced to a single aspect of their fullness, or utilized for arguments so dramatic that a total context is forgotten. Something very like that has happened in the instance of Augustine's teaching about God's grace. The large and luminous light of grace permeates his writings. But the particular heresy he was called to combat has, for many, become normative for an understanding and assessment of his more comprehensive teaching. The general light of grace as Augustine affirmed has been reduced to a laser beam for cauterizing the Pelagian error.

---

thy Ware, *The Orthodox Church* (Baltimore: Penguin Books, 1959); N. Zernov, *The Church of the Eastern Christians* (New York: Macmillan, 1942); Jaroslav Pelikan, *The Spirit of Eastern Christendom,* vol. 2 of the projected five-volume *The Christian Tradition* (Chicago: University of Chicago Press). Volume 1, *The Emergence of the Catholic Tradition,* was published in June 1971.

It would be unfair, untrue, and irresponsible to affirm that a study of St. Augustine on the doctrine of grace would disclose him to have intended so narrow or purely topical a reduction. It is very clear, however, that almost exclusive attention to grace within the rubric of *sin* and grace has fated his teaching to have been understood in such a diminished way. In Western thought Augustine lives in preaching, in catechesis, in moral counsel, and in general theological instruction principally in the sin-grace problem. One can sense the malproportion of this outcome if he examines Augustine's writings upon the knowledge of God, particularly in the *Confessions,* and in the treatise on *The Holy Trinity.* In these texts the doctrine of grace has the same topical centrality, the same "energy," the same sovereignty as it enjoyed in the earlier period to which we have attended.

One has only to follow Augustine in his description of the absolute efficacy of grace in that interior drama of reintegration of the love of self to the love of God — in the course of which man's incurvature is bent back to its intention — to absolve Augustine of any *formal* diminution of the power of grace. Augustine declares that just as it is a light of grace that "lights every man who comes into the world," so it is this same grace that abides with man and saves him from intellectual despair. The desire to know *(curiositas),* the study and systematization of empirical fact enables men to rise above the animal creation and become constructively human by relating means to ends in an ordered scheme of life. But this "good" of science is limited: it fails to disclose an end other than that of mere adjustment. Indeed, in the natural sciences, these "adjustments" have become enormous and range far beyond the dreams of Augustine. But their inability to satisfy the appetite for felicity is not only not reduced by the magnitude of such achievements, it is made thereby the more sardonic and bitter.

This view of *sapientia* or Christian wisdom as a basis for the judgment of value marks a final revolt from the spirit and method of Platonic science. Verbally, Augustinian *sapientia* is the exact equivalent of Plotinian *nous.* For Plotinus, however, the function of *nous* was to communicate with the One which is beyond knowledge and beyond being, and which is thus revealed — only in ecstasy. Augustinian *sapientia,* on the other hand, is emphatically not ecstatic and it presupposes no such detachment from the material world. As the judgment of value it is, indeed, "independent" of science and of the scientific discipline. That independence, however, serves merely to establish its right to supplement the deficiencies of science, by providing a fresh vision of the cosmos and of man's place in it. In the light of *sapientia,* man no longer sees himself over against a "nature" conceived anthropomorphically whether as "thought" or "mechanism." On the contrary, he *sees himself and his universe together* (underlining mine) as an expression of beneficent activity, the activity of the creative and moving principle — in the language of religion, as a "creature" whose origin, nature, and destiny are determined by the will of God.[32]

Augustine was a bishop. He was responsible for instruction and guidance. In the exercise of that responsibility he could not always honor symmetry of presentation above the precision and force required by the moment's need. And the need of the moment in his century was to address the gospel of grace to two issues. The one was political, the other moral.

The political problem was to present to his age — in which the old power of the idea of the empire, now waning, was no longer able to give unity and motive to men's energies — a total vision of the origin, meaning, and destiny of political communities. The image of the city of God was alone large enough and deep enough to accomplish that.

Professor C. N. Cochrane gives a broad, superbly articulated, and theologically sophisticated account of this achievement,[33] and brings together the Christian faith and the moral and political threat to the life of antiquity.

The moral problem was to clarify and propose a love adequate to the imperious loves of men — a love with which we are beloved, which should expose the futility of all lesser loves, relate them to itself, and redeem their egocentric curvative into that adoration which is both right will and true knowledge.

32. Charles Norris Cochrane, *Christianity and Classical Culture* (New York: Oxford University Press, 1944), pp. 435-36.

33. Cochrane, *Christianity and Classical Culture,* chapters "Regnum Caesaris, Regnum Diaboli," and "Nostra Philosophia."

In this concentration of his thought upon grace for political reconstruction of the community of men, and upon grace for the moral renovation of the perverted will and the futile loves of men, Augustine does not use the language of that cosmic Christology which had been so clearly utilized in the tradition before his time. The substance is there, however, and one has only to recall the fullness of his meditation upon that "light that lighteth every man that cometh into the world" and the "light which not only falls upon things but is also within the eyes with which things are beheld" to know this. Augustine's task was to speak to a historical crisis and to a moral lostness. For that reason the relation of grace to the world-as-nature does not receive from him an explicit discussion. But Augustine's teaching about the formation of the possibilities of knowledge in relation to the transegocentric love of God by which man's loves are elevated, and the formation of a new will in this process, clearly operates with an understanding of grace which is continuous with the earlier tradition.

All of the preceding is by no means a pedantic fussing around with ancient doctrines of grace. The effort is rather to locate and administer, in continuity with the church's faith and in ways useful for our time, the reality of a gracious God. That reality is always a disclosure creative of a response, and the point or theater of its effective impact changes with man's self- and world-understanding. In a following chapter the implications of this fact will be dealt with. A concluding concern of this chapter is to point to aspects of contemporary theological reflection that attest how radically man's new situation in relation to the world-as-nature is determining his response-capacity to traditional proposals of the grace of God.

The Dis-graced World

In the West two large patterns, descriptive of how grace and man's nature are related, have controlled Christian thought: a pattern based upon the analogy of being, and a pattern drawn from the primal divine activity of the Word of God. The first presupposes interior relations of possibility that the second does not necessarily suppose. But both are deeply in trouble. The analogy of being, in its older forms, draws checks on a metaphysical account that is exhausted; the second draws checks on an account that, while not exhausted, is presently undergoing such hermeneutical accounting that the checks are held up because of radical unclarity about what funds are really there.

In the meantime a new and earthy mode of analogy is emerging, and in its emergence is providing a different context and substance for all statements about the grace of God and man's response and possibility. Books bearing such titles as *Process and Reality, Faith and Culture, Christ and Cosmos, Redemption and Revolution, Ecological Man,* etc., suggest the natural context for fresh articulations of the Christian faith: it is an analogy rich in data drawn from man's embeddedness in nature, and assumes the truth of man's evolutionary identity as empirical fact. The creation, the Incarnation, and the natural world as place of grace — within that triangulation is the only present possibility for an intelligible grammar of grace and a rhetoric able to give it praise.

To the "crucial moments" already alluded to, several soundings into the sea of contemporary reflection about this issue may prove enlightening.

What characterizes very many modern efforts at christological reformulation is the direct, sometimes passionate probing for a Christ-understanding that shall speak to men within the grip of a twofold threat: (a) a disintegration of personhood so profound that the very realities of bond, covenant, respect, justice, and human preciousness are themselves no longer available for help, and, (b) an absurd, earth-destroying, life-mutilating, future-canceling, and brutal attack upon the resources and life-supporting materials and processes of man's ancient place, the earth itself.

When he was Vicar of Great St. Mary's parish in Cambridge, Dean Hugh Montefiore declared that we need to redefine creatively the Chalcedonian terms of "nature" and "person." The paradox of grace is proposed as the best analogy by which the relation of the human and the divine in Jesus can be understood today.[34] The ancient notions of "nature" will no longer serve; and ancient ways of speaking about God's grace in Jesus Christ must attend to this fact. Montefiore's simplest statement is, "Jesus revealed the fullness of divine activity in human personality. In Jesus Christ the pattern of divine activity was revealed in

34. Cf. the article "Theological Table-Talk" by John J. Carey in *Theology Today* 27, no. 3 (October 1970): 315-31.

a single historical life of a fully human person."[35] What is significant about the statement is not its substance (D. M. Baillie had earlier said much the same), but that it should have been forged out of the two central concerns of the essay in which it appears — the crisis of love and regard among persons, and man's growing insensitivity to and positive abuse of the good earth. The realm of the "divine activity" (cf. Gregory Palamas's "energies" of Christ) is identical with all loves and perversions and operations of man's engaged life with the world beyond the self; its center is "you are accepted in grace": its range and imperative is the gracious ethicizing of all the operations of the self.

Rosemary Ruether argues that that too narrow understanding of Augustine of which we have spoken, has indeed had fateful consequences:

> . . . Augustine's stress on man's depravity tipped the balance of the Eastern view in the direction of an identification of man with his depravity. This disrupted the sense of man's continuing grounding in the grace of the original creation. The underlying continuity between the original creation and God's saving grace was disrupted, and grace became discontinuous and antithetical to nature. Man mounted up to God by cutting his ties with what was below and behind him. The ultimate direction of this concept of man could only end in a final rejection of that view of nature in which nature was seen as the gracious icon of God's face; and it could only result in a substitute view which made nature an enemy to be ruthlessly put under man's feet![36]

During the writing of this chapter Professor John Black published his *The Dominion of Man*,[37] a superb historical account of the grace-nature issue in Western thought and practice. The entire book is a parallel, but much more detailed and fully documented, account of the same shift to which Rosemary Ruether's article is addressed.[38]

---

35. Carey, "Theological Table-Talk," p. 325.

36. Rosemary Ruether, "Critic's Corner," *Theology Today* 27, no. 3 (October 1970): 337.

37. John Black, *The Dominion of Man* (Edinburgh: The University of Edinburgh Press, 1970).

38. At about the time Professor Black's book appeared, a headline in *The New York*

One gathers material for theological reflection wherever he can find it, and much can come from places one is not looking for or at. Additional data for insight into that expansion of the realm of grace, and the longing to find the total meaning its bestowal promises, can be derived from the words and works of the artistic community.

For several years I was chairman of a commission representing many churches and assigned to inquire why it is that American artists are, for the most part, alienated from the terms, concepts, episodes, and symbols that set forth the Christian story. That they are so disengaged is both indubitable and strange. For this story, in its own terms and in its creativity within Western culture, has for many centuries been steady material for the exercise of the artistic vision, and for the translation of such vision into palpable forms. No generation before the present one would have thought of creating a commission on religion and the arts. Indeed, to have done so would have been regarded as a humorless bureaucratization of the obvious, like having a committee to study the relation of water and fish!

Our commission expected the artists to express alienation. We did not expect that the causes for such alienation would be so clearly and forcibly expressed, nor did we anticipate that such expressions would disclose so quickly and clearly the untheologically stated theological focus of the problem. The artist, painter, printmaker, dancer, actor, sculptor, novelist, poet, and musician is most commonly not only indifferent to the Christian story and without expectation that it has anything to say to him as an artist, he is angry about the churchly transmitters of that story.

Long exposure to the statements, eloquent nonstatements, disgusts, gestured feelings of the artist, and reflection upon these, has disclosed what I think is the heart of the matter. The artist carries on a lover's quarrel with the world; he is fascinated by the vivacity, variety, conflicts,

---

Times on the day the huge tanker *Manhattan* broke through the hitherto unpenetrated Arctic ice, read, "Man's Ancient Enemy Overcome!" This statement is an illustration both of the depth of the perversion that popularly prevails as regards man's living bond to nature, and an instance of what Professor Hugh Iltis of the University of Wisconsin calls "ecological pornography." That a vast and life-preserving ecosystem of ice, tundra, permafrost, and animals, all supportive of an ancient culture and way of life should be regarded as an "enemy to be overcome" — this uncalculated language is witness to a stupor of mind which is more perilous *because* uncalculated.

delights, and torments of life, and he is maddened into creativity by the endless effort to give this reality "a local habitation and a name." He sees his work as the patient and alert evocation of a secret. He is the midwife of the elusive, the siren of the timid, the articulator of the silent, the telltale of forms of life en route to becoming.

The artist loves the palpable and the immediate, the forms, shapes, colors, textures, movements, and the mad or recurring intersections of life. It is this very recalcitrance of the given actualities before his attack which is both his allure and his problem. And, rightly or wrongly, he feels that this living stuff of natural life is either indifferently regarded or negatively assessed by the community which is Christ's church. Or, if it is not rejected, both it and the artist are *used,* which is, in his judgment, a mere commodity-evaluation and utilization of the stuff of his dedication. The church, says the artist, thinks itself spiritually above the gross materialities of the artist's shop, or theater, or lonely place of struggle. But it has nevertheless managed, despite this transmaterial spirituality, to have got on very well in this world. The church seems to him unmoved by the artist's effort to bring to the surface those inchoate allurements of unity and significance, those secrets eloquent of our common human reality, which constitute both the pathos and the glory of mankind. The "spirituality" of the church appears to the artist as an abstraction when affirmed apart from the "spirituality" enfolded in things and persons and natural vitalities. He has an understandable feeling that all exposure of the real serves the truth; and if the truth of the Christian faith be indeed not *identical* with artistic truth, no "higher order" of truth ought despise the actual. It is precisely this negative assessment which the artist gathers from what I have called the "use" of the labor of the artist. The church "hires" the artist to paint, design, or write, but with the superior assumption that the bundle of palpable immediacies with which the artist works must serve a higher order of truth before their own truth and integrity can be accredited.

The artist who has

. . . heard inside each mortal thing
Its holy emanation sing[39]

39. W. H. Auden, "New Year Letter," *The Collected Poetry of W. H. Auden* (New York: Random House, Inc., 1945), p. 270.

is not a preacher of the gospel of the divine grace; it is quite possible that he may be the tongue to that living voice and form of "common grace" which, in terrible knowledge of what will *not* suffice, "goes before the face of the Lord to prepare his way." For if, as the letter to the Ephesians asserts, "in the futility of our minds . . . we are darkened in understanding," "alienated from God because of ignorance produced by callousness and hardness of heart" (Ephesians 4:17-18), then all that serves to lighten darkness, inform ignorance, sensitize callousness, and pierce hardness serves grace — without the name or intention so to do.

CHAPTER 4

Grace in Post-Reformation Culture

The purpose of this chapter is so to lead the reader from the biblical and early church reflections about God's grace and through the intervening centuries as to set him before the meaning and the problems of grace as that meaning, or lack of it, confronts the mind and sensibility of our time.

The foregoing discussion makes it now possible to attempt such a general statement about grace as shall sum up biblical and early Christian thought: grace is an action and gift of God whereby there is made possible a relationship to God that is otherwise impossible; what man *is* and becomes by the grace of God is not identical with what he could become simply in virtue of his existence as a human being. Catholic theology has often regarded creation itself as a gracious gift; the redemption of man within sustained existence is a further gift of grace. Man lives, that is to say, as a creature of a "double gratuity."

This understanding of grace as a gift of a new God-relationship has been variously understood in the several theological traditions, but central to all of them are three points which have been succinctly specified by Professor Eugene TeSelle:

140

At its origin, grace is the favor of God toward men, a free decision of love in their behalf. Grace is also the communication of this divine decision to men, whether the emphasis falls upon historical events (as in much of modern theology), or upon human words whose content is heard as revelation and thus becomes the power of God for salvation (as in classical Protestantism), or upon men (as is usual in Catholic theology). Whatever the means may be, the original divine decision is effectively communicated to man. Considered at its goal, grace is viewed as the intended aim of the divine decision and its communication to man.[40]

That paragraph about the origin, communication, and goal of grace, while clear and responsible, nevertheless puts the reader promptly before the problem of all theological speech about grace. For the terms "origin," "communication," and "goal" are not static-substantial but dynamic-historical terms. Grace is indeed commonly postulated as the elemental character of God in his relation to all that is not God. That postulation roots the reality of grace, not in some ontology of God, but in the confessed witness to God as he is understood through men's interpretation of historical and experiential encounters. Grace not only communicates a God so understood; grace is that God-as-communicating nothing less or other than himself as Presence. And the goal of grace is not accurately designated by the old phrase "state of grace." It is better put when the relational and continuing character of the work, goal, end, purpose, and gift of grace is understood as creative of a new relationship of all things to God, who gives himself in grace, new relationship to the fellowman (who is the fellow creature bound to God in a covenant of grace), new relationship to the nonhuman creation within which grace also resides and because it, too, is God's creation.[41] How grace, thus understood, addresses contemporary man will be the effort of the essays to

40. Eugene TeSelle, "The Problems of Nature and Grace," *The Journal of Religion* 45, no. 5 (July 1965): 239.

41. It is this relational character of the concept itself which has made even more inappropriate older notions of "infused" grace, "habitual" grace, "regenerative" grace. Such terms sought faithfully to testify to the absolute gratuity of grace, but the language, suggestive of substantial and even subpersonal operations, assumes an ontology that is otiose and an anthropology that is radically inadequate.

follow this chapter. Three intermediate and preparatory topics require discussion at this point.

Reformation Precision about Grace

If one were to have in mind the complex of forces that constituted the Reformation of the sixteenth century, and were to make an effort to pierce through the ecclesiological, doctrinal, political, social, economic, and personal data in order to specify the fundamental affirmation enunciated by those convulsive decades, one could defend this general statement: the Reformation was a vehement witness to the freedom of God in his grace.[42] A second statement could be defended as true of what followed upon the truth and vehemence of that central affirmation: that the precision of the reformers and the Reformation-born confessions about grace restricted the scope of that very grace which they so faithfully specified as central to Christian faith and life.

How did this diminishment of the scope of grace come about?

Throughout the whole of Western Christendom, from a time at least as early as Augustine, the reality of grace had been explored and explicated within the rubric of *sin* and grace. When the reformers and, following them, virtually all of classical Protestant theology spoke of the grace of God they meant

> . . . the free and unmerited disposition and activity of God for the benefit of the sinner, overcoming his bondage to sin (in Luther, sin,

42. I shall not argue this conviction. An immense literature discloses that seventeenth- and eighteenth-century assessments of the Reformation as a virtually detached theological and ecclesiastical phenomenon were followed in the succeeding centuries by studies which radically and justly complicated all simplistic interpretations. This second phase was followed by a third, characterized by new historiographical perspectives and richly supplied with critical editions of the works of the leading reformers. This third phase, honoring and utilizing all the accomplishments of the scholars represented by the second, inaugurated and has sustained a magnificent record of research by scholars on the continent of Europe, in Great Britain, and in the United States. That the freedom of God in his grace is indeed the core of the complex called "reformation" is admittedly a judgment. But it is a judgment made in knowledge of the enormous labors of one's historical and theological betters, and not in ignorance or defiance of their work.

the law, death, and the devil), restoring him to the life for which he was originally intended.[43]

There were reasons for this intense concentration of the meaning of grace at the point of sin. Among them, these: the reinforcement of the morally mordant strand of Christian teaching by the disorder, violence, economic misery, and disease-vulnerability that stalked the common life; the waning of a meaning-giving order in thought and feeling and sensibility in all aspects of common life as the medieval world of the West played out to the end the images, ideas, and institutions that had formed it for a thousand years; a slowly rising sense for the reality and authenticity of personal judgment, experience, and thought as the force of the immediately and experimentally known collided with an ever more formalized voice of a deepeningly politicized and bureaucratic church. The realities of grace were identified with and available only through a sacerdotalized clergy, a substantialized sacrament, and almost mathematized procedures for the achievement of redemption.[44]

The reality of the freedom of God in his grace is at once the charter of the church, the treasure of the church, and the interior corrective to all triumphalism, both doctrinal and institutional. Where sin is the heart of the problem the gospel of the freedom of God in his grace toward sinners is the answer. That sin was the heart of the problem in the fifteenth and sixteenth centuries, and that the proclamation of the primacy of grace was the effective answer is attested by that time's popular moral theology, books of meditation, religious, secular, and popular art, hymnody, morality plays, and legends. Therefore, the absolute concentration of the reality of grace at the point of Christ as that action of God in whom sinners are forgiven *sola gratia. Sola gratia* was not only a true but a tactically necessary focus for the doctrine in that time and situa-

43. TeSelle, "The Problems of Nature and Grace," p. 238.

44. There is no suggestion here that the great tradition of Roman Catholic theology is to be characterized by what popular understanding and practice actually did with that tradition. Unhappily, however, the depth, balance, and comprehensiveness of a great tradition is not usually maintained across the chasm that separates theological reflection and popular statement, understanding, and practice. The tradition is not justly represented by what Tetzel for instance, preached about sin, merit, or indulgence. But the common people heard Tetzel — not Augustine, Ambrose, or Aquinas.

tion. For the *sola* spoke both of the source of grace and of the place of its encounter.

Whether that precision and absolute accent is equally appropriate for another time and a quite different situation is a separate problem to which we shall return in a later section.

Enlightenment Displacement of Grace

Back of the Enlightenment, and necessary to an understanding of its amazing redirection of Western man's thought and action, stands that equally amazing and vivacious phenomenon called the Renaissance. The personalities, events, discoveries, and developments that are episodes of the Renaissance and suggest its scope and force are admirably summarized in a paragraph from John Addington Symonds. The modern reader will have undergone experiences that cause him to smile over the humanistic expansiveness of the passage. But the sardonic smile in the present is as educative for us as the sonorous confidence of the late nineteenth-century essayist is reportorial of a cast of mind entirely representative of one powerful strand of nineteenth-century confidence and expectation:

> . . . we cannot refer the whole phenomena of the Renaissance to any one cause or circumstance, or limit them within the field of any one department of human knowledge. If we ask the students of art what they mean by the Renaissance, they will reply that it was the revolution effected in architecture, painting, and sculpture by the recovery of antique monuments. Students of literature, philosophy, and theology see in the Renaissance that discovery of manuscripts, that passion for antiquity, that progress in philology and criticism, which led to a correct knowledge of the classics, to a fresh taste in poetry, to new systems of thought, to more accurate analysis, and finally to the Lutheran schism and the emancipation of the conscience. Men of science will discourse about the discovery of the solar system by Copernicus and Galileo, the anatomy of Vesalius, and Harvey's theory of the circulation of the blood. The origination of a truly scientific method is the point which interests

them most in the Renaissance. The political historian, again, has his own answer to the question. The extinction of feudalism, the development of the great nationalities of Europe, the growth of monarchy, the limitation of the ecclesiastical authority and the erection of the Papacy into an Italian kingdom, and in the last place the gradual emergence of that sense of popular freedom which exploded in the Revolution; these are the aspects of the movement which engross his attention. Jurists will describe the dissolution of legal fictions based upon the False Decretals, the acquisition of a true text of the Roman Code, and the attempt to introduce a rational method into the theory of modern jurisprudence, as well as to commence the study of international law. Men whose attention has been turned to the history of discoveries and inventions will relate the exploration of America and the East, or will point to the benefits conferred upon the world by the arts of printing and engraving, by the compass and the telescope, by paper and by gunpowder; and will insist that at the moment of the Renaissance all these instruments of mechanical utility started into existence, to aid the dissolution of what was rotten and must perish, to strengthen and perpetuate the new and useful and life-giving. Yet neither any one of these answers taken separately, nor indeed all of them together, will offer a solution of the problem. By the term Renaissance, or new birth, is indicated a natural movement, not to be explained by this or that characteristic, but to be accepted as an effort of humanity for which at length the time had come, and in the onward progress of which we still participate. The history of the Renaissance is not the history of arts, or of sciences, or of literature, or even of nations. It is the history of the attainment of self-conscious freedom by the human spirit manifested in the European races. It is no mere political mutation, no new fashion of art, no restoration of classical standards of taste. The arts and the inventions, the knowledge and the books, which suddenly became vital at the time of the Renaissance, had long lain neglected on the shores of the Dead Sea which we call the Middle Ages. It was not their discovery which caused the Renaissance. But it was the intellectual energy, the spontaneous outburst of intelligence, which enabled mankind at that moment to make use of them. The force then generated still continues, vital and expansive, in the spirit of the modern world.[45]

The energies, goals, and accomplishments so amply detailed in this passage were, in the period of Enlightenment that followed, organized by empirical reason. Men resolved to make themselves fully at home in the world of time and space. In the passion of that resolution there developed a way of thinking and feeling that gave birth to all that is characteristic of modernity. The opening sentence of the essay "Enlightenment" in the Encyclopaedia Britannica reads:

> . . . a movement of thought and belief, developed from interrelated conceptions of God, reason, nature and man, to which there was wide assent in Europe during the 17th and 18th centuries. Its dominant conviction was that right reasoning could find true knowledge and could lead mankind to felicity.

The intention of the term "displacement" as the designation of this section can be made instantly clear by setting over against that encyclopedia statement some memorable words from the liturgical prayers of the church during the seventeen hundred years that preceded the period of Enlightenment. What did common men and women in a hundred thousand village parishes and cathedrals understand, assess, and mean when they spoke of the grace of God? Whence and by whose gift was that power and presence in which men trusted to ". . . lead mankind to felicity"? The language of these prayers is, indeed, often an Elizabethan English translation of Latin Collects; but as that *cantus firmus* sings on beneath the changes of formal theology, no one with any sense for the stubborn continuity of devotion can miss in these words the catholic substance of faith.

> O God, the strength of all them that put their trust in thee: Mercifully accept our prayers; and because through the weakness of our

---

45. John Addington Symonds, *Renaissance in Italy,* published in 7 volumes between 1875 and 1886. The edition here is from the Modern Library edition (New York: 1935), vol. 1, pp. 3-4.

mortal nature we can do no good thing without thee, grant us the help of thy grace. . . . (Collect for First Sunday after Trinity)

Lord, we pray thee, that thy grace may always go before and follow after us, and make us continually to be given to all good works. . . . (Collect for Sixteenth Sunday after Trinity)

That the grace of God, preceding, attending, judging, consoling, enfolding, was the elemental context of the ever so ambiguous Christian culture of the West marks also the Prayer for the Dead. In this prayer grace is the guarantor and content of that felicity which, in Enlightenment culture, was differently located.

Almighty God, with whom do live the spirits of those who depart hence in the Lord — and with whom the souls of the faithful, after they are delivered from the burden of the flesh, are in joy and felicity: We give thee hearty thanks for thy grace bestowed upon thy servants, who, having finished their course in faith, do now rest from their labors. . . .

The point is clear. The fundamental conviction of Enlightenment culture was that ultimate human felicity was attainable and was to be sought in the strength of rational thought and action. The grace of God was acknowledged, celebrated, and even called upon, but the effectual reality of it was displaced from the center of the human story, and gradually replaced by another confidence, another possibility for fulfillment, and another center of hope. It is not necessary to detail here the steps of that process or cite the spokesmen for it. Our present purpose is but to recognize and assess the theological requirements placed upon us by the outcome.[46]

46. Cf. Joseph Haroutunian, *God With Us* (Philadelphia: Westminster Books, 1965), p. 136. This statement by the late Professor Joseph Haroutunian is the bluntest and most succinct I have encountered.

Contemporary Man and
the Relocation of Grace

Under this topic, looking back to the mainly biblical and historical substance of the foregoing discussion and looking ahead to a concrete description of the context of life today, it is both possible and necessary to
sketch out the fundamental lines of an expanded Christian doctrine of
grace. To have attempted that earlier would have left the argument arbi-
trary and hanging in midair; to defer the effort longer would leave the
following pages without an interpretive focus for the reader.

Two observations must precede the effort. The first observation is notice served upon those who stand theologically to my left that I find the
juicy vocabulary of joy, celebration, dancing, and feasting, to be an en-
gaging but rootless body of admonition unless the ancient, steady reality
of the *hilaritas* of a gracious God is its ground and its exhaustless energy.
The second observation is notice to those who stand theologically to my
right that when, in the sections to follow, I reflect about grace "beyond"
the language, concepts, images, propositions, and contexts of the Scripture, that reflection is a product of the Scripture whose modes I find it
faithful to transcend. Such reflection "beyond" Scripture does not mean
that the what, and the from-where, and the energy-born witness to grace
is "beyond" what Scripture affirms; it does mean that how, in the Bible,
men grasped by the reality of God beheld and understood and dealt with
themselves, their fellowmen, and the world is a fact that must be stated
"beyond" the biblical mode if God and grace and contemporary men and
their world are to be served.[47]

---

47. This necessity to reflect "beyond" ought properly be explicated. But to do that
with the required fullness would entail so extended a detour as virtually to halt the argument. A compromise, full of suggestive force, may be achieved by quoting some sentences from a paper read to a faculty conference in the Divinity School of the University
of Chicago by Professor Paul Ricoeur in the spring of 1971. The statements are such a
succinct contribution to the present probing for an adequate principle of interpretation
of texts (including the biblical text) that the content of the term "beyond" is given substance and direction.

> The sense of a text is not *behind* the text, but in *front* of it. It is not something
> hidden but something *disclosed*. What has to be understood is not the initial sit-
> uation of discourse, but what points toward a possible world, thanks to the non-

1. *The Meaning of Grace*

All Christian theology appeals to the reality of grace to specify its central intention when it speaks of God. This is as true of Christian philosophical theology as it is true of biblical, dogmatic, and moral theology. The God of A. N. Whitehead is as fundamentally a gracious God as the God of Karl Barth. To speak of God as gracious is to say that what we mean by God is a creative and redeeming reality, presence, energy, and allure, and that all manifestation of this reality, whether clear or masked, unequivocal or ambiguous, so ultimately discloses God — not fully to knowledge, but sufficiently in faith — that the reality of God as loving, sustaining, and fulfilling power for the life of the world is the central confession of the community of faith. One of the forces that inwardly demanded the formulation of Trinitarian confessions about God was clearly the necessity to ground the enpersonalized, incarnated, and historical incandescence of grace in Jesus Christ absolutely within the reality of God. "Grace . . . came by Jesus Christ," but grace was not created by Jesus Christ. The substantive, *grace,* functions historically in the verb

---

ostensive reference of the text. Understanding has less than ever to do with the author and his situation. It wants to grasp the world-propositions opened up by the reference of the text. To understand a text is to follow its movement from sense to reference; from what it says to what it talks about. . . . What we have said about the depth-semantics which structural analysis yields invites us rather to think of the sense of the text as an injunction starting from the text, as a new way of looking at things, as an injunction to think in a certain manner. . . .

The text speaks of a possible world and of a possible way of orienting oneself within it. The dimensions of this world are properly opened up by, disclosed by the text. Disclosure is the equivalent for written language of ostensive reference for spoken language. It goes beyond the mere function of pointing out and of showing what already exists, and in this sense the function of ostensive reference is linked to oral language. Here showing is at the same time creating new modes of being.

. . . it is not the initial discourse situation which has to be understood, but that which, in the non-ostensive reference of the text, points toward a world toward which bursts the reader's situation as well as that of the author. . . . Beyond my situation as reader, beyond the author's situation, I offer myself to the possible modes of being-in-the-world which the text opens up and discovers for me.

came. God, who is gracious, once took this way of actualizing his grace. And the Spirit who "leads into truth" is the functioning of the reality of grace in time-occasioned, but not time-bound, and ever-fresh ways.

Grace is the fundamental ascription that Christian faith must make in the God-relationship. It is that particular "attribute" or reality, or energy, essence, or substance of the God of Abraham, Isaac, and Jacob, and of Jesus Christ; and every theological method that would seek to be reflectively and reflexively adequate to the faith of the community founded by faith in this God must probe and grope for concepts to designate and a language to distinguish and celebrate this particularity. The church's experience of and reflection upon the reality of grace could not stop short of a doctrine of the Trinity for the reason that what that experience disclosed could not be confined to Jesus in his individuality, or to the spirit as ". . . the Lord and Giver of Life, Who proceedeth from the Father and the Son, . . . Who spoke by the Prophets." All is of grace, and the One God is a God of grace.

This recollection of the Trinitarian amplitude of the church's explication of the meaning of grace suggests what must be the scope and effective arena of grace.

2. The Place of Grace

The reality of grace defines the place of grace. If grace is postulated of God the Creator, God the Redeemer, and God the Sanctifier, then the presence and power and availability of grace must be postulated with equivalent scope. There has never been a time in the church's history when this requirement has been formally denied; there have been times when the point has been effectually forgotten, or when situations arose that tempted to such exclusive accent upon the christological or the Spirit-focus that grace and the creation were suppressed into practical denial.

It is exactly the point of the foregoing paragraphs to suggest that the entire life-experience of post-Enlightenment man demands the recovery of catholic comprehensiveness in the doctrine of grace. The assertion that the reality of grace must be "relocated" in the spheres of creation where contemporary man's operational actuality is most clearly evidenced, and amidst those tormented movings of the Spirit toward a transtechnical realization of men's common humanity in personhood fulfilled in justice, peace, and mutual recognition, is not a "relocation" that proposes a novelty; it is, rather, an appeal for the restitution of an almost forgotten dimension.[48]

This relocation of grace within the actuality of man's life within history and nature, and amidst the most common and formative episodes of experience, is not only a formal requirement of the interior energy of the plenitude of grace itself; it is an absolute requirement arising from the post-Enlightenment embeddedness of man's mind, self-assessment, and operational life in the world. If, therefore, the proposal of grace is not made to man in the matrix of his life-situation, the proposal is either unintelligible or uninteresting.

This "embeddedness" has generated enormous reportorial attention; the literature descriptive of the secular man, and the responses of the religious community to the process of secularization is abundant. But it is necessary for theological analysis to go beyond both such tracings of historical causation and of sociological description of behavioral changes. Theology must ask: What has happened within the mind of modernity that changes how that mind and sensibility *hears* the term "grace"?

When our fathers heard the word grace, they *heard* it from within a thought- and world-structure that had existed fundamentally unchanged for centuries. Grace, originating in the will of God, concretized in a historical appearance, was a sovereign holy resource for the overcoming of man's sinful alienation from God, a therapy for souls in the custody of the church. The very term "the means of Grace" confirmed the notion of grace as a gift and a power from God given to men.

That word of grace, in that mode of proposal, is no longer either clear or persuasive. The entire hearing-situation has changed because of the complete shattering of the anthropology presupposed in it. The place for the encounter with grace has to be relocated within that self- and world-

48. In Chapter 5 a necessarily fuller and more concrete content is given to the meaning of these assertions. The purpose at this point is a "formal" one: to ground the doctrine of grace and such explications as I shall later attempt into those traditional potentials which lie, although neglected, richly in tradition.

knowledge and understanding which is the huge and accumulating story of Western culture from Galileo to the present. The possibilities-of-intelligibility are given by and within the powerful presupposition about self, world, and their relations. *That* is what has changed. Terms which for hundreds of years presupposed our model of world-origin, -structure, and -process, and were thus a matrix within which a language could be shaped to articulate both man's need and God's grace, have been either annihilated or have gone silently out of mind.

An illustration of this cultural emptying of language and the refilling of the evacuated space by new fundamental notions can be gained by attention to a statement from Alfred North Whitehead. The statement gains force by remembering that it predates the recondite mathematical and physical sciences research by which its speculative vision was later substantiated. What Whitehead was saying softly and to the very few who had the knowledge to understand him in 1933 is now a commonplace in high school classes in general science.

The philosopher is speaking of the changed meaning of the word "location." He writes:

> Modern physics has abandoned the doctrine of Simple Location. The physical things which we term stars, planets, lumps of matter, molecules, electrons, protons, quanta of energy are each to be conceived as modifications of conditions within space-time, extending throughout its whole range. There is a focal region, which in common speech is where the thing is. But its influence streams away from it with finite velocity throughout the utmost recesses of space and time. . . . For physics, the thing itself is what it does, and what it does is this divergent stream of influence. Again the focal region cannot be conceived as an instantaneous fact. It is a state of agitation and differing from the so-called external stream by its superior dominance within the focal region. Also we are puzzled how to express exactly the existence of these physical things at any definite moment of time. For at every instantaneous point-event within or without the focal region, the modification to be ascribed to this thing is antecedent to, or successive to, the corresponding modification introduced by that thing at another point-event. Thus if we endeavor to conceive a complete instance of the existence of the physical thing in

question, we cannot confine ourselves to one part of space or one moment of time.[49]

In such language is communicated that radical shift of world-understanding which has created the difficulty of "hearing" the old language of the old tradition when its affirmations are made in the old way. What things and forces and realities might be, how they operate, where they must be specified at work if they are to be conceived at all — these are proposals for reflection that are dead upon utterance if they fail to intersect with the mind's primal cognitive vocabulary. That vocabulary may be most generally designated as a vocabulary of reality-in-relations. Things are what they are, and do what they do, and have the force they have because they are *where* they are in a vast and intricate ecosystem. Just as the "where" of a thing demands systems-models for its adequate explication, so the nature and force and the promise of an energy (like grace) cannot even be proposed-for-faith if the proposal stumbles over discarded concepts.

Grace is not nature and nature is not grace. But grace and nature are related. No description of that relationship can of itself impart grace, but an unintelligible proposal can impede the mind's hearing of what is proposed for faith. The "relocation" of the reality of grace within the Trinitarian plenitude of God-proposal is here advocated because the God of grace *is* a God of grace in the fullness of his being as Creator, Redeemer, and Sanctifier. Such a relocation is not a diminution; it is rather a restoration of the place of encounter to the amplitude of the life-theater in which man actually lives, experiences, thinks, wonders, and works. The "grace of the Lord Jesus Christ" is like the ". . . focal region which, in common speech, is where a thing is." The region of grace is all that is, has been, and will be; that is exactly what is meant by the New Testament ascription of Alpha and Omega, ". . . the first and the last, the beginning and the end." When, in the concluding verse of the eleventh chapter of Romans, the "gracious gifts of God" (verse 29) are recalled as of such scope and power to evoke the total response to total mercy in the paragraph beginning "O depth of wealth, wisdom, and

49. Alfred North Whitehead, *Adventures of Ideas* (New York: Macmillan, 1933), p. 201.

knowledge in God," the occasion and focal point of this mercy is indeed the gospel of Christ. But the focal region of God's grace is not less than the whole creation. "Source, Guide, and Goal for all that is — to him be glory for ever. Amen" (NEB).[50]

3. The Occasions of Grace

If "the freedom of God in his grace" is a right designation of the central substance of the Christian confession, then any systematization of the modes, operations, intersections, and redemptive powers of that grace within man's historical existence must be appropriately modest. If, to put the matter another way, we postulate freedom of God in his disposition of grace, we must reciprocally postulate an open, incalculable, nonpredictive structure for man's encounter with and joy in it.[51] This is

50. Is it not possible that the twin confessions, the Oneness of God and the Christocentric confession of the Lordship of Christ, might find in a "regional" and "focal point" conceptuality a uniting, discriminating, and clarifying speech which could accomplish for the twentieth-century "hearer" of the Word what the metaphysical alliances of the Nicene and Chalcedonian Fathers accomplished for their time and situation? And is it not further possible that the relational-dynamic concepts of contemporary physics and biology might be peculiarly apposite to the uses of biblical language? The God-man relationship in the Bible is regularly expressed in vital terms. God is the source, origin, and fountain of life, food for hunger, water for thirst, restorer of the broken, returner of the lost, redeemer of the enslaved, Savior of the captive, light for darkness, reconciler for alienation. Just as the situation of man is in terms of his being before God in the wrong place, so that the work of grace whereby he is placed by God in the right place is not by a hypodermic injection of a "substance" but by an encounter with a possibility that judges misplacement and redeems by restoration. The biblical mode of speech about God and man is relational in fundamental structure and image.

51. In the literature of Christian proclamation known to me there is no more sonorous and astonished apostrophe to this freedom of God in his grace than in the following portion of a sermon preached by John Donne in the year 1624 in London. The quotation is added here for another reason; it illustrates the meaning of the term "occasion" in its theological usage in relation to the freedom of God's grace.

God made Sun and Moon to distinguish seasons, and day, and night, and we cannot have the fruits of the earth but in their seasons: But God hath made no decree to distinguish the seasons of his mercies; In paradise the fruits were ripe,

only to say that in theology, as in other realms of discourse, the systematization of freedom is a perilous undertaking.

Such an understanding grounds the choice of the term "occasions" for this section. For the term suggests and recalls the lively unexpectedness of the bestowals of grace in the Gospels: "And suddenly," ". . . and on the way he met . . . ," ". . . now it happened that . . . ," ". . . there stood before him a man. . . ." In the midst of the many-threaded, wild unsystematic of the actual, the not-expected was crossed and blessed by the not-possible.[52]

Such an understanding of the surprise, the might-not-have-been, the indeterminable quality of God's grace, so episodically rich in the Gospels, has been made difficult of recovery by a theological tradition that has made of grace a "datum" or a "state" or a steady and stable "quality" or "attribute" of God. If, on the contrary, grace is understood as the energy of love, having its origin in the freedom of God who finds "occasions" for the bestowal of that love, not in the regularities of *law*, but in and by the instant and uncalculated response to man in the matrix of the historical madness of human cussedness and glory, that is, according to

the first minute, and in heaven it is alwaies Autumne, his mercies are ever in their maturity. We ask, *panem quotidianum,* our daily bread, and God never sayes you should have come yesterday, he never sayes you must againe tomorrow but *today if you will heare his voice,* today he will heare you . . . God (hath) mercy and judgement together: He brought light out of darknesse, not out of a lesser light; he can bring thy Summer out of Winter, though thou have no Spring; though in the ways of fortune or understanding, or conscience, thou have been benighted till now, wintered and frozen, clouded and eclypsed, damped and benummed, smothered and stupified till now, now God comes to thee, not as in the dawning of the day, not as in the bud of the spring, but as the Sun at noon to illustrate all shadowes, as the sheaves in harvest to fill all penuries, all occasions invite his mercies, and all times are his season.

52. If there is any consensus at all among the great company of scholars who have given themselves, since the days of Schweitzer, to a reinvestigation of the role of the miracle story in the life and faith of the first-century Christian community, it is surely this: that the stories are there because they specify, serve, and characterize the radicality of the "kingdom," and point beyond themselves via the shock of their content to a God-possibility in history which is piously evaded when such stories are made into metaphors of intersubjectivity and its analgesic or salvatory potential, or so "spiritualized" as to make their intent a kind of literary paradigm for untapped human psychological or other resources.

the dynamics of *gospel,* then the "occasion" of grace must be thought of in fresh ways. The common life is the "happening-place" of it, and man as man in nature and in history supplies its normal occasions.

There is an absolute distinction between the cause of grace and the occasions of grace. Destruction from a gas explosion is not caused by a spark; it is occasioned by it. Nothing natural is the cause of grace; anything natural (or historical) may be an occasion of it. The disclosure of grace in the enormous paradox of the cross is the "focal point" for man's encounter with grace. The grace of God is humanly, historically, and episodically incandescent in Calvary. That occasion, indeed, was and is so crucial an occasion that the mind and devotion of the devout is tempted to forget, in its grateful Christocentrism, that Jesus was not centered in Jesus at all. He is called the Christ precisely because of that. Our theology can be Christocentric as regards the reality and crucial occasion of grace precisely because that Christology lives within the grace of the Holy Trinity. The holy occasion of the discovery of the grace of God may indeed be the mountaintop experience, but the place and content of the experience is not identical with the experienced in its origin and fullness and destiny. That is why the occasion must be both absolutely valued and absolutely qualified. For the decisive context of life is time as continuity and not time as moment; continuity, not break; steadiness, not staccato; what goes on and not only what shakes up.

All of this is but a way of saying that the reality of grace is the fundamental reality of God the Creator in his creation, God the Redeemer in his redemption, and God the Sanctifier and Illuminator in all occasions of the common life where sanctifying grace is beheld, bestowed, and lived by.

Is it possible to lay aside for the moment the quite proper Christian acknowledgment of grace as primarily an overcoming of alienation from God by God's action of forgiveness, and ask what is grace as a sheer phenomenon? That is both possible and necessary. When we do that, we see that what we mean by the term, pre-theologically and conceptually, is grace as the sheer *givenness-character* of life, the world, and the self — the plain *presentedness* of all that is. The underside of this sheer gratuity, the givenness quality of things, supplies the subjective vocabulary by which that unaccountability is recognized; it is surprise, wonder, Tillich's "ontological shock." The term "gratuity of grace" includes both the knowledge of the gift and the astonishment that all that is is "gifted."[53]

This appeal to the phenomenological core of grace-as-such, and an effort to specify that core as "sheer givenness," is not to be easily dismissed as an instance of pantheism, panentheism, or, in general, a theological procedure tinctured by poetic sensibility. The appeal proceeds rather from a hardheaded Trinitarian assumption that, as St. Thomas says, "God is above all things by the excellence of his nature; nevertheless he is in all things as causing the being of all things." It does not follow that man can move from nature to grace. It does follow with immutable force that he must move from the focal point of the incarnated embodiment and disclosure of grace to the creation as a theater of grace. The Christian doctrine of redemption stands alongside the Christian doctrine of creation. Both doctrines postulate meaning; both specify that meaning in relation to the doctrine of God. The reality of God is working itself out, as it were, in both realms — the world-as-nature and the world-as-history. And these two "mighty workings" must be related. If there is postulated a logos-toward-redemption at work in history, and if the Lord who is disclosed there is postulated as the Lord of all that is, then this same comprehensiveness must inhere in an adequate Christology. Indeed, the earliest Christian communities, as we saw in an earlier chapter, felt the force of this momentum in their ascriptive doxologies to Christ and expressed it. Nature, that is to say, is an "occasioning" context, an interlaced web of origin and sustenance without which man is not. Where, in the eighth chapter of Romans, St. Paul sings his great song of redemption, he cannot halt the reality of it short of the creation itself — trapped indeed in futility, but waiting in longing and expectation.

This very notion of a primal "givenness" about all that is is a difficult

---

53. There are abundant signs that contemporary reflection, informed by phenomenological ways of analysis, is again becoming aware that the mind does not stop when nothingness is the verdict of its reflection about self and thought and meaning. For *something* is — our environing world encompasses us about with actual beings, structures, and processes. Out of that shock, so Heidegger suggests, comes afresh the surprise of something — "just there," the bald naked thingly givenness of things, and of a world. Out of this proceeds the possibility of what this philosopher calls a "letting-be," a "releasement toward things," a surprised beholding of a world-presented.

one for a scientific and technological culture to apprehend. When analysis, classification, control, and management of fundamental components of natural life — atoms, cells, chromosomes, genes, etc. — has become ordinary, taken for granted, the blunt datum that all of this is sheerly "there" and "given" is an elemental fact that is muted or forgotten in and by virtue of the operations with it. What we do with the given is so astounding that the given-as-given becomes all unthought starting place for thought, a no longer surprising datum awaiting scientific transformations. The mind filled with the excitements of what men do with the components of the world works to blunt primitive astonishment before the fact that there is a world to do something with and men to do it.

Efforts of conceptual, systematic speech either to disclose this blunting of awareness or to correct it are futile. The hauteur of theologians toward the work of those who seek a language to give a "local habitation and a name" to that surprise-in-things which slips through the coarse net of generalizing language does nothing to help and much to hinder. To suppose that "occasions of grace" can be specified without a language that catches that bright and absolutely *particular* which shocks the mind into astonished awareness, and to that startled thankfulness for things that are, is to suppose the impossible.

Without apology, therefore, and in the conviction that theological repudiation of factic speech is a stupefaction that constitutes the problem rather than a sterile purity of intellection that might help toward a solution — and in the spirit of E. E. Cummings's blazing ascription:

> i thank You God most for this amazing
> day: for the leaping greenly spirits of trees
> and a blue true dream of sky; and for everything
> which is natural which is infinite which is yes.[54]

I adduce the quieter evidence of another poet to the joy and gratitude that is evoked by the primal and the factic. The poem is called "Objects"; from the end of the third stanza it reads:

---

54. E. E. Cummings, "i thank You God," from *Poems 1923-1954* (New York: Harcourt, Brace, and Co., 1954), p. 464.

. . . Among the wedding gifts

Of Herë, were a set
Of golden McIntoshes, from the Greek
Imagination. Guard and gild what's common, and forget
Uses and prices and names; have objects speak.

There's classic and there's quaint,
And then there is that devout intransitive eye
Of Pieter de Hooch: see feinting from his plot of paint
The trench of light on boards, the much-mended dry

Courtyard wall of brick,
And sun submerged in beer, and streaming in glasses,
The weave of a sleeve, the careful and undulant tile. A quick
Change of the eye and all this calmly passes

Into a day, into magic.
For is there any end to true textures, to true
Integuments; do they ever desist from tacit, tragic
Fading away? Oh maculate, cracked, askew,

Gay-pocked and potsherd world
I voyage, where in every tangible tree
I see afloat among the leaves, all calm and curled,
The Cheshire smile which sets me fearfully free.[55]

55. Richard Wilbur, "Objects," from *The Beautiful Changes and Other Poems* (New York: Harcourt, Brace, and Co., 1947).

CHAPTER 5

Grace and a Sense for the World

It has been the latent but controlling supposition of the entire preceding discussion that intelligible proposals of the grace of God presently require a reconstitution of theological and religious language; that such a reconstitution must include both the language for specifying the faith which we believe as objective to the mind's beholding, and the faith whereby we believe as interior to the beholding mind. It is a further presupposition that such a reconstitution and relocation of language is not advanced by the multiplication of fervent pleas that it be done, or by a frantic recoloration of ancient terms in ever so psychedelic hues transferred from the paint box of merely contemporary sensibility.

The task is harder than that. Fundamental terms must be retraced to their multiple roots in the subsoil of a rich and varied tradition, their possibility for new life and force and clarity *as proposals* reassessed in terms of what ultimate pointings, structures, and possibilities of meaning inherent in them exude, bear forth, and freshly address contemporary knowledge, need, modes of cognition, and feeling-for-fact.

The "grace of God" is a term that demands such a procedure.

In the several sections of the present chapter we shall look at some of the components that make our time a literally new time in man's experience, and in such an excursion try to designate, in events of art, literature, and common experience, materials for reconstitution that lie at hand.

In the carrying out of that task a double-movement is required at every point: (a) the powers, intersections, and liberations of grace — because these were first witnessed to in episodes whose surprising nature both specified the reality and named it *grace* — must be honored by absolute attention to their historical particularity; (b) the holy and the human potential for the bestowing and the receiving of grace must not be limited to the various *mythoi* of its bestowal, acceptance, recognition, or of its accumulated fiducial burden in past acknowledgments.

The preceding chapter ended with a poem. The lines of the poem in themselves, and the use of those lines as a tactic for the advancement of the argument of these pages, are deliberate and intentional. For men do "guard and gild what's common." To inquire with the mind why they do that, and rejoice with delight and a lifting of the heart because they do that, is to place oneself at the center of what this chapter aspires to illuminate, a "sense for the world." We want to ask, for instance, what it means that Van Gogh so paints a pair of old shoes that there is evoked from the beholder a deep sense of both the terror and the dignity of man's common humanity, and a smiling sense of our fellowship with it; that Edward Hopper can so paint a figure enclosed in solitariness, sitting upon a stool in a garish, neon-brilliant corner of an all-night eating-joint starkly contrasted with the immense darkness of the midnight city, that the call of loneliness to loneliness is "guarded and gilded" in an iconography of recognition; that in all ages mighty works of literature ". . . traffic not with cold, celestial certainty, but with men's hopes and fears and breakings of the heart, all that gladdens, saddens, maddens us men and women in this brief and mutable traject . . ." of life in the creation which is our home for a while, the anchorage of our actual selves.[56]

The purpose of these paragraphs is not simply to state but to illustrate that nature and grace, perception, experience, and wonder, the creation as the habitat of our bodies, and the divine redemption as the Word of God to our spirits, must all be held together in thought as indeed they occur together in fact. And if, in the elaboration of this notion, the sober statement of the artist is adduced as useful, the absence of a theological label upon such evidence is of no significance. If the occasions of grace are incarnate, both in Israel's experience and in the testimony of the Christian community — for Israel in her historical experience of liberation and God-heldness, for the Christian community in the "glory" of God beheld in "the face of Christ Jesus" — the place of grace must be the webbed connectedness of man's creaturely life. That web does not indeed bestow grace; it is necessarily the theater for that anguish and delight, that maturation of longing and hope, that solidification of knowledge that can attain, as regards ultimate issues, not a clean, crisp certainty but rather the knowledge that:

56. Condensed from a long paragraph in Sir Arthur Quiller-Couch's volume, *The Act of Writing* (New York: G. P. Putnam and Sons, 1916).

We who must die demand a miracle.
How could the Eternal do a temporal act,
The Infinite become a finite fact?
Nothing can save us that is possible:
We who must die demand a miracle.[57]

This turning to experience is not a way to account for grace; it may well be a prolegomenon to the possibility of what Karl Rahner calls a "transcendental anthropology," by a way the artist affirms in his own concrete and earthy vision. Joseph Conrad, for instance:

> He [the artist] speaks to our capacity for delight and wonder, to the sense of mystery surrounding our lives; to our sense of pity, and beauty, and pain; to the latent feeling of fellowship with all creation — and to the subtle but invincible conviction of solidarity that knits together the loneliness of innumerable hearts, to the solidarity in dreams, in joy, in sorrow, in aspirations, in illusions, in hope, in fear, which binds men to each other, which binds together all humanity — the dead to the living and the living to the unborn.[58]

Or Henry James:

> Experience is never limited and it is never complete, it is an immense sensibility, a kind of huge spider-web of the finest silken threads suspended in the chamber of consciousness, and catching every air-borne particle in its tissue.[59]

57. W. H. Auden, "For the Time Being: A Christmas Oratorio," from *The Collected Poetry of W. H. Auden* (New York: Random House, Inc., 1945), p. 411.

58. Joseph Conrad, preface to *The Nigger of the Narcissus,* in *A Conrad Argosy* (New York: Doubleday, Doran, and Co., 1942), pp. 81-82.

59. Henry James, *The Art of Fiction* (New York: Oxford University Press, 1948), p. 10.

Grace and the Independence
of the World-as-Nature

This section is interposed at this point because the issue of the status of the universe must be rightly put if any proposals about God, or grace, or "occasion" within human life and nature are credibly open to the interpretations of faith. If the status of the universe is assessed to be a "closed system" then we are called upon to understand it without reference to anything outside it.[60]

But the universe is not closed to God's agency. The basic issue of the universe itself has not been settled, and there seems to be no possibility that it can be settled. Among many philosophers it is said that we do not know whether the universe is the sort of thing that has a reason for its existence. The question of its *status* is an open question.

The enormous and growing body of knowledge about the structure and processes of the universe has caused contemporary theology to become silent about an issue that once preoccupied theologians. The "proofs" for the existence of God really were intended to establish the dependence of the universe upon God. These "proofs," ancient and modern, are in disarray; as a result, the place and scope for any agency of God is restricted to the realms of the historical, the social, and the solitary personal.

At the very moment such a contraction of the realm of meaning is acquiesced to, one is aware that the scope of satisfactory meaning has been isolated from the massive context within which the *question* of meaning arises, and apart from which its urgency cannot be quieted. In a world known by cosmology, anthropology, biology, and virtually every other basic discipline, the mind's demand for proposals of "total meaning" is the matrix of the question.

It is, therefore, of high importance that, in the midst of ordered, growing, and verifiable knowledge about the structure and process of the universe we remain clear about the question theology asks, and must always ask. Diogenes Allen puts the matter as follows:

60. This entire section to follow is so directly dependent upon a superb essay ("Theological Reflection on the Natural World," in *Theology Today* 25, no. 4 [January 1969]: 435-45) by Professor Diogenes Allen that I shall make slight effort to rephrase what is there so succinctly put, and no effort at all to excuse my eager filching of its argument!

We may ask, "Is there a reason for the order of the universe?" and get two types of answer. One is to go outside the universe to account for its order; another is to account for its order by scientific explanations and perhaps in addition metaphysical ones which remain within the universe. In either case the question is answered. But with the question of *existence* of the universe, we do not know whether there is a reason for its existence or not. It is not a matter of a dispute over what the reason is, or of the type of reasons required, as with the order of the universe; in this case we do not know whether or not there is a reason for the *existence* of the universe.[61]

When, that is to say, one cannot ever dismiss from his mind that child-like but not childish question which has forever been the primal forest of wonder, "Why is there something rather than nothing?" the multivaried and detailed rejoinder of the descriptive sciences that things that are seem to be constructed in such and such a way, and seem to operate in such and such predictable regularities, etc., etc., quite misses the point. Or if, as is likely the case, the researcher in the natural sciences and, often, the philosopher say of the question that it is a "useless question," they should not be surprised that many in our time who retain a primal curiosity about total-meaning dismiss their dismissal as a perilous sickness. These others come to a conclusion, so clearly articulated in the literature, art, and drama of this generation, that if that question should cease to form, define, and ever freshly reconstitute the human person, then mankind is indeed an absurdity, a "useless passion," an exquisitely bitter joke of cosmic proportions. For, says Professor Allen, "One is not asking how the universe operates or why the universe operates as it does, but what its status is; one is concerned to know whether it is ultimate or not, regardless of its ways of operating and its contents."[62]

61. Allen, "Theological Reflection on the Natural World," p. 441.
62. Allen adds, "A conspicuous example of reflection on nature in America is process theology, which has developed largely from the stimulus of Whitehead. Whitehead himself, however, was concerned to understand how the universe operates. To achieve this understanding he found it necessary to postulate God. But his work is still an immanent type of metaphysics; for it is concerned with understanding how the process operates, even though it includes teleological elements in its account; and God, however

The question about the status of the universe, so airily dismissed in the days of the regnancy of the logical positivists, is returning to roost again among the philosophical fraternity. But no answer seems to be forthcoming. "We cannot specify why the totality should have a reason for its existence, but on the other hand there is nothing known to preclude it from having a reason."[63]

If, then, one is to advance beyond the incessant question, "Is the universe ultimate or not?" the question must be raised in the company and context of other considerations. In the final chapter I shall suggest such considerations and propose a context which has a size and nature appropriate to the question. Such suggestions will not, to be sure, make it logically necessary to conclude that the universe is not ultimate, that the universe is indeed dependent. But they will be, I think, such clear and reasonable "suasions" as to invite the mind to suppose that the universe may be dependent, and give universe-intrinsic grounds for that judgment.

Grace, Its Content in Nature and in History

Just as, then, a "sense for the world" is prevented from gathering appropriate fullness because of the logically unwarranted assumption that the independence of the universe is scientifically verifiable, a second impedient oversimplification must also be considered.

The issue can be put thus: the phrase "a sense for the world" proposes reflection about the double context within which all acts of perception and reflection take place. The huge categories, nature and history, are no longer clearly defined or capable of being cleanly set over against each other. If by history we mean most simply the realm of human action, and if by nature we mean the not-self as the given theater within which such actions occur, then it is clear that as historical life witnesses broad and deep advances in knowledge about and interference with natural life the interpenetrative and modifying energies of this transaction will

---

different he may be from the rest of the universe in his system, is still an item within the universe" (p. 440).

63. Allen, "Theological Reflection on the Natural World," p. 441.

present an ever more subtle situation. And the appropriateness of the relatively distinct older use of the theological categories of nature and of grace will have to follow the facts and reformulate their meanings. The suggestion here is that practical anthropocentrism, the tyranny of the historical, may arise and take command with so Olympian a certainty that the world-as-nature actually ceases to impact upon consciousness with steady force. Professor Loren Eiseley writes:

> There is something wrong with our world view. It is still Ptolemaic, though the sun is no longer believed to revolve around the earth.
>
> We teach the past, we see further backward into time than any race before us, but we stop at the present, or at best, we project far into the future idealized versions of ourselves. All that long way behind us we see, perhaps inevitably, through human eyes alone. We see ourselves as the culmination and the end, and if we do indeed consider our passing, we think that sunlight will go with us and the earth be dark. We are the end. For us continents rose and fell, for us the waters and the air were mastered, for us the great living web has pulsated and grown more intricate.[64]

Most cultural history of Western reflection since the Enlightenment obscures the truth of that observation in efforts to disclose it. For such studies assume that the world-as-nature, following the work and thought of Galileo and Copernicus, has been the focal point of man's attention. It is precisely the vigor of this investigating, systematizing, describing, and ultimately, the practical utilizing for man's purposes of the energies and processes of nature, which permit, indeed invite, this misunderstanding. That vast intellectual energies of post-Enlightenment man have gone into investigations of natural fact must not seduce us into the assumption that nature as such retains its actuality, force, and fundamental character as the determining reality of modern reflection. Nature as field of intellectual and instrumental operations is, indeed, the focus, both as material for reflection and as productive of a methodology for control. But in this process nature as a primal reality is subsumed under *nature as resource for historical*

64. Loren Eiseley, *The Immense Journey* (New York: Vintage Books, 1957), p. 57.

transformation. The central, operating factor in world-reflection since the Enlightenment has not been the world-as-nature; it has rather been the world-as-history, as this world, with man its primary agent, has been instrumentally anthropocentrized in fact.

Modern anthropocentrism has arisen as a function of this vast accomplishment of man-as-history operating *upon* nature; the life of nature has been drawn up into the volitional and fatefully decisional life of man-as-history. It is within the whorls of man's fiercely expanding managerial activity as historical actor that nature now presents itself to man for reflection.

But it is an illusion that man, in such a reflective life inclusive of rationalized, ordered, and used nature is really admitting the "creation" as such into his reflections. It is a fallacy to suppose that because we know about and think about atoms, genes, astrophysical space and organization we are thereby thinking about the creation. That fallacy arose out of the ironical fact that human exuberance about the knowledge of and control of aspects of nature has really little to do with nature-as-creation. *Creation* is a religious and philosophical term; it is not a term whose proper reference is simply the fact of, or the possible structure and process of, the world. The term "creation" contains and requires a God-postulation. Until we get this through our heads, and admit nature as the *creation* into our reflective nexus, and permit nature there to retain its intransigent reality, we shall neither theologize soberly nor be theologically guided to act constructively. Is it not likely that the reality of death — the event of it presently turned over to morticians, and grave reflection about it relegated to the comparative obscurity of poets and short story writers — has become in popular culture a dirty cheat, a surprise, almost an illegal and unmannerly interruption of the carefully planned party *because* the inexorable periodicity of the world-as-nature has been muted by the drama of man's historical accomplishments?

Several years ago Michael Harrington, engaged in a round-table discussion of current utopian ideas, recalled the epigram of a Russian revolutionary thinker to the effect that "the function of socialism is to raise men from the level of a fate to that of a tragedy," and added:

> . . . Utopia is not going to solve everything by any means. As a matter of fact, I have thought for a long time about Marx's prediction

that in a society where men are no longer murdered or starved by nature, but where nature is under man's control there would be no need of God because God is essentially man's projection of his own fears and hopes — a curious image. In contrast to that, I wonder whether, at precisely the moment all economic problems disappear, there could not be a great *growth* in religion rather than a decline. It is a possibility, because we would have a society in which men would die not from floods or plagues, or famines, not from their own idiocies about the economy. They would die from death. And at that point the historical shell around the fact of death would be broken. For the first time society would face up to death itself.[65]

Have not humanistic studies which one might suppose capable of exposing this humorous and ironical diminishment of the nexus of human reflection actually participated in the shrinkage? For these studies, also, anthropocentric and sometimes excruciatingly acute in their exposition of awareness, sensation, and introspection, have invited the mind of modernity to fold itself inward upon its own and its fellows' cerebral and emotional past and present, and by the very virtuosity of that accomplishment diminished the reality of unregarding and ever-persistent nature. The questions men ask (and in theology the questions God puts) are thus dealt with by a reflective capacity shriveled by the very attentions which constitute its pride.

Let us as an exercise in imagination suppose that one curiously unshrunk in primal naiveté falls into reflection while standing in the midst of a great, proud, modern city. Its very form, structure, vigorous systematic of production, consumption, and communication, is a microcosm of a triumphant technology fashioned upon scientific knowledge as its base. Let one suppose further that by catastrophe or plague all human life were in a moment annihilated. Within decades all the piled-up accomplishments of man would fall into dissolution — rotted, fallen into debris, dissolved, their slowly disappearing remnants covered over by the creeping greenness of a fecund and luxurious nature. Chartres would become a squat mound with vines entwined about broken frag-

65. Michael Harrington et al., *Cacotopias and Utopias* (Santa Barbara, Calif.: The Center for the Study of Democratic Institutions, 1965), p. 21.

ments of interesting shapes, and Rembrandt canvases soggy strips of fungus-splotched fiber. The waters of the man-defiled Rhine, Hudson, and Thames would run again to the sea sparkling and clean and their banks resound to the calls of the returning birds.

If men accept an understanding of the world as independent, there is no place for God's agency, and the notion of grace is not credible; if men so radically historicize their understanding of the world as to bring all dynamics of world-happening within the orbit of man's determination, there is no place for God's agency, and the notion of grace is not credible. Further, if men's sense of reality, identity, worth, and function is overwhelmingly defined by their place and role and function within the world-as-nature *technologically* organized, a third force is at work to transform their sense for the world.

Perhaps a new designation is needed to point to the dominant sensibility of men as they are defined, and are tempted to define themselves within a technologically organized world. The entire world, to be sure, is not so organized; but the parts and peoples of it that are not seem to wish they were. "Undeveloped" is the term used to describe them.

In seeking for such a new designation one remembers how men of other times have generalized about the particularity of the human species. He has been called *Homo sapiens,* the creature who reflects; or *Homo politicus,* the creature who creates institutions, makes laws, and orders the powers of life for public purposes; or *Homo faber,* the creature who makes tools to extend his powers and multiply his hands; or *Homo ludens,* the creature who, standing apart from himself, can be amused by himself.

But many a new man of our new time might be designated as *Homo operator.* His procedures are often at a distance, removed from actual things, persons, purposes. He sits at a desk covered with papers that represent things, not at a bench covered with real things. Actualities come before him in their mathematized or otherwise symbolized equivalents. He is teller, broker, retailer, distributor, operator of a part of a system. He sits in an office in Boston and sells State of Maine potatoes, which he has never seen, to a wholesaler who is an "account" and a voice on the telephone and who lives in Chicago. He crouches over levers of a crane and guides it to lift stone from Indiana, which he has never touched, to the top of a construction job in Omaha, where it is fixed in walls he need not look at, designed for purposes he has nothing to do with, by men whose names he does not know and whose faces he never sees.

The pilot of a modern aircraft is *Homo operator* in an almost absolute sense. Every natural reality that makes his plane go and holds it up arrives to his sense and procedure via gauges, indicators, lights, and meters. *Numbers* tell him the state of his airy world: elevation, velocity, the condition or status of engine, wing, tail, fuel, and water. Distance is transposed into time: Atlanta is ninety minutes from Chicago. Visual fact is transposed into interpretive signals on a dial; the actual, and the responses necessary to conform to it, is taken out of the agency of personal judgment and transferred to computerized adjustments appropriate to a complex of factors that require neither hands nor eyes.

The point here has nothing to do with the value, trustworthiness, or even the necessity of such instrumentation of natural fact. The point is rather to enforce the truth of the argument that technology as such, and quite apart from one's assessment of its promises and perils, profoundly changes *Homo operator*'s sense for the world. One is reminded of Professor Paul Tillich's "technical reason," which provides means for ends but provides no guidance for the determination of ends. Production, or plain continued operations, become frantically involved with ever more sophisticated means, and the tools which are used in the process create a "second nature" above physical nature which subjects man to itself, and proves as unpredictable and destructive as nature itself. Indeed, there have been perceptive questions as to why the recent vehement determination of the young to change the priorities of America's national life has so precipitously collapsed. The force of Professor Tillich's assertion that technology injects a "second nature" into man's reflective life is certified by a typical student outburst: "What can we do? Where can we grab hold of what's fixed and set and rolling along? The whole damned thing has a life of its own: it runs by itself!"

This changed sense for the world demands two quite fresh responses to a world so organized in mind and practice.

The first of these is a vast expansion of the notion of nature itself. For the reference of the term must now go beyond the given nonhuman world of land and sea and forest and wind and rain and petroleum and the entire range of plant and animal life. *Homo operator* is as ultimately dependent upon this primal nature as man has always been: but the *sense* for this dependence is distanced and muted in virtue of the astounding transformations science-based technology has wrought. The "made" world that has come into being following the work of the chemist, the physicist, the biologist, the engineer, is closer to the common life of the millions than the "natural" world of his fathers. Forests meet him as paper and plywood; oil and coal as energy, saran wrap, tires, and pharmaceuticals.

Nor can the argument that this transformed, artifactual world constitutes a primary factor in contemporary estrangement really be sustained. There is an estrangement, to be sure, but observation forces one to locate its causes elsewhere. For so adaptable is man to the world that science has made possible and technology has realized that in this new, "made," extrapolated world most men feel at home. Here he "belongs," in the company of fellow operators in the world he finds his "natural" community; here he feels secure, for he knows the rules of the game; here he sees and works with astounding fabrications out of primal nature and deals with them with familiar, even playful, recognition.[66]

If, then, we are required to expand our notion of the natural to include man's transformation of it, we are also required to relate grace to nature in ways appropriate and adequate to nature so understood and so brought within man's operational existence. The advancement of this theological task cannot be accomplished by theology working in a specialized, reconceptualizing disengagement from other areas of men's sensibility.

For the reality of grace must be encountered, specified, named, and known in *whatever* perceptions carry upon and within themselves the

---

66. Very responsible descriptions of this process of at-homeness in the technological world are many. For a theological treatment of the matter see Dietrich Von Oppen, *The Age of the Person* (Philadelphia: Fortress Press, 1969). For a sociological study see Victor Ferkiss, *Technological Man* (New York: Braziller, 1969). For a blunt factual account see William Kuhn, *Environmental Man* (New York: Harper and Row, 1969).

But, better still, simply look, feel, think! It is a matter of fact that to the generation born since World War II the outer-space explorations, so dreamlike and mind-boggling to the older generation, have become simply uninteresting. The intersection of many refined technologies represented in these events are, to the younger generation, simply routine, expected, completely "natural" in the sense that each represents another notch in a method of organizing data and energy that is taken for granted.

impact and quality that resonates back to that fountain, origin, and actor-in-grace who, in the tradition, is called ". . . the God of Abraham, Isaac and Jacob . . ." and ". . . the Father of our Lord Jesus Christ." This interior resonance of recognition, begetting, or evoking praise and thanksgiving, is a function of the particularity of grace itself. For grace has its marks. Whenever men encounter grace it is the shock and the over-plus of sheer gratuity that announces the presence, as indeed, it invented the name. By gratuity is meant a primal surprise, the need-not-have-been of uncalculated and incalculable givenness. "Amazing" is the only adequate adjective; wonder is the ambiance. For amazement, wonder, and grace occur together: ". . . they were amazed at the graciousness of his words. . . ."

But the very capacity for wonder can become callused, covered over with the scar tissue that forms when experience abounds in the new, the marvelous, the fantastic. Operational man presents a hard case for the voices in our day that plead for a "rebirth of wonder." A generation reared on the TV extravaganza has been so visually and aurally bombed and banalized that efforts to reach and touch into life the shrunken sense of gratuity must find fresh ways. There can be no doubt that the church, the community that lives by the recognition of grace, is beginning to understand this and grope for such ways as shall celebrate the "difference" in her sense for the world, and signalize this known difference by exterior signs. The movement is all in one direction — to announce the amazing in, with, and under the common; to beckon to wonder via the close and the usual; to divest the wonderful of the habiliments of elegance and reclothe adoration in simplicity. In architecture the churches cannot out-big the world: therefore the direct, the honest, the unostentatious. In vestments the church cannot outdo Countess Mara; therefore the plain bluntness of common texture. In the language of worship the church cannot longer allure by sonorities of the half-understood; therefore the crispness of clear statement. There is a student congregation known to me in which the general prayer is responded to no longer with the traditional "Amen" but by the rejoinder "We really mean it!"

This moment toward the domestication of the occasions of grace is neither a denial of its source in God nor a diminishment of its power; it is rather a relocation of the encounter amidst those operations which constitute the level-usualness of lived reality. It is a fresh realization of the deeply evangelical truth that the Incarnation of grace, precise in a person, is creative of a sense for the world which is total in its scope, near at hand in its invitation to recognition, adoration, and service, and beseeches and judges us in infinite love through the mortal eyes of human need.

The critical problem of Jesus' use of the "Son of man" term cannot be used to evade the terrible clarity of Matthew 25:31ff. For it is God the Father who here assesses and judges. When the Father's blessing is declared upon those who cared for the hungry, thirsty, lonely, naked, sick, imprisoned, and when, astonished, men asked where and when it was that the Father was thus encountered, the identification of a gracious God with the anguish of men is absolute. "I tell you this: anything you did for one of my brothers here, however humble, you did for me."

To relegate this saying to the field of ethics is a fateful misunderstanding. For the reality of grace is not severable from that web and bundle of life out of which the human emerges and is defined, within which the negatives of need and anguish and death, as well as the affirmative vitalities of beauty and joy burst forth, to which the Incarnation of grace came, and which, in the numberless occasions of experience, constitutes the theater of man's redemption by grace.

Grace and Man's Identity

In this section we shall inquire what relation may actually exist between the grace of God and man's sense of identity. The task may well be opened by recalling an aphorism of Professor Karl Rahner, variations of which occur often and with growing enrichment of meaning throughout the accumulating volumes of his *Theological Investigations*.[67] "All truth cannot be less than the truth that specifies my being."

It is certainly true that a capital fact that "specifies my being" is simply that a person is not a person by himself. My late colleague, Professor Joseph Haroutunian, gave the last years of his dedicated life to a criticizing of the Christian vocabulary by bringing central terms under the disclosive illumination of that fact. He wrote as follows:

67. Karl Rahner, *Theological Investigations* (Baltimore: Helicon Press, 1961).

173

We must take another look at "human nature" upon which the grace of God or God himself is said to act. It is not at all obvious that *human* nature or humanity is what a man is born with, so that one can study and describe it as the individual's private equipment. We know human beings in actual intercourse with their environment and in their actual communion with their fellowmen. Characteristic activities of human beings, such as speech, thinking, willing, loving, and hating, do not occur and are unthinkable apart from an interpersonal setting. Even perceptions, feelings, emotions, and actions occur in a social context, and these are what they are as responses in the common life men have with their fellows.

. . . We have no ontological status prior to and apart from communion. Communion is our being; the being we participate in is communion, and we derive our concrete selves from our communion. The old controversy between the realists and the nominalists about universals and particulars is incongruous with the ontology of communion. We have to do, not with universals, but with our neighbors, not with particulars, but with particular fellowmen. We do not participate individually in Being, and Being is not by our own being individually. There is no individual to participate in Being or to make Being to be. In the beginning, by God's creation, is the *fellowman,* and the fellowman is by loving his neighbor. The apparently universal notion, at least in the Western world, that *one* man can *be* and that he can have a nature suggests an alienation that gives us, not *a human* ontology, but one from which the human manner of being is excluded. In the beginning is communion and not being or Being. For this reason, in Christian philosophy, traditional ontology is a source of misunderstanding and confusion.[68]

Just as the understanding of the self must be pervaded by the knowledge that selfhood as a notion is incapable of specification except as the fellow self in communion with selves, a second contextual matrix for the achievement of identity must be grasped with equal resolution and insight. The natural world, within which men thus socialized in self-

68. Joseph Haroutunian, *God With Us* (Philadelphia: Westminster Press, 1965), pp. 148ff.

understanding actualize their being, must be acknowledged not simply as "out there" but a self-constituting datum operative in deep and steady interiority.[69]

The explication of interiority entails recollection and illustration. When, for instance, I consider my life and the million-faced coruscations of meaning, illusive but unforgettable, which light up or break out of the sheer factic *thereness* of the physical world, I am astounded by the number and the force of them. They include childhood's personification of animals and trees and clouds and all dumb things; the relentless allure of the sea in Homer, in Melville, in Conrad; Shakespeare's use of analogies from nature to pierce to the heart of the pathos of passingness:

That time of year thou mayst in me behold
When yellow leaves, or none, or few, do hang
Upon those boughs which shake against the cold,
Bare ruin'd choirs where late the sweet birds sang.

Does it mean nothing for our reality as persons that the natural world which is not human is yet *to* the human a life-sustaining placenta of self-consciousness? Is it without force that metaphors drawn from that world have been immemorially necessary when men have sought to find a language ample enough and powerful enough to celebrate or lament the "glories of our blood and state"? John Milton was quite clear about the Reformation doctrine of grace; he was quite aware that nightingales are not sources of grace. He was also quite certain that the God of grace encountered in redemption was not without such manifestations of care and beauty in the world of the creation as to constitute it an occasion of grace. And therefore:

69. The so-called Romantic Movement, ever since the earliest writings of Karl Barth, has been generally regarded as a sub-Christian if not anti-Christian exploration of the human spirit. It is no accident that in these days of awareness of environmental catastrophe the principal figures of that movement — Wordsworth, Coleridge, Hegel, Schelling — should have returned to haunt and trouble the mid-twentieth-century intellectual community. For a magnificent discussion of the theological roots of the questions the romantics were asking and the returning theological relevancy of the relations between selfhood and nature that they were proposing, see M. H. Abrams, *Natural Supernaturalism* (New York: W. W. Norton and Co., 1971).

Now came still evening on, and twilight gray
Had in her sober livery all things clad;
Silence accompanied, for beast and bird,
They to their grassy couch, these to their nests.
Were slunk, all but the wakeful nightingale;
She all night long her amorous descant sung.

(*Paradise Lost,* Book IV, lines 598f.)

In an earlier chapter, reference was made to the enigmatic verses (19-25) in the eighth chapter of the Epistle to the Romans. The amount of exegetical perspiration that has been exuded in Protestant efforts to privatize and spiritualize these verses, to make them exclusively cultic and ecclesiastical, has all the marks of a dogmatic tradition whipping recalcitrant dogs into line. Why should holy meaning be so dogmatically restricted to the *historical* drama of life as presumptuously to sweep clean of meaning the entire vast, cosmic, all-engendering, and all-enfolding matrix without which that life is literally inconceivable?

Paul made no such effort; and while there is in Paul no developed theology for nature, there is, in this *loci* and elsewhere, just such "an opening of the mind toward possibility" as demands that postbiblical reflection for which Professor Ricoeur (as quoted earlier) so urgently calls.

The scope of the salvific force of grace may be affirmed as identical with the creation by reflection upon the condition set by the very structure of personal identity. That structure specifies what are the interior possibilities of that "consummation" that faith is promised. For *consummation* of identity must be in some relation to the *constitution* of identity. It follows that inasmuch and insofar as man's transactions with nature, spiritual and operational, are powerful constituents of identity, the consummation of life in Eternal Life cannot annul or structurally distort the very constitution of life. By "constitution" is here meant not the accidents or individual fortunes that affect my personal history, but rather those primary relations, appetites, needs, self-disclosing and self-maturing factors that constitute the human as such.

Even a consummation that goes beyond "what ear hath heard or eye seen" cannot so absolutely transcend in elevation or amplitude as to be utterly discontinuous with these structural factors of the personal. Otherwise consummation would not be consummation; it would be rather so totally a "new being" as to be unrecognizable by the historical being who, *in* the world of the creation and the divine redemption, learned to envision, and to long for newness of life and consummation.

Redemption means life with God. Faith means to accept what God gives, himself as giver and himself as the gift. To be a Christian means to accept, know, enjoy, and live on this acceptance of our acceptance. This acceptance of an accepted life is not bestowed, known, experienced, or loved in capsulated privacy: the very structure of knowledge, experience, and love close that possibility. This redeemed-life is given and matured in time and space and matter, among my fellow creatures, human and nonhuman. One cannot speak of this life apart from participating in and receiving identity-forming powers from those orderings of community, symbolizations of meaning, conceptual accruals and specifications of form and substance and energy which make up the actual life of intellection.[70] As a man-participant and inheritor of all this, I announce my "membership" in a body which is trans-self in all delighted or mordant moments of recognition which occur when, in literature, art, and music, I find formal distillations of curiosity, creativity, loss, gain, ambiguity, frustration, play, fear, love, hate, hope, and far-dreaming.

This life I have as redeemed into life-with-God is Eternal Life. I have it now; it will never cease to be. If one is redeemed he is "hidden with Christ in God," and God does not die. When, therefore, I am saddened by the knowledge of my mortality, that sadness is both real and quali-

---

70. When these essays were in process of formulation I had thought to include among them an extended discussion of the poetry of Gerard Manley Hopkins, not as a contribution to literary studies (for this I have not the competence), but as an acknowledgment of the debt I owe to that amazing poet for his contributions to theological reflection.

That task, if ever I get around to it, will have to await another occasion. But let this footnote be my notation of gratitude to my colleague and friend Nathan A. Scott Jr., who, through the years in conversation and writing, has confirmed my conviction that theological anthropology steadily and almost proudly starves its perception and thins out its categories by neglect of the human dialogue with the natural world as this dialogue is movingly alive in so very large a sector of literature, old and new. A single instance of the enrichment that might accrue to theological reflection is Professor Scott's most recent volume, *The Wild Prayer of Longing* (New Haven: Yale University Press, 1971), and particularly the section devoted to the work of the late Theodore Roethke.

fied. I am saddened by the understandable regret that so significant a person as I am should cease to enliven mortal history. But the sadness is decisively qualified by the center of faith — that the redeemed are with God, and that God does not die.

But what could such an eternal life with and in God possibly mean for a person whose personhood came to be, and is, as a total function of residency in the total creation?

It follows from the logic of life in the only way the term has meaning for a person, that the entire creation — within which and as a part of which I am, have an identity, and without which I cannot conceive of being an identity at all, but only an emptily potential entity — must be the sufficient object of the divine redemption. It follows that for a person among persons and things, redemption into a world-of-relations of some transformed relational-complex is the only possibility of redemption that can have meaning, value, and fulfillment, or even interest.

Because men exist and are as relational entities, only a redemption *among* can be a real redemption. Only, that is to say, when the meaning and act of redemption is within the web of creation can a salvable identity be "saved" in any sense that makes sense. It is only in such a self-world context that I have a body, a mind, a memory, a spirit, expectation, response. What and who might be a person apart from this web? A no-thing.[71]

---

71. The "sense" of the church has always been sympathetic to the "sense for the world" articulated in this chapter. The church has permitted her children to sing some things the church has not ventured to make propositions out of; she has, in fact, created the songs the children sing. However muted may have been any consistent or strong theology for nature, the church has clearly affirmed that the Lord of the Creation and the Lord of Redemption are one Lord; she has intuited and sung and prayed beyond her doctrines. The grace she affirms in her doctrine is postulated as related to nature — even if this postulation, frightened perhaps by pagan absolutizations of nature, has squeaked into her life via liturgy, paratheological documents, and hymnody. In the Prudentius hymn *Corde Natus Ex Parentis* we are called upon to "Let Creation Praise Its Lord, Evermore and Evermore"; the legends of Christmas include into the circle of a freshly manifested but ancient grace of God the cattle, the donkeys, and the sheep; the robin, in one fable, has its breast of red because he stood long at a fire, beating it into flame to keep the Christ-child warm.

Just as at the Nativity of the Christ the whole creation is involved in the nascent redemption, so at the death of Jesus the sense of the church has projected a gracious "sense

The redemption of the *world* must be permitted to mean what it says, or it will cease to mean anything meaningful. In a bluntly human sense *my* redemption must include the possibility of redemption of everything. For I am no-thing apart from everything. The poet Richard Wilbur asks:

> . . . What should we be without
> The dolphin's arc, the dove's return,
>
> These things in which we have seen ourselves and spoken?
> Ask us, prophet, how we shall call
> Our natures forth when that live tongue is all
> Dispelled, that glass obscured or broken
>
> In which we have said the rose of our love and the clean
> Horse of our courage, in which beheld
> The singing locust of the soul unshelled,
> And all we mean or wish to mean.[72]

CHAPTER 6

Christian Theology and the Environment

The preceding chapters are among the things I have thought, recalled from tradition, and have been forced to reassess en route to the concrete and urgent matter which is the substance of this chapter. The environmental problem, that is to say, has been the issue that started and pow-

---

for the world" in the natural convulsions that attend the passion narratives in the Gospels, and in the many legends of the Glastonbury-thorn genre (see, for instance, the magnificent Northumbrian poem "The Dream of the Rood").

72. Richard Wilbur, "Advice to a Prophet," from *Advice to a Prophet and Other Poems* (New York: Harcourt Brace Jovanovich, 1959).

ered the reflections there recorded about God, Christ, Grace, and the interpretation of Scripture. In this closing chapter the relation between environmental fact and Christian ethics, and the grace of God, must be more tightly drawn. That effort will be made under two headings.

The Context of Ethical Discourse

Fundamental ethical categories — responsibility, obedience, love, integrity, and others — have not lost their Christian imperative force. But as the range and context of contemporary man in knowledge and operation has steadily widened, the setting of ethical reflection, the options open to decision, and the complexity of the facts that must be respected in the act of decision have multiplied. The physician treating illness has at his command therapeutical and procedural devices that no previous age has had, and his decisional situation is thereby complicated.[73] In every field of science and technology, ecological fact is presently so clear and the results of its ignoring so catastrophic that older guides to action are either useless or positively perilous. Sociology, which is but the ecological understanding of man's life among and within groups and institutions, is quite aware of the uncalculated and perhaps incalculable tremors that originate in private and group action and profoundly modify areas of life distant from that originating center. Psychological studies have long since gone far beyond experimental work in perception, sensation, memory, etc., and have so rooted the beheld data in familial and other primary contexts that these researches are an illustration of the fundamental postulate of ecology — that anything is related to everything. The very *field* of ethical reflection is in ever more complex and interactive motion.

Nor is this expansion of field the only factor that constitutes the difficulty for contemporary Christian ethics. The traditional center of such reflections remains the center — the reality of God and his will as embodied in and illuminated by Jesus Christ. But that force and figure is clearer as *center* than as content-for-ethics. Biblical and historical studies have made clear that (a) there is probably no historical or other road to

73. Cf. Paul Ramsey, *Fabricated Man* (New Haven: Yale University Press, 1971).

the precise recovery of the "intention" of Jesus; (b) that what we can be quite clear about because it seems most general and pervasive is that that "intention" was an eschatological act and message for and about the kingdom of God.

But even that relative clarity exacerbates the problem of defining what might be for us in our time a "starting point" for a Christian ethics centered upon Jesus. The "eschatological" as a formative ambiance for faithful self-definition and action, as this worked in an earlier period to organize thought about the relation of God to time and space and history and nature, is not easily translatable into the mind of an era that lives ever more consciously out of knowledge of beginnings, developments, forces, and transformations, ascribes absolute agency to immanental vitalities, and understands destiny to be a secret folded within the coils of human history within the vast theater of cosmos.

This historical distancing from originating events begot a process of demythologizing into various categories — subjective interiority, radical symbolization, etc. The entire movement has had a profound effect that is designated by the title of this section, "The Context of Ethical Discourse." And necessarily; for the fortunes of men's minds follow the fortunes of their bodies with absolute seriousness; their reflections reenact the orbits of their operations. When men's bodies walk upon the moon their questions about the meaning and intention of Jesus, and of faith's Christ, will not be content to swing within the older orbits of self, family, nation, church, or even the "historical" as exemplified the career of humanity as a particular species busily managing or mismanaging life in the thin biosphere that surrounds a particular heavenly body. Men seek patterns of meaning that are correlative in scope to the magnitude of their questions.

We may, to be sure, so "historicize" reality as to shrink its data to a size more comfortable for our anthropocentric inclinations. But such a decision is counterproductive for our children, who, for better or worse, *do* have their hands upon the very large — in astrophysical investigations — and upon the very small — in subatomic and genetic researches.[74] A generation whose "world" is of that size and complexity, and known to be bound together in an ecological web of some astonish-

74. Cf. Clifford Grobstein, *Strategy of Life* (San Francisco: W. H. Freeman, 1965).

ing subtlety, will not cease to ask about God and Christ and grace in terms that have an equivalent magnitude.[75]

It will not suffice for the present scope of meaning-reflection to deal with a world so known (however imperfectly) by appeals to the New Testament's clear distinction between the world as cosmos and the world as historical drama *(kosmos* and *aion).* Both nature and history are mute as regards God and meaning; and the life of nature has been so drawn up into the energies of history in virtue of man's science-based manipulations of nature, that these categories, useful and legitimate in the biblical worldview, are no longer of the same categorical efficiency.

Nor will it do, either, to elaborate an ethics that bows in the direction of the good that is made possible for individuals and society by modern "operational" man, but does not take seriously the absolute necessity to relate the grace of God to the disclosure of this good and men's joy in it. *Theological* ethics, that is to say, must address man in his strength as well as his weakness, in his joy as well as his sorrow, and in his accomplishments — to direct them and hold them in proportion to larger goods — as well as in his failures — to forgive and console them.

When men experience as a positive good the activities of their lives, the range of the work of their brains and imaginations and hands (what they feel in the discovery and reorganization of novel substances and energies and the excitement accompanying the never before put-together), they do not feel either sinful, pretentious, or subhuman. They know, rather, that it is precisely in such work and works that some healthful re-

---

75. Illustrative here is the work of Sir Herbert Dingle of the British Academy of Science, as reported in the *British Journal for the Philosophy of Science* 2 (1951): 86, 95. ". . . the Victorians looked upon the progress of science as a process of accumulation. . . . Our view today is different . . . the picture of the whole which we form in our attempt to express its interrelations undergoes unceasing transformations. . . . We can no longer say, the world is like this, or the world is like that. We can only say, our experience up to the present is best represented by a world of this character; I do not know what model will best represent the world of tomorrow, but I do know that it will co-ordinate a greater range of experience than that of today."

The late Percy Bridgman, a Harvard Professor of the Philosophy of Science, affirmed that there is no necessary connection between the thoughts in our minds and the way things are! See P. W. Bridgman, "The Way Things Are," in *The Limits of Language,* ed. Walker Gibson (New York: Hill and Wang, 1962), pp. 38-49.

ality of their nature is being fulfilled in joy and creativity, some significant element in their constitution as men is being realized.

The theological requirement of this anthropological fact is clear and commanding. The grace of joy and creativity, the possibility of life-understanding and life-enhancement thus experienced, the sense of a self-transcending engagement with the allure and power and mystery of the world refuses to be identified as absolutely separate from the grace and joy and new possibility given to human life in that Christically focused grace, greater than all, which is the forgiveness of sin. Precisely here is disclosed the theological and pastoral necessity to speak of the grace of the Triune God in a way that breaks out of the Protestant disposition to enclose the total reality of grace within the focal point of the second article of the doctrine — of Christ and redemption.[76]

For while nature and history may be mute about both the reality of God and meaning in life, man's experiences engender prehensions which become occasions within which the announced presence of a gracious God in the divine redemption is, by a necessary momentum, postulated as the meaning of the creation. Israel's faith produced Deuteronomy (that record of historical occasions when a gracious God was encountered) before it produced Genesis (the story of the creation of the world by God), and that sequence is of significance. It affirms that the God who is man's Redeemer dare not be acknowledged as other or less than the Creator of the world. The scope of Lordship dare not be specified as less than the scope of all that is. Indeed, Psalm 104, firmly fixed in that conviction, is literally a cosmic-ecological doxology.

That faith should forever have to risk the act of investiture of the whole in the power of the experienced redemptive occasion — is this not of the profoundest character of genuine faith? The eighth chapter of Romans tormentedly pushes through to such a conclusion. And more — for precisely in the ambiguity and often hiddenness of the gracious presence of God in nature and in history lies the inexhaustible and generative power of faith. All occasions that promise but do not suffice, and in a way that leaves the power of the promise unabated by the insufficiency, constitute a "negative" testimony to a possibility. Glimpses that unfor-

---

76. For a difficult yet rewarding essay on this point see Karl Rahner, *Nature and Grace* (London and New York: Sheed and Ward, 1963).

gettably allure but do not focus into clarity or satisfaction constitute a witness by the very pathos of their partiality. Meanings that beckon, slip, and slide amidst the patterns of history, form a mind and sensibility that can neither dismiss them as of no worth nor combine and accumulate them into the solidarity of certainty. Faith, that is to say, when it becomes maturely conscious of the risk-character of its demand, is always an act of investiture of total reality with that vision, value, and meaning which has been granted to us in our encounters with the deepest, highest, and holiest. When that deepest, highest, and holiest is the presence and power of grace, and when the occasions of its life-sustaining gift are granted to man within his historical life among his fellows as well as within his residency within the nonhuman world-theater of his existence, the place and scope for the ethical is given along with the realm of the gracious.

This effort to draw our regard for the world-as-nature into organic relation with the reality of grace is not a merely theoretical exercise; its intention is practical. Unless some huge, primarily religious, and commanding vision of the future of the world can seize, release, and exalt our spirits free of our unregarding, arrogant, and ultimately suicidal operations with the creation, we shall continue to be bombarded by the awesome data of ecological disaster, but remain unsupplied with a theological indicative as big as the issue and an ethicality unexpanded to appropriate dimensions.[77]

77. These essays are a monograph about a neglected and presently urgent *aspect* of grace; they are by no means a comprehensive treatise. It is necessary to stress this limited intention in order that the realm of the *human* as the primary realm for ethical response to God's creation shall not be understood as of lesser pathos and importance. Richard Neuhaus's *In Defense of People: Ecology and the Seduction of Radicalism* (New York: Macmillan, 1971) is a powerful and passionate statement of this primary realm of Christian ethical obedience that literally screams in anguish for ". . . the manifestation of the children of God." Even Mr. Neuhaus's attack upon the ecological movement as "diversionary" from the humanly demanding task for the poor, the powerless, the unjustly trapped — even his insightful pages about the slick operations of corporate monsters who, having had a large role in the raping and pollution of the earth, are now cashing in on the profits to be made from ameliorating the effects of their depredations, and disguising this tactic by a rhetoric of engagement and concern that approaches linguistic ethical pornography — must be heard and honored as the truth.

I share the main thesis of the Neuhaus book. Its appearance indeed makes it unnec-

Ethicality and Verification

In the course of his journey to Jerusalem he was traveling through the borderlands of Samaria and Galilee. As he was entering a village he was met by ten men with leprosy. They stood some way off and called out to him, "Jesus, Master, take pity on us." When he saw them he said, "Go and show yourselves to the priests"; and while they were on their way they were made clean. (Luke 17:11-14 NEB)

I wake to sleep, and take my waking slow,
I feel my fate in what I cannot fear,
I learn by walking where I have to go.

This shaking keeps me steady, I should know.
What falls away is always, and is near.
I wake to sleep, and take my waking slow.
I learn by going where I have to go.[78]

The New Testament episode and the poem make the same point: action may sensitize cognition. We do not do what we should only after we are clear about all the facts; we also learn about facts when we go the way we must. The doing of the required illuminates and multiplies the possible; it draws the mind forward into fresh cognitions. Walking where one "has to go" discloses hitherto unregarded relations. The incessant pressure of the question, "What ought I to do?" decisively modifies and

---

essary to say again what he has said so well. But Mr. Neuhaus knows very well that the human brutality he records is of a piece with the less dramatic and quieter fault to which attention is called in these essays: i.e., that all abuse is a distortion of right use, for persons as for all things. What is not regarded as a grace will be disgraced into use without care.

This is the proper place to take notice of and record gratitude for Paul Santmire's *Brother Earth* (New York: Thomas Nelson, 1970). Summoning to his argument theological resources other than those I have called upon but equally well warranted in tradition and Christian confession, Mr. Santmire, too, has aimed at a renovation of Christian theology at its neglected center.

78. Theodore Roethke, "The Waking," from *Words for the Wind* (Bloomington: Indiana University Press, 1971), p. 114.

opens the epistemological question, "What can I know?" The ten lepers were cleansed "on the way" to an indeterminate and clinically absurd obedience. As old as Augustine is the relation between how I regard a thing and what is possible to know about a thing. Love opens to knowledge. *Non intradit veritatem nisi per caritatem* — there is no entrance to truth save by love.

This symbiotic coexistence and interaction of the risk of faith, the consequent investiture of the creation with a gracious possibility in virtue of the Incarnation of grace in time, space, matter ("born of woman, crucified under Pontius Pilate"), and an ethicizing of our regard for and our transactions with nature as *still,* despite man's rapacity and despoliation, a field of grace — this is proposed as a Christian theological pattern of a magnitude that matches the misery of our environmental debacle.

Can the affirmation that God is gracious, and that God's creation must be enjoyed and used as a gracious gift, have the power to accomplish that radical change in "the spirit of our minds" that the problem of man and environment demands? Two considerations are in order as we ask that question. First, if the Christian community is to go beyond a mere adding of its numerically modest voice to the urging of that issue, that community under the guise of public morality will betray its responsibility. A change in the "spirit of our minds" requires something vastly more than a combination of frightening facts and moral concern. There is sufficient evidence that men are quite capable of marching steadily into disaster fully equipped with the facts. Pride, comfort, and an idolatrous and brutal hardness of heart have for several generations permitted the American nation to stare straight into the face of poverty, injustice, and the calcified privilege of the powerful — and leave national priorities unchallenged.

Against that fact one must assess realistically the sanguine assumption that knowledge of fact can by itself create change. Fundamental changes are evaded by the dramatization of small ones; faults at the center of a system are obscured or dismissed by cosmetic operations on the surface. A political and an economic system develops a rhetoric of celebration about its accomplishments that is capable of an act of seduction on a national scale. Rigor mortis is celebrated as stability.

Ecological rationality, and the creation of public law appropriate to justice and care for the clear and clamant needs of persons — these right ends of social purpose are regularly shattered against inherited and clearly no longer effective laws governing uses of property, the exercise of legally defended autonomy in land use, and definitions of corporate responsibility bent to the advantage of the strong.

The second consideration is this: the Christian community exists in the power of events, presences, and visions that are betrayed when its total and holy understanding of man and God, man and the neighbor, man and God's creation are translated down from their fiercely elevated and dynamic, steadily revolutionary reality. That the care of the earth is rational, necessary, aesthetic — the convulsive and renovating and never-to-be-quieted torment and glory of the story of God and Abraham, God and Jesus Christ, God and our recalcitrant spirits — does not have to be invoked for *that*. The community of the people of God, who live by and are held within God's grace, has another and wilder thing to do. They are a people caught and held by a vision of a King, a kingdom, and a consummation — and by the massive contexts of culture, history, nature, as fields of its holy disturbance.

It is not an accidental fact that utopias have been formulated only where the historical dynamism inseparable from Christian faith has been exercised. But there is a decisive difference between utopias and the visions of human life and possibility that the faith relentlessly explodes into fresh forms. Utopias owe their character and force to the vigor of the "see what is possible!"

The Christian vision is fundamentally different; its vision of what is possible is engendered both by the realities of human existence and the promises of the God of its faith. Christian vision believes out of both possibility and promise. Its fundamental trust is not in the allure or energy of the possible (these collapse, wane, frustrate) but in the Giver and Promiser who does not abandon what he has given or renounce his promises. Just as one's hope for eternal life in God is a correlate of the reality of the promises of the God of his faith, and does not ultimately rest upon either man's desire or man's hope — so man's vision of the New Creation is a product of God who is affirmed in faith to be a Creator of the world, Redeemer of the world, and Sanctifier of the world.

The one comprehensive reality of this Trinitarian God is grace; the place of encounter with this grace of the Triune is the given and modified arena of creation, the alienated arena of redemption, the envisioned arena of the future of man, the Spirit, and the world.[79] It is in the power of that argument that this entire effort has been undertaken.

Is there, however, apart from the sheer momentum inherent in the reality of grace itself, and the formal necessity to postulate the grace of the one God as present and at work in the work and presence of the one God, evidence from the facts of life that faith's investiture of everything experienced and reflected about with the supreme meaning-as-grace is an intelligible act?

The theme of this final section is ethicality and verification. By ethicality is meant the necessity for the organization of life toward continuation, care, and enhancement if life is to be at all. That life is like that and that its fundamental drive is in that direction I take to be a nonarguable datum. When in Chapter 5 it was argued that knowledge about the structure and process of the universe does not preclude reflection about the status of the universe — dependent upon God or not — an issue was raised which, regardless of what scientist or philosopher may think, cannot be left hanging for faith. When grace is postulated as the reality of God, as the reality of the life of the Father in the Son, witnessed to by the "internal testimony of the Holy Spirit," then literally all that is must be invested with an interpretation congruent with that postulate. By ethicality, then, is meant not only a way of acting in accord with and as an actualization of that faith, but a way of understanding that begets the possibility to assess all things from that center.

By verification is meant a warrant for the adequacy, coherence, and truth of such an understanding.[80] What warrant is there for such a faith-

---

79. Professor Carl Braaten's *Christ and Counter-Christ* (Philadelphia: Fortress, 1971), while not focused upon the doctrine of grace, so elaborately details the theological and practical vitalities resident in the recovery of apocalyptic as central to Israel's faith, as the setting and transformed presupposition of the event of Jesus, and the promise, vision, and thrust toward liberation in history, that what is said here about "vision" is given in that volume a very extended and variously illustrated treatment.

80. The extensive literature produced by logicians, linguistic analysts, and others, in search for a principle of verification of statements, suggests that the term "verification" may be too precise and too strong. I think the term is open to the charge. But the deepening complexification of the meaning of "verification" itself as the debate has moved into a more accurate specification of the ambiance of words and sentences, the indeterminate intentionality of statements, the cultural "career" of statements that tran-

investiture? What evidence from the world of fact invites the mind to suppose and supports the mind in supposing that the grace of the Creator is a principle of the creation; that a primal regard for things in terms of the marvel and particularity of their "being there" at all is somewhat more than an imposition, or an unwarranted extrapolation from the superheated theological fancy untroubled by intrusions of verifiable fact?

If things cannot continue to be at all except men deal with them with due regard for their given structure and need, then there is certainly rational warrant that assessment of things according to their transutilitarian "good" is an appropriate recognition of an intrinsic "good" in things that are. If a postulate about the source, status, and transpersonal actuality of the world-as-nature (that it is of God, and a theater of his grace) begets an assessment of that world and a consequent use of it consistent with the assessment then, by an empiricism-of-outcomes, the postulate is logically and experientially warranted. Or, to put the proposal another way: what is necessary for the continued existence of things and essential to prevent the perversion or distortion of the given nature of things may be reasonably postulated as congruent with the truth of things. Indeed this "postulate" moves toward the status of a principle if conditions for the very existence of men and things are *absolute* conditions.

If the realm of nature is regarded and used under the rubric of grace, and responds as if one had discovered her true name, and along with God's human creation "delights" to have a name and to have been given freedom to be, the ancient image of "the morning stars sang together, and all the sons of God shouted for joy" returns with something more than poetic force. If, for instance, Lake Michigan is assessed according to its given ecological structure as a place for multiple forms of life, by nature self-sustaining and clean, available for right use and delight, then in a blunt and verifiable way we are "justified" by grace even in our relation to the things of nature. The opposite of justification is condemna-

---

scend ostensive reference in virtue of horizons "of possibility," etc. — this entire discussion seems to me to give leave to ordinary reflection to reclaim the idea of verification now that the "angels" who fear not to tread in that recondite region are stomping one another in multiplication of qualifications.

tion, and there is an empirically verifiable condemnation that works out its slow but implacable judgment in the absence of such "gracious" regard for nature. If a lake becomes a disposal-resource, or a dump, or a source for water to cool ingots with, or a bath to flush out oil bunkers (both instances proper to legitimate use and technically subject to restoration to cleanliness) then a repudiated grace that "justifies" becomes the silent agent of condemnation.[81]

> For he has made known to us in all wisdom and insight the mystery
> of his will, according to his purpose which he set forth in Christ, as a
> plan for the fullness of time, to unite all things in him, things in
> heaven and things on earth. (Ephesians 1:9-10)

81. This illustration is an extension of the truth and meaning of the doctrine of justification into the area of material things; it is by no means a transposition of the ground and origination of that doctrine in the freedom and will of God whereby men are justified by nothing other than the grace of God.

The Scope of Christological Reflection

It is now eleven years since, at New Delhi, at an assembly of the World Council of Churches, I set forth in very general terms what seemed to me a legitimate and necessary way to speak of the Lordship of Christ.[1] The appeal on that occasion was to the theological community to reassess the nature, scope, and richness of reference of the christological ascriptions and images in the New Testament and to inquire how the intersection of some of these with contemporary man's engagement with the natural world might draw christological thought into orbits of meaning coordinate with the magnitude of modern man's transactions with the natural world.

The address was regarded as interesting but esoteric; legitimate as individual speculation and private vision but tangential to solid and established ways of thinking about the meaning of Christ.

Since that time there has been rapid, even convulsive, movement in very fundamental notions in theology proper, in biblical studies, in philosophical theology, in social anthropology. The momentum of these has added up to vigorous investigation of the theme which I have made the title of this essay. I should like, therefore, to set down what these "movements" are, adduce the substance and weight of them to a firmer

1. Joseph Sittler, "Called to Unity," *The Ecumenical Review* 14 (January 1962): 177-87.

securing of the original proposal, and relate the resulting accumulation to a task that urgently confronts us all — the development, in contemporary terms and in recognition of ecological fact, of a christological, doxological speech which intersects the actuality of the world as modern man knows it and deals with it.

The first fact to be recognized is this: Contemporary theology is necessarily giving fresh attention to the doctrine of creation. In a single journal, *Theology Today,* and within a period of two years, major articles have signalized this attention and skillfully focused it.[2] Both take seriously the statement:

> The word "God" is used meaningfully only if one means by it the power that determines everything that exists. Anyone who does not want to revert to a polytheistic or polydaemonistic stage of the phenomenology of religion must think of God as the creator of all things. It belongs to the task of theology to understand all being in relation to God, so that without God they simply could not be understood. This is what constitutes theology's universality.[3]

The thrust of these and other essays[4] is quite clear. Just as in the Bible the doctrine of creation is a necessary correlate to the doctrine of the divine redemption, so in contemporary theological efforts to articulate a doctrine of Christ which shall have a magnitude competent to declare his Lordship over all things, the creation of the world by God (since Schleiermacher, interpreted as meaning only the sustaining and preserving of the world) must again be made a fundamental dogmatic affirmation if Christology is to be unfolded to the dimensions of its intrinsic fullness.

2. Diogenes Allen, "Theological Reflection on the Natural World," *Theology Today* 25 (January 1969): 435-45; George Hendry, "The Eclipse of Creation," *Theology Today* 28 (January 1972): 406-23.

3. Wolfhart Pannenberg, *Basic Questions in Theology,* trans. George Kehm (Philadelphia: Fortress, 1970), vol. 1, p. 1.

4. Cf. Vilmos Vajta, ed., *The Gospel and Human Destiny* (Minneapolis: Augsburg, 1971).

II

Augustine's aphorism that God has formed us for himself and that therefore our hearts are restless until they rest in him is no longer an adequate delimitation of the realm of theological speech. The *Lebenswelt* (the realm of man's experience of the world-as-history) no longer specifies the world dimension demanding understanding. For how can anything "mean" if everything doesn't? And because man now knows that he is from, of, within, inextricably a product and function of that energy and process whereby everything that exists *is* — the categories for self and human explication cannot be extruded solely from his *Lebenswelt*. Indeed, efforts to do that presently appear to be faintly absurd. The history of nature is the context of the nature of history; the immense journey that Loren Eiseley ponders is the context of the troubled historical awareness and activity of *homo sapiens, homo faber,* and *homo politicus.* The astrophysical sciences suggest that the macrocosm — whatever model of it may presently be deemed most adequate — is the context of microcosm. From galaxy to atom is a pattern reflective of a single energy and structure; and that aware bundle called man must ask the questions he asks within that context.

There is something ironical in the fact that material pollution seems at the moment to trigger theological expansion! Anxiety about dirt begets awareness of ecology as fundamental. And the reality of the physical as an ecological web begets the recognition of the anthropological in a cosmic web. By a strange and invincible necessity the mind that starts with pollution cannot find categories adequate to define or confront the problem short of asking the very question that much of theology for a hundred and fifty years has laid aside. That question is the one Diogenes Allen asks in the essay alluded to: ". . . not . . . how the universe operates or why it operates as it does, but what its status is; one is concerned to know whether it is ultimate or not, regardless of its ways of operating and its contents."[5]

The moment one puts the question that way — and I would insist that the momentum of absolute relatedness of all things, as freshly dramatized in the environmental crisis, permits no other way to put it — he is on a theological ski run from which there is no exit short of the end of the slope. In this regard one may further expect that just as the recog-

5. Allen, "Theological Reflection on the Natural World," p. 440.

nition of man's actuality within nature as creation has forced the question of creation center stage, so the effort to elaborate a Christology to the size of *that* ecological placement of man will not be able to stop short of a fresh go at the venerable doctrine of the Holy Trinity.

The doctrine of the Trinity arose precisely because of the magnitude of the Christian community's claim about Christ. The community knew that if God is subtracted from Jesus the remainder is not Jesus. And nothing in the post-Bultmannian biblical, historical, or theological efforts of the past two decades comforts the mind with any exit from that welded relationship. The theologians of hope, by reflecting *forward* to God, are trying to accomplish by the facts and energies of world-historical categories precisely what the fathers of the church, including the writers the New Testament, sought to accomplish by reflecting *backward* upon the events and energies of Israel's historical experience. The first efforts were necessary; current efforts are no less so. But to suppose that the subtleties of *Lebenswelt*-analysis dissolves or sufficiently enfolds into silence the *world-status* question is an illusion. We have come to the end of the Schleiermacher road, not because the statements of Schleiermacher are erroneous, but because the world placement of the person who asks the questions about God and Christ and himself is no longer an inhabitant of Schleiermacher's world.

It would be possible, given space enough, to detail the forces that have annihilated that world. This essay assumes knowledge and experience of these and will attend only to several which are indigenous to the biblical-theological enterprise itself. And chief among them is the counterpoint between exegesis and systematic theology — with focus upon Christology.

This relationship is a marvelous combination of support and demolition. Christological statements have always purported to be proposals that are distillations of witnesses. And because the primary witnesses are the documents that comprise the New Testament, any profound disturbance in the understanding of those documents eventually transmits shock waves throughout the entire structure. The time-lag between a disturbance at the base and a shudder at the doctrinal apex gets steadily shorter. The accumulation of critical studies indicated by the names Reimarus, Wrede, Schweitzer has reached a methodological consensus among New Testament scholars in the short span of about seventy-five years. In the history of theology that is not very long. But when "the eschatological" as a possible perspective within so short a time begets redaction criticism as a fundamental exegetical method, and when this interior biblical and theological development coincides with and occurs within the *general* intellectual passage indicated by the names Max Planck, Albert Einstein, and Enrico Fermi, the pressure of the context for reformulation of the content is enormous.

Nor has christological reflection been unaffected by this massive erosion of the traditional way of moving from event to witness to systematic statement. One of the clearest indications of this enlargement of the scope of experience to which the doctrine of Christ must be addressed can be discerned in the interesting succession of topics under which ecumenical Christology has carried on its studies in faith and order. The doctrine of Christ was a central inquiry in the movement at Oxford and Edinburgh in the nineteen thirties. In 1951, at Lund, the rubric was expanded to "Christ and the Church." Since the New Delhi Assembly in 1961 the dimensions of the study have been specified as "Christ, the Church, and the World."

Man's place in nature, the penetration of even the scientifically untrained and uninformed mind by a sense for the immense dimensions of time and space within which man exists and has come to be, has established an a priori context for thought about Christ which inwardly determines the dimensions of reference which *any* intelligible ascription of significance must occupy.

This expansion of the theater of reflection has been simultaneous with profound disturbances in the very psyche of the reflector. My late colleague Joseph Haroutunian once said that the fortunes of men's minds follow the fortunes of their bodies with absolute seriousness. And that epigrammatic statement, better than any other I know of, puts its finger upon the heart of the problem. For the piety that could once sing "Jesus, Lover of My Soul" as an adequate designation of trust, loyalty, and meaning is not saying enough about Jesus, love, or persons now that portions of interstellar space bear man's footprints.

"The psyche of the reflector," is as deeply formed by nature knowledge as by the impact of historical events. The prejudice of theology in favor of the historical as determinative of the emergence, substance, and forms of confession of the Christian faith is fully disclosed by any analy-

195

sis of contemporary man's identity crisis. The force and importance of the convulsive and disclosive historical events of this century are not to be discounted. But to suppose the agenda of these to be sufficient to account for contemporary man's fractured sense of self is to ignore the context of identity itself — and fatefully. Social psychology is a true descriptive discipline. But not true enough. I am what I am not only as one with, among, and in self-forming transactions with men; I am who and what I am in relation to the web, structure, process and placenta of nature. And because and insofar as contemporary theology ignores that — as the anguished and complex convolutions about hermeneutics in which it is presently involved testifies — its reflections about the adequacy of redemption in Christ will be uninteresting because insufficiently real. Contemporary linguistics, to cite but one avenue of study, clearly indicates that the scope of reality that language encompasses, refers to, and releases is incommensurable with Cartesian notions of selfhood. If the self is to be redeemed by Christ, *and if that self is unspecifiable* apart from its embeddedness in the world as nature, then "the whole creation" of the Book of Genesis and of Romans 8 is seen as the logically necessary scope of christological speech.

There is a mass of evidence — to which the professional theological community has not seriously attended — which attests the force of man's sheer animal fixedness within the natural world of the not-self as profoundly constitutive of his sense of identity. There is a straight line from modern man's manipulative and awesome transformation of nature, his accelerating technological astro-turfing of the earth, and his deepening anxiety about his own identity. For thousands of years he has specified his selfhood among, alongside (even under) the things, forces, natural processes, periodicities, mutations of earth, sky, animal, and plant life. So profound has been this fellow-creature sense of place-among-and-with, that the very metaphorical structure of his language has been determined by it. Shakespeare can give absolute expression to that pathos of passingness and the closing circle of man's mutability only in appeal to the leafless tree now black against the winter sky from which the birds of summer have flown:

> That time of year thou mayst in me behold
> When yellow leaves, or none, or few, do hang

Upon those boughs which shake against the cold,
Bare ruin'd choirs where late the sweet birds sang.

And a constant theme in contemporary literature is the question how man's identity, so long formed by a sense of belonging to a God-intended world of persons and things, can survive a world of meaning-lessness. Literature, to be sure, does not commonly put this issue in terms of the death of God. But Christian theology must ask what relation there might be between this "aloneness in the world" and an utter historicizing of the meaning and presence of Christ isolated from the creation and moralized in terms of radical privacy.

Furthermore, there is within biblical study itself what might be called a momentum and directionality which, in conjunction with modern hermeneutical theory, brings together the preceding paragraphs about the dimensions of selfhood, the quest for a Christology which shall be both continuous with the elevation and scope of the New Testament ascriptions and doxological statements, and is congruent with man's awareness of his ecological residency within the vast cosmos.

The history of exegesis makes clear what is referred to by the phrase "momentum and directionality" above. Redaction criticism has not only secured the fact that all of the New Testament writings are theologically formed; it

> . . . is concerned with the interaction between an inherited tradition and a later interpretive point of view. Its goals are to understand why the items from the tradition were modified and connected as they were, to identify the theological motifs that were at work in composing a finished Gospel, and to elucidate the theological point of view which is expressed in and through the composition.[6]

There clearly is a momentum and a directionality at work in the scope and variety of the New Testament witness to Jesus as the Christ. Its progress is from forms of doxological ascription which, to use C. H. Dodd's phrase, were "quarried" from the language expressive of the hope of Israel, onward and in widening circles of reference. This circle spins

---

6. Norman Perrin, *What Is Redaction Criticism?* (Philadelphia: Fortress, 1969), p. vi.

out in larger and larger orbits until, in Colossians, chapter 1, and in the great rhetorical passage in Ephesians, chapter 1, it enfolds "all things" as destined in Christ to be interpreted as existing to "the praise of His glory."

For a long time the extraordinary amplitude of Colossians 1:15-22 was reduced to dogmatically less embarrassing size by dismissing it as superheated rhetoric fashioned by the writer to relate Christian claims for Christ to the scope of Gnostic speculation, and indeed, possibly to have borrowed its images from that tradition. This tactic is no longer possible.

Professor Paul Ricoeur, in an unpublished paper read to the Divinity School faculty at the University of Chicago in the spring of 1971, spoke of exegesis and hermeneutics in a way that suggests another possibility. Having made a distinction between ostensive and nonostensive references of a text, Ricoeur indicated how hermeneutics in the service of theology can and must break out of the classical tasks of exegesis in justice to the text itself. He said,

> We now can give a name to non-ostensive reference. It is the kind of world opened up by the depth-semantics of the text. This discovery has immense consequences concerning what is usually called the *sense* of a text.
>
> The sense of a text is not *behind* the text, but in front of it. It is not something hidden, but something disclosed. What has to be understood is not the initial situation of discourse, but what points toward a possible world, thanks to the non-ostensive reference of the text. Understanding has less than ever to do with the author and his situation. It wants to grasp the world-propositions opened by the reference of the text. To understand a text is to follow its movement from sense to reference; from what it says, to what it talks about.
>
> Disclosure is the equivalent for written language of ostensive reference for spoken language. It goes beyond the mere function of pointing out and of showing what already exists and, in this sense, transcends the function of ostensive reference linked to oral language. Here showing is at the same time creating new modes of being.
>
> Therefore it is not the initial discourse situation which has to be

understood, but that which, in the nonostensive reference of the text, points toward a world toward which bursts the reader's situation as well as that of the author. Less than ever, understanding is not directed toward an author who is to be resuscitated. It does not even address his situation. It turns toward the propositions about the world opened up by the text's references. Understanding the text is to follow its movement from the sense to its reference, from what it says to that about which it talks. Beyond my situation as reader, beyond the author's situation, I offer myself to the possible modes of being-in-the-world which the text opens up and discovers for me.

What is suggested here is what almost the entire corpus of biblical study pushes toward but seldom articulates: that the New Testament is a document that stands between events — whatever their nature and quite independent of concerns of "verifiability" — that were constitutive of a unique community; that the center and "Lord" of this community was Jesus as the incandescence of the reality, power, presence of God among men; that faith as trust in him is redemptive of men in bondage to sin, death, and the demonic. The New Testament is a complex probing for adequacy in the reporting of this faith, in the explication of its interior nature, and in its deeply disturbing relation to all earlier forms of the God relationship.

In the course of working out such propositions, analogies, images, symbols this literature states its "belief" in the strength and according to the possibilities and limits of the worldview that was available to it, bequeathed to it by the Old Testament behind it, and to a lesser degree, by the forms of ascription, cognition, and recognition gleaned from the world around it.

In a current book Alistair Kee makes a distinction that is useful here.[7] *Beliefs* are to religion what *worldview* is to general language use. But faith is a *choice,* a determination to commit oneself. In this sense, and within this distinction, one can say that the New Testament is, because of its unique relation to constitutive events, a belief document probing for expressive and ascriptive adequacy for faith's reality and designation.

7. Alistair Kee, *The Way of Transcendence: Christian Faith Without Belief in God* (Harmondsworth, Middlesex: Penguin, 1971), p. ix.

When Ricoeur's description of the momentum of hermeneutical transactions with the text is conjoined with this understanding of the New Testament, one can see both the normative and the relative character of this witness of the primitive community. When, for instance, a writer speaks of Christ as the power, presence, and principle in "whom all things hold together," he may indeed be witnessing to a christological scope of meaning in terms taken over from the belief world of Gnosticism. But to point *that* out is not to the point. The energies of the faith world to the writer interiorly both permit and demand such a blooming of language to encompass a faith that the God who in "these later times" has encountered men in Jesus is no other and no less than the creator of the world.

The "intentionality" of the writer (even if we *could* fully recover it!) is not the limit of the life and energy and career of the *text* — as the doxological text moves through the centuries. In this sense a text opens up a world of possibility in which the faith elements that determined it must ever anew probe for ways to release, point, bear witness. Such a recognition by no means dishonors tradition or renders erroneous the belief statements of the past. Nicean and Chalcedonian christological statements intend what we, too, have *faith* in; they are, however, put in *belief* terms that require extensive historical and intellectual recoveries that make them less and less intelligible to the common life of the church.

The quest for a Christology that shall serve our time is given urgency by what is commonly called the environmental crisis. Knowledge of the extent of pollution, the dynamic equilibrium of the natural world, the ecological structure of all life is a kind of catalytic in awareness. This knowledge is with concreteness, clarity, and force causing all men to acknowledge that life is indeed a bundle, that "all things" is the context of anything, that physics by nature demands a metaphysics.

An ecological worldview will require belief statements appropriate to the dimensions of faith energies. And these belief statements, with an urgency that our fathers did not know, will have to swing in larger circles of specific reference than any from earlier times in the church's life. For they must address men not only in their religious, moral, and spiritual selves but also in their operational actuality. What men are doing, and by refinements of scientific knowledge expanded into technological procedures will in the future be able to do, with the natural world is a radically novel datum. No earlier time has had the knowledge or power to put its manipulative hand upon the dynamics of evolution or upon the molecular structures of matter and energy. But our times does, and a Christology that does not propose the power and presence and grace and judgment of God in Christ with an amplitude congruent with these power potentials as an operational mode of life deeply formative of technological man's personhood will be an unintelligible Christology, even an uninteresting one.

Evangelism and the Care of the Earth

A believer is an evangelist primarily by who he is and how he lives — not by what he says. What he says is important; but unless his speaking tallies with what he is and does, he had better keep quiet.

"For the worldly are more astute than the other-worldly in dealing with their own kind" (Luke 16:8 NEB), commented Jesus; and they are particularly, even unfairly, astute in their perception of the imperfection and inconsistencies of the "other-worldly." This is true in large part because they know very well that complete worldliness is not sufficient, and they dull the guilt of their own worldliness by cultivating a sharp eye for the faults of the "other-worldly." A crook can smell a crook a mile away — not because his righteousness gives him a better sense of smell, but because his crookedness has educated his nose. "It takes one to know one," as the saying goes.

A Christian is a person whose life is centrally gripped by the reality of God, and who has come to see the reality of this God most clearly in that fully God-grasped man, Jesus. This being grasped by God is never complete, and the Christian's life, in thought, word, or deed, is never fully obedient to this having-been-grasped. But he knows his life ought to be, and this "ought to be" is for him forever a gift of grace, a judgment, an allure, and an incompleteness.

In this grace, under this judgment, troubled toward the better by this allure, and simultaneously repentant and joyful in this incompleteness, he is always in motion: "I press on, hoping to take hold of that for which Christ once took hold of me" (Philippians 3:12 NEB), says Paul.

How does this man-in-motion live in the world? There has to be a difference! If there is no difference, there will be no evangelism (a calling out, as it were, to those who do not know God-in-Christ, to "come and see").

The difference has a thousand faces, ways of showing itself and thereby inviting others to "come and see." Among these ways is one that is as commanding as a holy summons, as clear as a bell at silent midnight, as visible as a bright light in a black place. The Christian is called to care for the earth! Well, isn't everybody? And shouldn't everybody? And are we not all on a collision course with catastrophe if we don't? Yes! — vehemently and demonstrably yes. But the Christian is called, commanded, interiorly obligated to care for the earth as a part of *being a Christian.* How is this? Let us try to unwrap that by reflecting upon four questions.

I. How is man constituted by God?

The great story on the first page of the Bible tells us the fundamental truth. According to that story, man is who and what he is and can become because he is constituted by three forces that cross — and he is who he is because these forces intersect in him.

First, man is formed by God. Man *is* because God is; God wills man to be. God is the Creator; man is created creature. Man's existence is subsistence; that is, another is, and wills man, and man is because of that.

Man may not like this, will this, want this — and, like Adam and Eve, he does strange things to change this. He wants to be by, for, with himself. But he cannot successfully buck the structure. He's stuck with God.

Second, man is formed by the fact that God made man *to be* among his fellowmen. God made one; then he made another. The one can't *be* one without the other. A solitary man is no man at all. I am who I am because I am a man-among. God made me; but he makes me as a plain biological entity by the communion of others. I have parents; I have children. All of us *are* because God creates out of the bundle of life. Absolute aloneness is not only pathetic; it is impossible.

Third, God makes man out of, within, and absolutely dependent upon the *whole* world that he has made. I can live without food for a month, without water for a week, without air for perhaps six minutes. I am stuck with God, stuck with my neighbor, and stuck with nature (the "garden"), within which and out of the stuff of which I am made. I may love God, hate God, ignore God. But I can't get unstuck from God. I may love my neighbor, hate my neighbor, or ignore my neighbor. But I can't get unstuck from my neighbor. And I may love the world, hate the world, or try to ignore the world. But I cannot get unstuck from the world.

II. Where does God place man?

We've already answered that. Man's place is the "garden," this world. Man is not alone in this world, not even when his aloneness is unalleviated by the companionship of the fellowman. For the creation is a community of abounding life — from the invisible microbes to the highly visible elephants, the vastness of mountains, the sweep of seas, the expanse of land. These companions of our creaturehood are not only *there:* they are there as things without which I cannot be at all! They surround, support, nourish, delight, allure, challenge, and talk back to us.

Take a look at the 104th Psalm, a veritable ecological doxology!

> Countless are the things thou hast made, O Lord.
> Thou hast made all by thy wisdom;
> and the earth is full of thy creatures,
> beasts great and small . . .
> All of them look expectantly to thee
> to give them their food at the proper time.
>
> (Psalm 104:24-25, 27 NEB)

III. What does God command man to do with this companion-world?

The Genesis story says that man is "to rule" (Genesis 1:26 NEB) the earth and "to till it and care for it" (Genesis 2:15 NEB). The "rule" is clearly a rule by "caring."

One can rule in many ways. One can rule by "careless" domination;

one can rule by subjecting everything to oneself; one can rule by assuming that everything that isn't oneself is good and has value only as it helps oneself. The first is brutish, the second is arrogant, the third is cynical. That kind of rule, in the creation as in a family, is a kind of ruling that is catastrophic. It ultimately destroys the ruler.

But man is to "rule" the earth as God's earth, not man's. It is *for* man, supports man — but it isn't *man's.* Man, who didn't make himself, is placed in a garden that he didn't make, and he is commanded to care for that garden so that God's creation may *be,* so that he himself and his neighbor may *be.* The command to care is gentle; the results of not caring are violent and fatal.

IV. How does God bless caring, and how does he judge not-caring?

We read that the judgments of God are "true and righteous altogether" (Psalm 19:9 KJV). We also read, and we know by experience, that those judgments may be in a coinage we don't expect, and the pace of them of a slowness, a patience, a toleration we don't deserve. Nature's God — her Creator, source, ineffable life — is astoundingly patient with the avaricious romping around of the children in the garden! *Bury My Heart at Wounded Knee* is the actual, sickening account of American extermination of Indian people and culture. *The Frail Ocean* is an account of man's pollution of the clean and life-supporting seas of the earth. *Oil on Ice* is a study of what is likely to happen when the oil reserves of Alaska's north slope are hot-pipelined across the habitat of Eskimo and caribou, over the fecund but delicate tundra of the north. *The Limits of Growth* tells us that Americans, 6 percent of the earth's population, consume about 45 percent of the earth's goods. And so the story goes, a story of incredible carelessness under the divine command to "care for and till the earth," and an even more incredible account of the patience of nature under man's rapacity and stupidity. If we believe that the judgments of the Lord are "true, and righteous altogether," dare we suppose that he will keep his anger forever? Or that he who marks the fall of the sparrow will forever withhold the fateful working-out of the forces that created, sustain, and make rich and various the life of both created garden and created and loved children?

And what, you may now well ask, has all of this to do with evangelism? Remembering the true statement with which we began, we ought quickly to see the inevitable and powerful connection. "A believer is an evangelist primarily by who he is and how he lives — not by what he says!"

If *in piety* the church says, "The earth is the LORD's and the fullness thereof" (Psalm 24:1), and *in fact* is no different in thought and action from the general community, who will be drawn by her word and worship to "come and see" that her work or salvation has any meaning? Witness in saying is irony and bitterness if there be no witness in doing.

Nature and Grace in Romans 8

I consider that the sufferings of this present time are not worth comparing with the glory that is to be revealed to us.

For the creation waits with eager longing for the revealing of the sons of God; for the creation was subjected to futility, not of its own will but by the will of him who subjected it in hope; because the creation itself will be set free from its bondage to decay and obtain the glorious liberty of the children of God.

We know that the whole creation has been groaning in travail together until now; and not only the creation, but we ourselves, who have the first fruits of the Spirit, groan inwardly as we wait for adoption as sons, the redemption of our bodies.

For in this hope we were saved. Now hope that is seen is not hope. For who hopes for what he sees? But if we hope for what we do not see, we wait for it with patience.

ROMANS 8:18-25 RSV

It ought to be of some comfort to many lay people who have difficulty penetrating all the meanings of the Bible that through 45 years I have calculatedly ducked preaching on the eighth chapter of Romans. I always found it possible on this Sunday to preach either on the Gospel or on the Old Testament text, and thus did not have to come to terms with this immense and meaningful lesson, because I was not certain I had a good grasp of what it means.

This should be of some comfort to many lay people who think, "Well, I don't understand this very well, but the pastor knows all about it. He's been trained in biblical studies, so even though I don't understand, he certainly does." Let me assure you, many times he or she doesn't. It belongs to the magnificence of Holy Scripture that meanings in the lessons, episodes, stories and counsels resonate with a depth which a lifetime of reflection — even by those who turn professionally and full-time to that reflection — does not fully and fundamentally discharge. There are levels within levels and wheels within wheels.

Who has believed what we have heard? And to whom has the arm of the Lord been revealed? For he grew up before him like a young plant, and like a root out of dry ground; he had no form or comeliness that we should look at him and no beauty we should desire him. He was despised and rejected by men; a man of sorrows, and acquainted with grief; and as one from whom men hide their faces he was despised, and we esteemed him not.

Surely he has borne our griefs, and carried our sorrows; yet we esteemed him stricken, smitten by God, and afflicted. But he was wounded for our transgressions, he was bruised for our iniquities; upon him was the chastisement that made us whole, and with his stripes we are healed.

All we like sheep have gone astray; we have turned every one to his own way; and the Lord has laid on him the iniquity of us all. (Isaiah 53:1-6 RSV)

Think, for instance, of that great passage where old Isaiah says, "There was no beauty that we should desire him," and, "We hid our faces from him, and the Lord laid upon him the iniquity of us all, and by his stripes we are healed." I know the meaning of the surface statement, but the interior resonance of meaning that comes out of those mighty metaphors a lifetime does not suffice to unfold.

Think of other statements. For example, there is a passage of St. Matthew which still haunts me. Jesus is speaking about children, "And I say unto you that in heaven their angels do always behold the face of my Father" (Matthew 18:10). What is he saying about the nature of new, fresh and unspoiled life? I do not know for certain what the metaphor of the childlike means, but it is of the essence of Scripture that what we do not fully comprehend remains to haunt us.

The study of Scripture recalls what the poet John Keats wrote to his brother: "A huge and alluring vision strides just before me." This is true of any serious inquiry into any profundity, this groping after language with which to enclose and stop and make clear what is fundamentally ineffable.

So it is when we come to the eighth chapter of Romans. It is probably fair to say that never before or since in the history of literature has such a group of powerful, enormous notions and concepts been compacted into so small a space. Having said that a thing is in some ways inscrutable, I shall not try flat-footedly to unscrew it. If it is not fully clear, let me not talk about it as if it were. But some things in the statement are not totally obscure either.

The first statement which is quite clear is that, in Paul's understanding, nature is not complete. The world is in motion, and there are to be unfolded events which have not yet occurred. We know from sheer, observed fact that this is true. Every element and structure and process in nature is always moving toward profounder complexity. It always seeks somehow to transcend itself; it is never content to be static. This is no religious judgment, but a purely scientific one. This is true of everything from viruses and bacteria to the structure of the human brain. The whole creation is in movement; and it is moving *toward* something. The metaphor by which that something is vaguely indicated does not open itself absolutely to our conceptualization, but the point is available.

And humanity also! Humanity embedded in nature shares nature's lack of fulfillment, an incompleteness in the shape of a bud tightly folded, which eon after eon opens and opens and opens. This is not the old idea of progress. One has only to understand how primitive humans dealt with nature, how the American Indians lived on this continent, and compare them to contemporary land developers, to realize that progress is a very dubious notion. But *we,* not nature, have done this. Nature itself, and humanity in some aspect of our being, is still unfolding. Ours is an incomplete and unfulfilled world.

209

The second relatively clear idea from the passage is that this incompleteness is not simply a law of nature. The scientist may regard it in this way and has every legitimate right to do so, but the religious — specifically the Christian — point of view, following Paul, would say "and God has subjected it in hope."

What does this mean? That God somehow did not give us in the Creation a finished job, a static world with all things in immutable place. "God has subjected it in hope" (Romans 8:20). In Hebrews the words meaning "to wait" and "to hope" have the same root. Things have an interior possibility that God both plans and draws toward some ultimate unfolding.

The third identifiable point in the lesson is that, as suggested above, we are related to this process. Humanity is not to be set over against nature and understood purely as the consciousness and awareness of intellectual creatures who dream and create concepts. No, our being is deeply imbedded in the ground of nature, so that the whole Creation and we ourselves are "groaning in travail, waiting."

The picture is not only of an untroubled opening toward God's fulfillment, but of a tumultuous and a painful opening. The episodes which we might regard as disruptive of the human community may be the groaning of nature and history to bring forth a future justice.

I recall when a late undistinguished vice-president went about the country bewailing "the weakening of the moral fiber" of the young. What he called "the weakening of moral fiber" were the riots and disruptions and screaming of people who had been systematically deprived of a decent humanity.

There is a groaning and travailing, but it brings forth a better child. Not all troubles are negative; not all disruptions necessarily require the FBI; not all disorders are against a better order. The birthing of the better involves the groaning and travailing of the less good. The respectable static will always be pained by the emerging better. The whole Creation, including humanity, is subjected in hope, waiting.

This passage is in the context of a great speech about the nature of the spirit of God, which is the whole eighth chapter of Romans, and that will be dealt with presently. But first, what may we say this message says on a very practical level? It says many things, some of which I am sure I do not understand. But one of the things our forebears in the

Church felt it was saying was indicated by the other lessons. The Psalm has to do with the green and fecund earth, the joy that people should find in it and the care they ought to have for it.

I wish to conclude with a proposition. Finally, as regards really important issues, the visionaries of this world are more practical than the self-announced pragmatists. Practical people, in the long run, foul up the situation regularly. Practical people know that there is cheap meat available for dogs and cats if they chase down the remaining three hundred sperm whales in the world's oceans. And so they do, and soon there will be no more of what the Psalm called "that great leviathan in whom the Lord delighteth" (Psalm 104:26 KJV).

The easiest, cheapest, most practical way to get coal is to rip off the topsoil and jerk it out of the earth. Oil companies know quite surely that there is a lot of oil under the earth, but no matter how much there is, it is a finite amount. Yet they say that if we give them more money to pump it and transport it more quickly, we will solve our energy crisis. Thus we solve the problem of a non-replaceable resource by using it faster!

As regards such realities, Paul in the eighth chapter of Romans is not a religious man dreaming when he says, "The whole creation groans in travail, waiting for the revealing of the sons of God." Can this mean that a serious "son of God" should really mean it when he says that "the earth is the Lord's and the fullness thereof"? And really mean it when he reads that Adam was put in the garden in order to tend it? The present use of the word "development" has nothing to do with tending. "The whole creation, and we, too, groan in travail, waiting." Could it be waiting for the children of God to begin to act like they are?

Along with this dreamer in the text, let us for a moment dream of this. What might it mean if 80 to 90 million nominal Christians and Jews in the United States of America really believed what they said? Suppose that in private reflection, private behavior, familial practice as regards basic public issues we really believed that the rape of the earth is not only irrational, impractical, and stupid, but blasphemous? Suppose we really believed it?

> There is therefore now no condemnation for those who are in Christ Jesus. For the law of the Spirit of life in Christ Jesus has set me free from the law of sin and death. For God has done what the

law, weakened by the flesh, could not do: sending his own Son in the likeness of sinful flesh and for sin, he condemned sin in the flesh, in order that the just requirement of the law might be fulfilled in us, who walk not according to the flesh but according to the Spirit. For those who live according to the flesh set their minds on the things of the flesh, but those who live according to the Spirit set their minds on the things of the Spirit. To set the mind on the flesh is death, but to set the mind on the Spirit is life and peace. For the mind that is set on the flesh is hostile to God; it does not submit to God's law, indeed it cannot; and those who are in the flesh cannot please God.

But you are not in the flesh, you are in the Spirit, if the Spirit of God really dwells in you. Any one who does not have the Spirit of Christ does not belong to him. But if Christ is in you, although your bodies are dead because of sin, your spirits are alive because of righteousness. If the Spirit of him who raised Jesus from the dead dwells in you, he who raised Christ Jesus from the dead will give life to your mortal bodies also through his Spirit which dwells in you.

So then, brethren, we are debtors, not to the flesh, to live according to the flesh — for if you live according to the flesh you will die, but if by the Spirit you put to death the deeds of the body you will live. For all who are led by the Spirit of God are sons of God. For you did not receive the spirit of slavery to fall back into fear, but you have received the Spirit of sonship. When we cry, "Abba! Father!" it is the Spirit himself bearing witness with our spirit that we are children of God, and if children, then heirs, heirs of God and fellow heirs with Christ, provided we suffer with him in order that we may also be glorified with him. I consider that the sufferings of this present time are not worth comparing with the glory that is to be revealed to us. (Romans 8:1-18 RSV)

Some texts present a single question, and some present a double one. Some texts are quite clear, and the point of the sermon is simply to get people to do what the text says. But there are other texts — and the eighth chapter of Romans is filled with them — which present a double problem. The language is compacted and the images are so rich that one must first undertake clarification of the several layers of meaning in the text, and only then ask that we hear and obey. So it is with verses 1-18.

It would be folly to suppose that one could deal adequately with even a piece of it in a short space, but I want to reflect upon the resonance of the word "Spirit," and how it works in this text.

Perhaps there is no other word in the Christian vocabulary which is in our day more confused or subject to dismayingly inadequate understanding than this word, Spirit. There are those who declare that the Spirit is a kind of private pipeline to God, and that it is possible to have "inputs" of the Spirit which in an ineffable, mysterious, and supernatural way grant to the blessed children of that gift an insight and relation to God which is not available to the common run of humanity.

Not an ounce of evidence in the Bible defends this as the fundamental word about the Holy Spirit. If it were true, the Christian community would be a kind of spiritual coterie of the especially gifted, and there is no evidence that that is now, or ever has been, the case. The power and the enthusiasm of the charismatic movement in our day have legitimate aspects and must not be denied, but that movement could only gain by being enlarged to the dimensions of the Spirit as understood in the eighth chapter of Romans.

Observe the first word in the chapter, which is a piece of characteristic Pauline connective tissue: "therefore." It makes small sense to try to describe what lies this side of the "therefore" without knowing the argument to which the word is the apostolic reply. What lies back of the "therefore"? The letter has a concentrated single statement when, after reviewing the situation of mortal, finite, sinful humanity in the midst of a world filled with evil, demonic power and death, Paul cries out, "O wretched man that I am! who shall deliver me from the body of this death?" (Romans 7:24 KJV).

This cry has often been understood as an ejaculation out of the deepest level of Paul's exquisite conscience. It is no such thing; there is no evidence at all that Paul had an exquisitely sensitive conscience. He could say, "As before the law, I am blameless." Paul did not take it lying down when he was accused of being worse than other people. What then could he mean by calling himself a wretched man? He means something that we all know, knowledge of which does not depend upon exquisite sensitivity or moral consciousness. He means that good or bad, fairly righteous or not so righteous, we are all within the grip of three mighty structures which are transpersonal, everlasting, and universal.

The first of these is the fact of evil. In our deepest selves, even the devout, the pious, the sanctified, those on the way to glory, know that evil is a thing we always fight but never destroy. It often dogs the steps of the pious with more seductiveness than it does those of sinners. Second, we live in the midst of demonic forces. When the Epistles talk about "principalities and powers," they don't mean simply the obvious rottenness, nastiness, and aggressiveness of the world. They mean that there is something tending toward destruction, a negativity, a No in the midst of all the Yeses of this world. How shall an individual be delivered from that?

Third, who shall deliver us from the grasp of death? We can sing pleasant songs about this problem and create a mellifluous language about "passing away." We can do all kinds of things to mask it, but we all move toward death. Who shall deliver me from that structure which stands at a point in all life? Thus when Paul says "therefore," he's not talking about private piety and the little evils and sins — or even the major ones — that lay waste life. He is talking about the vast structures that imprison finite humanity, creatures with an infinite capacity for dreams, within time and nature and history.

Then Paul begins a mighty doxology in the eighth chapter, "Therefore, brethren, there is now no condemnation." He piles the whole thing up and then sweeps it away with a mighty gesture. There is no condemnation because of one thing only, and that to which Paul points is nothing less than the fact that God who created this world — and who knows it in the depth and power of all these structures — entered into all of them, went down under the worst of them, and came through and out of them alive.

"There is now no condemnation, if any man be in Christ Jesus" — and Christ Jesus is but the name for that action whereby God became the hell of this world, this life, and this imprisonment and was not thereby destroyed. If you are in Him, your open, pathetic destructibility by these forces is now hidden in the life of the One who was not destroyed by them. "There is therefore now no condemnation." And when in the lesson Paul talks about being free from the law he is not referring to statutes. The word law is used to mean just those structures of periodicity and of destructiveness. You are free from these if you are "in the Spirit."

Now what can Paul mean by Spirit, when he uses the concept in relation to Jesus, to God and to the Christian life? I want to address this issue by recalling a statement a student of mine once blurted out in class. He said, "If God is not enough God for everything, he isn't enough God for anything." The statement disclosed a typically modern mood: the student knows that a person, a human reality, has roots biologically, geologically, and historically in *everything* that is.

We are not just *homo sapiens* crawling across the surface of the world. We are *of the world.* We are produced by it. Therefore, any notion of God which is to come to us as a private word whispered into our individual ear — "Buck up, old boy, I'm on your side" — this is not enough. The only salvatory God must be a God who has the whole wide world in his hands. If he is not the God of everything, he is not an adequate God for my anything, no matter what that anything might be.

As we look further into the text, we find that the Spirit — which is a power of God whereby we are inserted into that victorious life of God — is spoken of in many ways. Let me refer to the usage in the Nicene Creed. Here in the fourth century the Church made a statement of its confession. This seems very early to us, but the Church was already quite old — older than the American Republic.

A mature Church said, "And I believe in the Holy Spirit, the Lord and Giver of Life." If we grasp that, we are very close to what the Bible means by the Spirit of God. The Lord's spirit breathed over nothing, and something was. The concept of spirit, in its profoundest sense, means God's creative action whereby there is a world; the creativity of God which is identical with life itself — not life in some aesthetic, philosophical sense, but the plain biological reality of cells and organisms which cannot be destroyed in their life history.

I want to refer to three points as a kind of suasion or analogy — not a proof — for what the creed referred to by the words, "And I believe in the Holy Spirit, the Lord and Giver of Life." In *The Lives of a Cell,* Lewis Thomas discusses the indestructibility of biological life, which apparently does not waste, but goes on. He offers the amazing word that to a biologist there is something unnatural about human death. Unnatural that life should cease at the moment of physiological death, says the biologist!

Another such instance I cite from the television program, *Nova,* when astrophysicists from Cambridge and elsewhere discussed the discovery of a gigantic new galaxy known as the Crab Nebula. It cannot be seen at all except with very powerful instruments, but its emission of power is so gigantic that the energy emitted from the sun is one forty-thousandth of the energy of this nebula invisible to the naked eye. The astronomer added that of course it was getting older, and in another four billion years it will collapse upon itself with such enormous energy that out of sheer pressure it will then re-explode, and a new galaxy will be born. "The Lord and the Giver of Life" — we must think of this in big enough circles.

I will add a third illustration. I once had a neighbor who was an investigator at Argonne National Laboratory, the atomic research center west of Chicago. One day he said to me, "You know, the bacteria are growing inside the reactor." Inside the reactor with its incredible heat and the dreamlike destructive power of splitting atoms! Still, the bacteria are doing their thing inside the reactor.

When we are led into the eighth chapter of Romans by the statement that there is no condemnation "by the law of the Spirit of life in Jesus," that phrase refers to the displacement of the absoluteness of the old structures. They are still there — we die, we do evil, we know the demonic — but their ultimate power has been destroyed. If you live within the law, in Paul's terms — that is, the mighty structure of the life of God which came and is illuminated in Christ — then there is another side to the whole story of finite human existence. When we baptize a child, that sacrament is the insertion of every new arrival into that life cycle and into that story of no condemnation.

A second verse to which I wish to call special attention is the following: "If the Spirit of Him who raised Jesus from the dead dwell in you, you also shall be raised with Christ" (8:11). The Spirit, then, is not simply what Jesus occasionally, or even extraordinarily, felt. "The Spirit that raised Jesus from the dead" means that something greater than death is the life of God, and it goes in, through, under and out of all dying; so the power of the Spirit is nothing less than the power that raised the dead.

When people talk about the Spirit, and describe "getting" the spirit at occasional important moments of their lives or asking God's Spirit to give them a clue as to whether they should make this or that decision, they are evidencing a banal reduction into ridiculousness of the majesty of this statement: "If the Spirit of Life in Christ Jesus that raised him from the dead reign in your bodies, you too shall be raised with him" (8:11).

Therefore, the Christian hope of eternal life — never a proof, but a *hope,* a kind of trust — is not an unreasonable one. The text refers to that when it says, "The Spirit bears witness with our spirit." Not without our spirit, not against our spirit, but *with* our spirit.

Is there that in our own spirit which is open toward this possibility? One paleontologist says that all living things move toward transcending themselves. That is true at every level of life right up to the human. All living things reach beyond themselves. With humans such self-transcendence may be that in our spirit which opens to hear the promise and believe it in trust. It comes out in a majestic line in one of the poems of Dylan Thomas, addressed to his father.

Do not go gentle into that good night.
Old age should burn and rave at close of day;
Rage, rage against the dying of the light![1]

What is it within humanity which rages against the dying of the light? Which knows that there is that which would transcend itself, which has a dreamlike capacity to envision another possibility?

To that possibility, Paul addresses the text, "There is therefore no condemnation," because what our spirit dreams as possible, the disclosure of God in Jesus Christ declares as actual.

We know that the whole creation has been groaning in travail together until now; and not only the creation, but we ourselves, who have the first fruits of the Spirit, groan inwardly as we wait for adoption as sons, the redemption of our bodies. For in this hope we were saved. Now hope that is seen is not hope. For who hopes for what he sees? But if we hope for what we do not see, we wait for it with patience.

1. Dylan Thomas, "Do not go gentle into that good night," in *Collected Poems* (New York: New Directions, 1957), p. 128.

Likewise the Spirit helps us in our weakness; for we do not know how to pray as we ought, but the Spirit himself intercedes for us with sighs too deep for words. And he who searches the hearts of men knows what is the mind of the Spirit, because the Spirit intercedes for the saints according to the will of God.

We know that in everything God works for good with those who love him, who are called according to his purpose. For those whom he foreknew he also predestined to be conformed to the image of his Son, in order that he might be the first-born among many brethren. And those whom he predestined he also called; and those whom he called he also justified; and those whom he justified he also glorified.

What then shall we say to this? If God is for us, who is against us? He who did not spare his own Son but gave him up for us all, will he not also give us all things with him? Who shall bring any charge against God's elect? It is God who justifies; who is to condemn? Is it Christ Jesus, who died, yes, who was raised from the dead, who is at the right hand of God, who indeed intercedes for us? Who shall separate us from the love of Christ? Shall tribulation, or distress, or persecution, or famine, or nakedness, or peril, or sword? As it is written,

"For thy sake we are being killed all the day long;
We are regarded as sheep to be slaughtered."

No, in all these things we are more than conquerors through him who loved us. For I am sure that neither death, nor life, nor angels, nor principalities, nor things present, nor things to come, nor powers, nor height, nor depth, nor anything else in all creation, will be able to separate us from the love of God in Christ Jesus our Lord. (Romans 8:22-39 RSV)

In the biblical faith and in early Christianity, something that tends to characterize our contemporary religious mood was almost unknown. This is the understanding that Christian faith, or indeed any religious faith, is a matter of absolute inwardness, intense privacy, and individual belief. While this sentiment characterizes modern religious faith, I do not find it in the Catholic tradition or in the Bible. Meaning is indeed personal; the personal, the inward, the individual is a rich realm of meaning. But ultimate meaning is not and cannot be personal, because my person is not identical with reality.

I come from a mighty universal process called nature. I live in that which transcends my individual life, called history. I have a long past as a biological organism, and I move toward an indefinite unfolding future. Therefore, any attempt to identify sufficient meaning with privacy is futile, but works against the very tradition we are here to glorify.

When Paul talks about faith, love, and trust, he reaches for a metaphor big enough to handle the bigness of it. He says that "the whole creation" somehow is a work of God signifying the presence of God, and then he spins the orbits of the fundamental terms of faith in the same dimensions as the whole creation, historically and naturally.

In the last part of the letter to the Romans, Paul has built up the great story of how into the futility, obscurity, and limited meaningfulness of human life, God has come with a clear, personal Word in the form of his own Self. He came among us in flesh and blood; and while we see always through a glass darkly, that we do see. Having built up this argument, Paul comes to a last condensed, difficult, even confusing, passage.

The mood is clear among us, that having religious faith or belonging to a religious community, or taking the central terms of faith seriously is a highly private affair. It has nothing to do with truth or the way things really are. It is somewhat like stewed prunes, all right for people who like that sort of thing, but there isn't much chance of their ever evoking universal approbation. Angkor Wat, Chartres, these are roofs that shelter the idiosyncrasies of a few people who were disposed to like that sort of thing.

If that were really true, the Christian faith would have ceased long ago. The only reason there is a continuing tradition whose symbols constitute not only some meaning but complete and absolute signals of meaning for millions of us is because we never made it an analgesic for privacy, an aspirin for solitude, or a kind of salve for pain. We believe it because it's true, because it points to that which constitutes deeper understandings of the nature of human life, transcendentality, cussedness, sin, communion, reality than any other story or set of symbols we know about.

Therefore, at the end of Romans appears a complex passage dominated by three terms: believing, waiting, hoping. Notice how Paul deals
with these. He lays out the story and the program of the Christian tradition, and then he says that we must trust in this. The word trust as used
in the New Testament is the same word as "to do believing" or "to believe." The word "believe" is both a substantive and a verb. As a substantive it means the substance in propositional form of what it is you say
you believe.

The Apostles' Creed, the Nicene Creed, the Westminster Confession,
the (Catholic) Baltimore Catechism, the Augsburg Confession are all
statements of what people believe and have believed. It is necessary to
make such statements, and we think that they are true and adequate in
their time and situation. That is belief used as a substantive.

As a verb, to believe means to *do believing* all your life — in your
head, your heart, your feet and your hands, to do with your whole action
what it is you *say* you believe. For many persons belief as a substantive
becomes a kind of soggy lump of unexamined propositions they heard
their parents utter. "And I believe in the Holy Spirit, the Lord and Giver
of Life." We say it solemnly every Sunday; but if you believe your belief,
then you won't look at the processes of biology, or geology, or history, or
ethics, or running a city in the same way. If the Lord is the giver of all
life, and he does this through the Spirit, then the Christian cannot turn
ethics over to the professors of ethics, or politics over to the politicians,
or war over to the generals, or the meaning of life over to the psycholo-
gists, the sociologists, or the philosophers. If you must "do believing"
out of what you believe, always unfolding it in relationship to what you
have to deal with now and now and there and there, then you are using
belief or trust as a verb, not just a substantive.

Believing and waiting. What is the fate of believing in this world?
Are we ever in this life in time and history, related to the object of our
faith — God — in such a way that we can say, "Now I know it absolutely! The argument is complete: the logic is infrangible; there is a
God, and he is thus and so, and what he wants me to do I can read as
clearly as I can read the telephone book, or even more so"? No, we never
experience God that way. God has us absolutely, in grace and judgment,
but we never grasp God as we are by him grasped. We see through a
glass darkly. Paul refers again to the phrase he used about nature and

says, *we too,* who have the first fruits of the Spirit, we groan inwardly with an anguish too deep for words.

Anyone who has been a pastor, or who has called upon others in anxiety or desolation or death, knows that this believing has always to skate on the ice of faith at every moment. At the death of a child, for example — one of the most horrible things to try to understand under the agency of a good God. Ivan in the *Brothers Karamazov* never does solve the problem. In fact, he says that if such a God rules this world, I respectfully hand him back the ticket.

But Paul adds a second word. We have this faith — this action of God for humans whereby he does not leave us alone — but we wait. In the Hebrew language, which Paul used, waiting and hoping are the same verb. What can it be to live one's whole life in waiting upon God, the God in whom you trust but whose actuality you cannot logically or empirically certify? But whether we like it or not, or wish it might be otherwise, that is the way it is.

An evidence of this is the magnificent history of the Jews. Something strange about the Christian community is that it almost never mentions the Jews except during Holy Week, and then as the rascals of the story. But the whole magnificent history of Judaism — at least six thousand years of it — is waiting, waiting, waiting.

If you have read Elie Wiesel's stories about the Jews of Central Europe during the Second World War, you know of the millions of Jews who, waiting upon a God against all the evidence, walked with the ancient prayers of their fathers straight into the gas ovens. The history of Judaism is the richest commentary I know upon the meaning of the words "to wait upon God."

Thus do we wait, but we do not wait simply in a vacuum. We wait in hope. If one sees that for which one hopes one doesn't have to hope, one sees. But Paul says that "If we see not that for which we hope, then do we with patience wait for it" (Romans 8:25).

Having said these things, Paul has tied himself up in a kind of knot, and it's rather humorous to watch him try to get out of it, and very elevating to see how he does so. He says that if God be for us, nothing is really against us. Then he apparently asks himself how this really works, and we get those tangled sentences which have sent theologians up the wall for a thousand years.

God calls us his children. If he calls us, he must predestine us; and those whom he predestines, he also justifies; and those whom he justifies, he also glorifies. That's a great apostolic ladder, but even Paul knows it isn't very clear. Even Paul knew he had a nut which he could not logically crack, and he got tired of the whole exercise. The next verse says, "What then shall we say to this?" Paul had got himself wrapped up in a logical effort to understand the mystery of God, and he did the best he could, and then looked at the whole business and swept it all away. "What then shall we say?" (Romans 8:31 RSV)

What Paul says next is not another rung on the ladder, but something quite different. He passes from doctrine to doxology. He goes from confusion to jubilation. He sweeps things off the table and goes straight from anxiety to adoration, the only possible step you can take when you come to the end of the logical possibilities. "What then shall we say" to this whole ineffable fact — that God acted in Christ and is trustworthy, even though we cannot understand the process of his life and his dealings with us, even though he remains off in a mystery?

What shall we say? Paul stops arguing and starts singing: He who did not hesitate to come into our situation himself, he may be trusted not to cast us off when the going gets rough. "Now I am completely confident" that nothing in life or death, in heaven or hell — none of the earthly powers or principalities which assault and make dubious and ambiguous and tragic this life — nothing can really destroy me because nothing ultimately destroyed Him. Therefore, Paul says, *nothing* shall separate us from the love of God which is in Christ Jesus our Lord (Romans 8:38-39).

The eighth chapter of Romans ends with that great lyrical passage; so do we end our reflections on this chapter and conclude with this: to be a Christian is not to know absolutely. It is not to have faith absolutely, not the faith with which we are beheld and beloved. We can never achieve that. Faith, as Luther loved to say, is *fiducia,* trust. It is to stand with the evidence that the God who did what he did is to be trusted in all the obscurities and darknesses of this life.

CONCLUSION

Sittler the Pioneering Ecological Theologian

STEVEN BOUMA-PREDIGER

"I have never been able to entertain a God-idea which was not inte-grally related to the fact of chipmunks, squirrels, hippopotamuses, galaxies, and light years."[1] In such words does Joseph Sittler declare that the Christian understanding of God must take the earth and its crea-tures into account. More precisely, Sittler states that "the center of my own theological work" is "the effort to fashion a more comprehensible and intelligible and relevant Christology to a quite new age, the twenti-eth century."[2] For Sittler the task is "to recognize that the traditional scope of christological understanding is under pressure to achieve vaster amplitude in virtue of contemporary man's apprehension of the world-as-nature."[3] The pressure to enlarge the scope of Christology also arises, Sittler insists, from the Bible.

> Positive theological work, it seems to me, must operate with the
> event of the Incarnation with a depth and amplitude at least as wide
> and far ranging and as grand as that of the New Testament. We may

1. Joseph Sittler, "Ecological Commitment as Theological Responsibility," *Zygon* 5 (June 1970): 173.

2. Joseph Sittler, "The Sittler Speeches," in *Center for the Study of Campus Ministry Yearbook 1977-78,* ed. Phil Schroeder (Valparaiso, Ind.: Valparaiso University Press, 1978), p. 29.

3. Joseph Sittler, *Essays on Nature and Grace* (Philadelphia: Fortress, 1972), p. 51.

not be able to go beyond Ephesians, Colossians, and the eighth chapter of Romans; but we dare not stop short of the incomparable boldness of those utterances.[4]

Whether on scientific or biblical-theological grounds, Sittler affirms the need to expand the scope of Christology. As he eloquently puts it in his famous New Delhi speech:

> The address of Christian thought is most weak precisely where man's ache is most strong. We have had, and have, a Christology for the moral soul, a Christology for history, and, if not a Christology for the ontic, affirmations so huge as to fill the space marked out by ontological questions. But we do not have, at least not in such effective force as to engage the thought of the common life, a daring, penetrating, life-affirming Christology for nature. The theological significance of cosmic Christology lies, for the most part, still tightly folded in the Church's innermost heart and memory.[5]

In short, a necessary dimension in the development of a "Christology for nature" is the articulation of a cosmic Christology. As Sittler asserts: "The way forward is from Christology expanded to its cosmic dimensions."[6] In such terms does Joseph Sittler stake out his theological agenda — to develop a cosmic Christology as a Christology for nature — and thereby prove himself to be a pioneering ecological theologian of the twentieth century.

As indicated above, Sittler turns to the Bible to ground his Christology for nature. And in so doing he squarely faces a crucial hermeneutical issue: How can one acknowledge the undeniable variety of the New Testament witness to Christ and yet also account for the apparent momentum in the New Testament toward a Christology cosmic in scope? As Sittler asks:

4. Joseph Sittler, "A Theology for Earth," *The Christian Scholar* 37 (September 1954): 374.

5. Joseph Sittler, "Called to Unity," *Southeast Asia Journal of Theology* 3 (April 1962): 12.

6. Sittler, "Called to Unity," p. 14; cf. Joseph Sittler, *Grace Notes and Other Fragments,* ed. Robert Herhold and Linda Marie Delloff (Minneapolis: Augsburg, 1986), p. 115.

Is it possible to speak of this variety in such a way as, on the one hand, to honor the warning against dogmatic "arrangement," and, on the other, to acknowledge that there is movement in this witness, that the referential amplitude is vastly wider in some voices than in others . . . ?[7]

On the one hand, "the New Testament witness to God and to Christ discloses a process . . . of fusion, transformation, and clarification" which admits of "no single or simple way of speaking of God and man and grace and the natural world."[8] If scripture is to be taken seriously and fairly, "the huge variety of the New Testament witness to Christ" must be acknowledged.[9]

On the other hand, Sittler claims that "it is possible and legitimate to see a growing magnitude in the christological utterances of the New Testament" — "an ever-widening orbit of christological meaning, scope, and force."[10] There are not only differences in the biblical testimony to Christ, argues Sittler, but "differences-in-motion" such that talk of a "christological momentum may be the most accurate term for what the literature of the New Testament discloses."[11] Especially in Paul there is a "christological momentum" or trajectory of thought toward a truly cosmic Christology.[12] In short, while Sittler acknowledges that there is in the New Testament witness to Christ a genuine plurality that cannot be systematized, he also insists that "there clearly is a momentum and a directionality at work in the scope and variety of the New Testament witness to Jesus as the Christ" — a momentum characterized by "widening circles of reference" until in Colossians and Ephesians "all things" are enfolded within the work of Christ.[13]

Sittler thus speaks of a "rhetoric of cosmic extension" in the Bible.[14]

7. Sittler, *Essays,* p. 29.
8. Sittler, *Essays,* p. 26.
9. Sittler, *Essays,* p. 28.
10. Sittler, *Essays,* p. 11.
11. Sittler, *Essays,* p. 29.
12. Sittler, *Essays,* p. 46.
13. Joseph Sittler, "The Scope of Christological Reflection," *Interpretation* 26 (July 1972): 334.
14. Sittler, *Essays,* pp. 36ff.

There is "an undilutable momentum, a 'blooming' of the language of Christ-testimony, in the New Testament" that has its roots in Israel's faith and finds its fullest expression in Colossians 1, Ephesians 1, and Romans 8.[15] As Sittler states in his New Delhi address — which actually is an extended meditation on Colossians 1:15-20, "the sweep of God's restorative action in Christ is no smaller than the six-times repeated *ta panta*."[16] Indeed, says Sittler, "all things are permeable to his [Christ's] cosmic redemption because all things subsist in him. He comes to all things, not as a stranger, for he is firstborn of all creation, and in him all things were created."[17] Redemption is as comprehensive and expansive as creation itself. As Sittler later puts it in summarizing the thesis of that famous address: "Only a Christology capable of administering the cosmic scope of biblical and catholic Christ-testimony would be adequate to the question about Christ and his meaning as it is necessarily put by men of modernity."[18]

Sittler also looks to the early Church, and especially Irenaeus, for examples of and resources for "a Christology of the total cosmos."[19] What attracts Sittler to "the cosmic Christology of Irenaeus" is "the idea that the Incarnate Word is in himself the unity and harmony not only of men, but also of the entire material universe," especially as Irenaeus works out that idea using the language of recapitulation.[20] In other words, "the God who is man's Redeemer dare not be acknowledged as other or less than the Creator of the world" and thus "the scope of Lordship dare not be specified as less than the scope of all that is."[21] Our Redeemer is our Creator — the Maker of heaven and earth. Sittler thus argues that "if there is postulated a logos-toward-redemption at work in history, and if the Lord who is disclosed there is postulated as the Lord of all that is, then this same comprehensiveness must inhere in an adequate Christology."[22]

15. Sittler, *Essays,* p. 30.
16. Sittler, "Called to Unity," p. 6.
17. Sittler, "Called to Unity," p. 6.
18. Sittler, *Essays,* p. 8.
19. Sittler, *Essays,* p. 55.
20. Sittler, *Essays,* p. 63.
21. Sittler, *Essays,* p. 116.
22. Sittler, *Essays,* p. 89.

An important implication for Sittler of this view of Christ is that it is precisely the earth that is the place where God's glory became flesh. "The Christian is to accept," says Sittler, "what God gives as Redeemer: the earth and all human life as the place wherein God's glory became flesh and dwelt among us."[23] And the presence of the glory of God implies the "indubitable, unassailable presence and action of God."[24] Hence the glory of God "is simply a sign of the ineffable which meets us through the effable, the material, the ordinary."[25] All creation is a sacrament — suffused with the weight of God's glory. The natural world is a sign of divine presence. So Sittler warns that "we dare not exclude as a theater of grace that same order of creation within whose form and substance God willed in Christ to make the place of his gracious presence."[26] Sittler's theology is thus an incarnational theology. As he insists, distinguishing his incarnational theology of nature from other theological perspectives, e.g., natural theology: "My theology is not one derived from nature; it is a theology of the incarnation applied to nature — which is quite different."[27] One does not properly start with the natural world and proceed to make inferences about the being and action of God; rather one draws conclusions about creation based upon the incarnation of God in Christ.

Given this incarnational perspective, it not surprising that Sittler claims "one finds nowhere in the Bible that strange assertion which one hears almost everywhere else — that God is concerned to save men's souls!" By contrast, he argues, "how richly, rather, is restoration there [in the Bible] presented in terms of men's material involvement in the world of nature." Hence Sittler boldly declares that God is "the undeviating materialist."[28] In sharp contrast to gnostic views of the person of Christ which truncate the work of Christ, Sittler's flesh-and-blood Christ goes hand in glove with a view of redemption as wide as his expansive doctrines of creation and incarnation.

23. Joseph Sittler, *The Structure of Christian Ethics* (Baton Rouge: Louisiana State University Press, 1958), p. 87.

24. Sittler, "Speeches," p. 21.

25. Sittler, "Speeches," p. 21.

26. Sittler, *Essays,* p. 132.

27. Joseph Sittler, *Gravity and Grace* ed. Linda Marie Delloff (Minneapolis: Augsburg, 1986), p. 67.

28. Sittler, "A Theology for Earth," p. 373.

It is of the heart of the Christian faith that this mighty, living, acting, restoring Word actually identified himself with his cloven and
frustrated creation which groans in travail. "The Word became flesh
and dwelt among us." To what end? That the whole cosmos in its
brokenness . . . might be restored to wholeness, joy, and lost love.[29]

And so Sittler the prescient ecological prophet concludes, in an article
published in 1954 — eight years before Rachel Carson's *Silent Spring* —
that:

The largest, most insistent, and most delicate task awaiting Christian theology is to articulate such a theology for nature as shall do
justice to the vitalities of earth and hence correct a current theological naturalism which succeeds in speaking meaningfully of earth
only at the cost of repudiating specifically Christian categories.
Christian theology cannot advance this work along the line of an orthodoxy — neo or old — which celebrates the love of heaven in
complete separation from man's loves in earth, abstracts commitment to Christ from relevancy to those loyalties of earth which are
elemental to being. Any faith in God which shall be redemptive and
regenerative in actuality dare not be alien to the felt ambiguities of
earth or remain wordless in the resounding torments of history and
culture. For the earth is not merely a negative illustration of the desirability of heaven![30]

Sittler draws numerous conclusions from this incarnational Christology for nature. Perhaps the most controversial is his claim that ecological degradation, from a Christian point of view, is not just socially inju-
rious and morally impermissible, but outright blasphemy. While it is
"difficult but possible" to get people today "to understand that pollution is biologically disastrous, aesthetically offensive, equally obviously
economically self-destructive, and socially reductive of the quality of
human life," Sittler observes that it is "a very difficult job to get even

29. Sittler, "A Theology for Earth," p. 373.
30. Sittler, "A Theology for Earth," pp. 373-74.

Christians to see that so to deal with the Creation is *Christianly* blasphemous."[31] Continues Sittler:

> A proper doctrine of creation and redemption would make it perfectly clear that from a Christian point of view the ecological crisis presents us not simply with moral tasks but requires of us a freshly renovated and fundamental theology of the first article [Creation] whereby the Christian faith defines whence Creation was formed, and why, and by whom, and to what end.[32]

For Sittler, ecological degradation is more than a moral issue; it is, strictly speaking, a theological issue of great importance. Sittler thus agrees with the current Orthodox archbishop of Constantinople, Patriarch Bartholomew: to degrade God's good earth is a sin.

By contrast, attending to and respecting those other creations of God's is the posture of those who see creation as the sacramental mystery it is. In this regard Sittler speaks of "beholding" our nonhuman neighbors.

> The word "behold" lies upon that which is beheld with a kind of tenderness which suggests that things in themselves have their own wondrous authenticity and integrity. I am called upon in such a saying ["Behold the lilies of the field"] not simply to "look" at a nonself but to "regard" things with a kind of spiritual honoring of the immaculate integrity of things which are not myself.[33]

Thus beholding a marmot or a meadow or a mountain is, for Sittler, an "acknowledgment of a fundamental understanding of man whose father is God, but whose sibling is the whole creation."[34] In language reminis-

---

31. Sittler, "Ecological Commitment," p. 179. Wendell Berry makes a similar claim on p. 98 of *Sex, Economy, Freedom, and Community* (New York: Pantheon, 1993): "We will discover that for these reasons our destruction of nature is not just bad stewardship, or stupid economics, or a betrayal of family responsibility; it is the most horrid blasphemy. It is flinging God's gifts into His face."

32. Sittler, "Ecological Commitment," p. 179.

33. Sittler, "Ecological Commitment," p. 175.

34. Sittler, "Ecological Commitment," p. 175.

cent of St. Francis of Assisi, Sittler often speaks of nonhuman creatures as brothers and sisters — fellow creatures made by God whose integrity we are called to respect.[35]

In this regard Sittler, following Augustine, carefully and properly distinguishes between use and enjoyment. Says Sittler: "To use a thing is to make it instrumental to a purpose, and some things are to be so used. To enjoy a thing is to permit it to be what it is prior to and apart from any instrumental assessment of it, and some things are to be so enjoyed."[36] Quoting Thomas Aquinas, Sittler affirms that it is the heart of sin that humans use what they ought to enjoy and are content to enjoy what they ought to use. So, for example, wine is to be enjoyed, not used; while charity is to be used, for the good of neighbor, and not enjoyed. Argues Sittler, with respect to matters ecological: "If the creation, including our fellow creatures, is impiously used apart from a gracious primeval joy in it the very richness of the creation becomes a judgment. . . . Abuse is use without grace."[37] Absent the virtues of attentiveness and respect, discernment and wisdom, we fail to see the world as it really is — a plethora of creatures with their own integrity and value — and consequently abuse it for our own illegitimate purposes. So, concludes Sittler, "Use is blessed when enjoyment is honored. . . . And a world sacramentally received in joy is a world sanely used."[38]

One final aspect of Sittler's Christology must, for our purposes here, yet be explicated. Sittler accurately perceives in modern life what he calls "the contemporary crisis of presence."[39] There is, says Sittler, a perceived absence of divine presence. The figure of Jesus is a "strange presence" amidst "the human diminishment and debacle of an 'absence.'"[40] And this felt absence of divine presence is compounded by "an increas-

35. See, e.g., "A Theology for Earth," p. 370, where Sittler refers to Francis and speaks of the earth as our "sister, sharer of his [human] sorrow."

36. Joseph Sittler, "The Care of the Earth," *Care of the Earth and Other University Sermons* (Philadelphia: Fortress, 1964), p. 95.

37. Sittler, "Care of the Earth," p. 97.

38. Sittler, "Care of the Earth," p. 98.

39. Sittler, *Essays,* p. 97.

40. Sittler, "The Presence and Acts of the Triune God in Creation and History," in *The Gospel and Human Destiny,* ed. Vilmos Vajta (Minneapolis: Augsburg, 1971), p. 98.

ingly impersonal culture."[41] Yet, states Sittler, the term presence "is nevertheless the term upon which must turn all speech about God in creation and in history."[42] There is a crisis of presence, and yet the very idea and, more importantly, experience of personal presence is a crucial requirement if religious language is to be meaningful since religious language is by its very nature, among other things, a language of presence.

For Sittler this crisis of presence finds its most profound expression in the "ineffable, inexplicable, almost unimaginable suffering" of Jesus.[43] In the cross one comes face-to-face with complete absence and utter abandonment. However, for Sittler the suffering of Jesus also represents God's response to the crisis of presence. Affirms Sittler: "The sufferer in the presence of the cross somehow knows he is not alone, that that which is ultimate, that which is the ground of all, is somehow engaged in the profoundest levels of his knowledge of his own humanity."[44] Pondering the logic of incarnation, Sittler argues:

Unless the God before whom we sit, and at whom we gaze, and about whom we think — unless that God has the tormented shape of our human existence, he isn't God enough. We ask, "Why did God become human?" And the answer is that the God who wants to be the source of our order must become the horror of our disorder, or he has no authority.[45]

In one of his earliest published articles, Sittler reflects on the brokenness and ambiguity of life — what he calls "the cruciform character of human existence."[46] He concludes that "because life itself is cruciform it must be addressed, if it is to be savingly struck, in an action which itself is cruciform."[47] The incarnation is such an action. Com-

41. Sittler, "The Presence and Acts of the Triune God," p. 99.
42. Sittler, "The Presence and Acts of the Triune God," pp. 98-99.
43. Sittler, "Speeches," p. 28.
44. Sittler, "Speeches," pp. 28-29.
45. Sittler, *Gravity and Grace,* p. 34.
46. Joseph Sittler, "The Cruciform Character of Human Existence," *The Chicago Lutheran Seminary Record* 54 (October 1949): 18.
47. Sittler, "The Cruciform Character of Human Existence," p. 20.

menting on John 1:14, Sittler expresses amazement at the words "The Word became flesh and dwelt among us." Declares Sittler: "Flesh — because that is *what* we are. Dwelt among us! — because that is *where* we are."[48] God took flesh and tented among us. The cruciform character of life has been addressed by the crucified Christ.

Such claims lie at the very core of the Christian faith. At the heart of the Christian story lies the bold and joyful insistence, incredible though it seems, that the Creator of the universe enters into our pain and undergoes our suffering. God tents with us. The cosmic Christ is a crucified God. In Sittler's words, only "the crucified God" is God enough to have "enabled generation after generation, century after century, to sustain so great a weight of human woe."[49] Only a crucifix "could absorb all of the worries and apprehensions heaped upon it."[50] As Sittler explicitly affirms with characteristic honesty and elegance:

> The cross is the symbol [of Christian faith] because the whacks of life take that shape. Our lives are full of abandonments, infidelities, tragedies. The affirmation is always crossed by a negation. The vitalities of life move toward death. And unless you have a crucified God, you don't have a big enough God.[51]

The cosmic Christ is the crucified God.

Given Sittler's cosmic Christology and Christology for nature, it is no surprise that Paul Santmire calls Joseph Sittler "a pioneering theologian of nature."[52] It is no wonder Moira Creede claims that what most distinguishes Sittler's theology and puts him "in the vanguard" of Christian theologians of his time was "his concern to provide a theological basis for the present ecological crisis."[53] As former colleague Jerald Brauer accurately states: Sittler had a "prophetic role in American theology" because "long before ecology became a household word in America, Sittler

---

48. Sittler, "The Cruciform Character of Human Existence," p. 20.

49. Sittler, *Gravity and Grace,* p. 33.

50. Sittler, *Gravity and Grace,* p. 33.

51. Sittler, *Grace Notes,* p. 118.

52. H. Paul Santmire, *The Travail of Nature* (Philadelphia: Fortress, 1985), dedication.

53. Moira Creede, "Logos and Lord" (Ph.D. dissertation, Louvain, 1977), p. 355.

was using the concept as a means of explicating Christian faith" — with respect to both the inner dynamics of faith itself and the presence of God in the natural world.[54] In our view, one of Joseph Sittler's unique and lasting contributions — his still prophetic legacy — is his Christology for nature — a Christology, Conrad Simonson remarks, "expanded to its cosmic dimensions."[55] In eloquence of word and depth of insight, Joseph Sittler sought to understand theologically the ecological crisis and to offer an expansive Christology as a prescription for our ailing earth, and in so doing trace the height and breadth and depth of God's love. In his theological labors, he has offered us, indeed, evocations of grace.

54. Jerald Brauer, "In Appreciation of Joseph Sittler," *Journal of Religion* 54 (April 1974): 100.

55. Conrad Simonson, *The Christology of the Faith and Order Movement* (Leiden: Brill, 1972), p. 94.

Joseph Sittler and Environmental Ethics: A Selected Bibliography

Works by Joseph Sittler

"The Grace Note." ("The Promise and Hope of American Life.") *Chicago Lutheran Theological Seminary Record* 56, no. 2 (April 1951): 2-4.

"God, Man and Nature." *The Pulpit* 24, no. 3 (August 1953): 16-17.

*"A Theology for Earth." *The Christian Scholar* 37 (September 1954): 367-74. [Reprinted as: "Meant for Each Other," *Motive* 16, no. 3 (December 1955): 6-9.]

"Commencement Address [May 8, 1959]." *Chicago Lutheran Theological Seminary Record* 64, no. 4 (November 1959): 34-37.

*"Called to Unity." *The Ecumenical Review* 14 (January 1962): 177-87. [Reprinted: *Pulpit Digest* 42, no. 290 (July-August 1962): 11-18; *Vital Speeches* 28 (15 February 1962): 281-85; *South East Asia Journal of Theology* 3 (April 1962): 6-15; *Currents in Theology and Mission* 16, no. 1 (February 1989): 5-13.]

"Urban Fact and the Human Situation." In *Challenge and Response in the City,* edited by Walter Kloetzli, pp. 9-20. Rock Island, Ill.: Augustana Book Concern, 1962.

*"The Care of the Earth." In *The Care of the Earth and Other University Sermons,* pp. 88-98. Philadelphia: Fortress, 1964. [Also appears in: *Sermons to Intellectuals from Three Continents,* edited by Franklin Littell, pp. 18-28. New York: The Macmillan Company, 1963.]

"Nature and Grace: Reflections on an Old Rubric." *Dialog* (Minneapolis) 3 (Autumn 1964): 252-56.

"Christ and the Cosmos — God's Work and Man's Search." *Mid-Stream* 3 (1964): 175-81.

"Report of Committee I, As Amended After Plenary Discussion: Creation, New Creation, and the Unity of the Church." In *Minutes of the Meetings of the Faith and Order Commission and Working Committee held at the University of Aarhus, Denmark 15-27 August 1964.* Paper No. 44. Geneva: World Council of Churches, Commission on Faith and Order, 1965.

"The Anguish of Christology." Chapter 3 in *The Anguish of Preaching.* Philadelphia: Fortress, 1966.

"The Principal Problem for Protestant Theology Today." In *The Word in History,* edited by T. Patrick Burke, pp. 60-68. New York: Sheed and Ward, 1966.

Untitled article. *Criterion* 6 (Winter 1967): 21-23.

*"The Role of the Spirit in Creating the Future Environment." In *Environment and Change,* edited by William R. Ewald, Jr., pp. 55-68. Bloomington, Ind.: Indiana Universtiy Press, 1968.

Review of *The Dominion of Man: The Search for Ecological Responsibility,* by John Black. *Zygon* 5 (December 1970): 370.

*"Ecological Commitment as Theological Responsibility." *Zygon* 5 (June 1970): 172-81. [Reprinted: *South Western Journal of Theology* 13 (Spring 1971): 35-45.]

"The Presence and Acts of the Triune God in Creation and History." In *The Gospel and Human Destiny,* edited by Vilmos Vajta, pp. 90-135. Minneapolis: Augsburg Publishing House, 1971.

"An Aspect of American Religious Experience." *Proceedings of the Twenty-Sixth Annual Convention of the Catholic Theological Society of America* 26 (14-17 June 1971): 1-17. [Abridged and reprinted as: "Space and Time in American Religious Experience," *Interpretation* 30 (January 1976): 44-51.]

"Components for Ecological Reflection." *Thesis Theological Cassettes* 2, no. 7 (1971).

"Two Temptations — Two Corrections." *National Parks and Conservation Magazine: The Environmental Journal* 45 (December 1971): 21.

Essays on Nature and Grace. Philadelphia: Fortress, 1972.

"The New Creation." Chapter in *The Human Crisis in Ecology,* edited by Franklin L. Jensen and Cedric W. Tilberg, pp. 96-103. [Philadelphia]: Board of Social Ministry, Lutheran Church in America, 1972.

*"The Scope of Christological Reflection." *Interpretation* 26 (July 1972): 328-37.

"Response to Johannes Metz." In *Hope and the Future of Man,* edited by Ewert H. Cousins, pp. 131-34. Philadelphia: Fortress, 1972.

"The Perils of Futurist Thinking." In *Shaping the Future: A Discussion at the 1971 Nobel Conference Organized by the Gustavus Adolphus College, St. Peter, Minn.,* edited by John D. Roslansky, pp. 67-82. Amsterdam: North Holland Publishing Co., 1972.

*"Evangelism and the Care of the Earth." In *Preaching in the Witnessing Community,* edited by Herman G. Steumpfle Jr., pp. 100-104. Philadelphia: Fortress, 1973.

"Christology and Grace." In *Center for the Study of Campus Ministry Yearbook 1977-78,* edited by Phil Schroeder, pp. 20-45. Valparaiso, Ind.: Valparaiso University [1978]. [Includes running sidebar, "Comments." One of several transcripts of talks given by Sittler June 12-17, 1977.]

Grace Notes and Other Fragments. Edited by Robert M. Herhold and Linda Marie Delloff. Philadelphia: Fortress Press, 1981.

"Return to New Delhi: A Lutheran Partners Interview with Theologian Joseph A. Sittler." Interview by Robert M. Herhold. *Lutheran Partners* 1, no. 4 (November/December 1985): 8-11, 25.

"Closing Address: Creating a Rhetoric of Rural Values." In "Preliminary Report: A Family Farm Action Agenda," pp. 37-47. Xeroxed booklet from "A Time to Choose: An Ecumenical Event on the Future of Family Farm Agriculture in Wisconsin," Madison, Wis., 8-9 March 1985. Madison, Wis.: Wisconsin Conference of Churches, 1985.

"Nature and Grace." Chapter in *Gravity and Grace: Reflections and Provocations.* Edited by Linda Marie Delloff. Foreword by Martin E. Marty. Minneapolis: Augsburg, 1986.

*"The Context: Nature and Grace in Romans 8" and "Language and the Bible." In *Faith, Learning and the Church College: Addresses by Joseph Sittler,* edited by Connie Gegenbach, pp. 15-26, 37-39. Northfield, Minn.: St. Olaf College, 1989. [Transcript of sermons given in 1975 at Augustana Lutheran Church, Chicago, Ill.]

Secondary Literature/Applications

Bakken, Peter W. "The Ecology of Grace: Ultimacy and Environmental Ethics in Aldo Leopold and Joseph Sittler." Ph.D. Dissertation, University of Chicago Divinity School, 1991.

———. "Joseph Sittler: A Bibliography." Typescript, 1994. [Available at Jesuit-Krauss-McCormick Library, Lutheran School of Theology at Chicago.]

Bouma-Prediger, Steven. *The Greening of Theology: The Ecological Models of Rosemary Radford Ruether, Joseph Sittler, and Jürgen Moltmann.* Atlanta: Scholars Press, 1995.

Bürkle, Horst. "The Debate of the Cosmic Christ as Example of an Ecumencially Oriented Theology." In *Indian Voices in Today's Theological Debate,* edited by Horst Bürkle and Wolfgang M. W. Roth (Lucknow, India: Lucknow Publishing House; Delhi, S.P.C.K., 1972), pp. 198-214.

Creede, Moira. "Logos and Lord: A Study of the Cosmic Christology of Joseph Sittler." Ph.D. Dissertation, Louvain, 1977.

Cromie, Thetis. "Feminism and the Grace-full Thought of Joseph Sittler." *Christian Century* 97 (9 April 1980): 406-8.

Gustafson, James M. *Protestant and Roman Catholic Ethics: Prospects for Rapprochement.* Chicago: University of Chicago Press, 1978.

Hall, Douglas John. *Imaging God: Dominion as Stewardship.* Grand Rapids: Wm. B. Eerdmans and New York: Friendship Press, 1986.

Hefner, Philip. "The Politics and the Ontology of Nature and Grace." *Journal of Religion* 54 (April 1974): 138-53.

Heggen, Bruce Allen. "A Theology for Earth: Nature and Grace in the Thought of Joseph Sittler." Ph.D. Dissertation, McGill University, 1995.

Santmire, H. Paul. "Toward a Christology of Nature: Claiming the Legacy of Joseph Sittler and Karl Barth." *Dialog* 34 (Fall 1995): 270-80.

Scott, Nathan A. Jr. "The Poetry and Theology of Earth: Reflections on the Testimony of Joseph Sittler and Gerard Manley Hopkins." *Journal of Religion* 54 (April 1974): 102-18.

Simonson, Conrad. *The Christology of the Faith and Order Movement.* Oekumenische Studien, no. 10. Leiden: E. J. Brill, 1972.

Index of Subjects and Names

Index of Scripture References